David Hillman
SHAKESPEARE'S ENTRAILS
Belief, Scepticism and the Interior of the Body

Anna Kamaralli
SHAKESPEARE AND THE SHREW
Performing the Defiant Female Voice

Jane Kingsley-Smith
SHAKESPEARE'S DRAMA OF EXILE

Katie Knowles
SHAKESPEARE'S BOYS
A Cultural History

Lori Leigh
SHAKESPEARE AND THE EMBODIED HEROINE
Staging Female Characters in the Late Plays and Early Adaptations

Rory Loughnane and Edel Semple (editors)
STAGED TRANSGRESSION IN SHAKESPEARE'S ENGLAND

Rob Pensalfini
PRISON SHAKESPEARE

Stephen Purcell
POPULAR SHAKESPEARE
Simulation and Subversion on the Modern Stage

Erica Sheen
SHAKESPEARE AND THE INSTITUTION OF THEATRE

Kay Stanton
SHAKESPEARE'S 'WHORES'
Erotics, Politics and Poetics

Alfred Thomas
SHAKESPEARE, DISSENT AND THE COLD WAR

R.S. White, Mark Houlahan and Katrina O'Loughlin (editors)
SHAKESPEARE AND EMOTIONS
Inheritances, Enactments, Legacies

Deanne Williams
SHAKESPEARE AND THE PERFORMANCE OF GIRLHOOD

Paul Yachnin and Jessica Slights
SHAKESPEARE AND CHARACTER
Theory, History, Performance, and Theatrical Persons

---

**Palgrave Shakespeare Studies Series Standing Order**
**ISBN  978–1403–91164–3 (hardback) 978–1403–91165–0 (paperback)**
(*outside North America only*)

You can receive future titles in this series as they are published by placing a standing order.
Please contact your bookseller or, in case of difficulty, write to us at the address below with
your name and address, the title of the series and the ISBN quoted above.

Customer Services Department, Macmillan Distribution Ltd, Houndmills, Basingstoke,
Hampshire RG21 6XS, England

# Imagining Shakespeare's Original Audience, 1660–2000

## Groundlings, Gallants, Grocers

Bettina Boecker
*Senior Lecturer, University of Munich, Germany*

First published 2015 by
PALGRAVE MACMILLAN

Palgrave Macmillan in the UK is an imprint of Macmillan Publishers Limited, registered in England, company number 785998, of Houndmills, Basingstoke, Hampshire RG21 6XS.

Palgrave Macmillan in the US is a division of St Martin's Press LLC, 175 Fifth Avenue, New York, NY 10010.

Palgrave Macmillan is the global academic imprint of the above companies and has companies and representatives throughout the world.

Palgrave® and Macmillan® are registered trademarks in the United States, the United Kingdom, Europe and other countries.

ISBN  978–1–137–37995–5

This book is printed on paper suitable for recycling and made from fully managed and sustained forest sources. Logging, pulping and manufacturing processes are expected to conform to the environmental regulations of the country of origin.

A catalogue record for this book is available from the British Library.

A catalog record for this book is available from the Library of Congress.

Typeset by MPS Limited, Chennai, India.

*For Martin*

# Contents

# Acknowledgements

Most of this book was written in my office in the Shakespeare Research Library at Munich University. I wish to thank the library's readers for their collective patience – they often had to wait for me to reach the end of the sentence before they finally got help with their queries. Of my Munich colleagues I want to thank first and foremost Andreas Höfele, who has been an exceptionally generous mentor over the years and who continues to inspire with his learning, his integrity and his sense of humour. Bastian Kuhl is among the most reliable and helpful people I know. Renate Schruff was a faithful go-between. A particularly big thank you goes to Kathleen Rabl for helping with my English, and with quite a lot besides. I would never have finished this book had it not been for the students who assisted in the day-to-day running of the library, and also with the technical aspects of this book. In particular, my thanks go to Diana Neiczer, Amelie Lutz and Silvie Baldauf.

I wish to thank Michael Dobson and Dympna Callaghan for including the book in this series. Participants in Stephen Purcell's seminar on 'The Origins of Original Practice' at the International Shakespeare Conference in 2014 provided valuable feedback. I have also benefited from discussions at various ESRA conferences, notably the ones in Utrecht and Krakow.

At Palgrave Macmillan, I want to thank Ben Doyle and particularly Tomas René for taking such good care of this book. Thank you Mychael Barratt for letting me use the etching on the cover!

Finally, I am grateful to my parents, Helga and Hans-Werner Boecker, to my brother Johannes and my sister, Anja Gisa, with her lovely family. I also wish to acknowledge the Deters clan, particularly my late grandfather, Theodor Deters. Above all, thank you Martin and Charlotte for bringing so much love and joy to my life.

# Introduction: *Those Nut-cracking Elizabethans*

In 1935, William John Lawrence published a collection of essays called *Those Nut-Cracking Elizabethans*.[1] To the specialist audience at which it is aimed, the fact that the book focusses on the Elizabethans in their capacity as theatregoers need hardly be mentioned: a nut-cracking Elizabethan is, by definition, located in the theatre. This assumption is part of a whole set of sometimes surprisingly specific and detailed beliefs about the Elizabethan audience current among both amateurs of and specialists in Shakespearean drama. Perhaps the most persistent of these tenets is that Shakespeare wrote certain passages (not necessarily his best) especially for those who had paid for standing room only – the notorious 'groundlings'. Over the centuries, a plethora of critics has claimed that this was a section of the audience of which he did not think too highly, citing the following passage from *Hamlet* as proof:

> *Hamlet*: [...] O! it offends me to the soul to hear a robustious periwig-pated fellow tear a passion to tatters, to very rags, to split the ears of the groundlings, who, for the most part, are capable of nothing but inexplicable dumb-shows and noise.[2]

Shakespeare, so this line of argument runs, is using Hamlet as a mouth-piece to vent his frustration with an audience essentially unworthy of his plays. That the dramatist addresses a confident 'Work, work your thoughts'[3] to the same audience in *Henry V* is a fact often ignored – or quoted in support of the counter-position, which conceives of Elizabethan theatregoers as particularly attentive and alert.

Since the re-opening of the theatres in 1660, Shakespeare criticism has produced many and often contradictory versions of those who frequented the theatres during the dramatist's lifetime. The comparative dearth of hard facts on theatregoers in Shakespeare's London has aided rather than abetted this process – even today, scholars acknowledge that when it comes to the Elizabethan audience, 'there is a point at which imagination must take over where evidence leaves off'.[4] The imagined audiences that result are not contingent. The discourse on Renaissance theatregoers is part of what Michael Dobson has called 'the making of the national poet'.[5] The early modern audience, as much as the Bard himself and, by extension, his age, are fashioned in the image of the later-born critic, reflections of the needs and sensibilities that are brought to Shakespeare as a site of cultural meaning. The 'reinvention'[6] of Shakespeare by each subsequent age or school of criticism goes hand in hand with a similar reinvention of his audience – an audience that is conceived as singular (in the sense of constant and uniform) rather than plural. With regard to the historical realities of Shakespeare's theatre, it is certainly apt to think of both *audience* and *audiences*: the one 'a collective entity – one that dramatists might know and appeal to', the other 'the variety of experiences and viewing practices that individuals brought to the early modern theatre'.[7] With regard to the critical discourse on Shakespeare's first receivers, however, this is not necessarily the case. To the extent that the Elizabethan audience is always an imagined audience, it is a fiction with a purpose: it explains, exonerates or extols the national poet. Shakespearean drama is what it is because its audience was what it was. This logical pattern is immensely complicated by introducing a plurality of audiences, hence a majority of critics over the centuries prefer to think of Elizabethan theatregoers as one stable entity.

Ever since the eighteenth century, the brunt of critical attention has been directed at the audience of the Globe. It is only comparably late that the indoor theatres and their customers enter the critical picture, and discussions of them are rarely as politically charged as the discourse on the open-air theatres. Because of the lower entrance fees, the latter were, at least theoretically, within the means of a larger share of the population – a continual source of irritation to the London authorities during Shakespeare's lifetime. This irritation has considerable resonances in the four hundred years of Shakespeare criticism that ensue, for in effect, the comparatively low cost of an afternoon at the Globe is at the core of a majority of the uses to which the Globe audience is put by later-born commentators. It has allowed for the Globe to be labelled as 'popular', a sobriquet that, though not unchallenged, remains firmly in place to this day. The question, of course, is just what the popular nature of the early modern theatre means to later generations. From the twentieth century onwards, it is usually presented as part and parcel of Shakespeare's greatness, of his claim to iconicity:

> Many people feel that the theatre of Shakespeare should be a kind of model. Though holding a mass audience, it was intimate, human, fast-moving, passionately real though without any fuss about stage illusion, and all this made it very democratic. Of course some critics want to refute the picture and prove that he wrote for the palace or for stately homes, but they still regard it in political terms.[8]

Whether public theatre or stately home, in both cases the issue is not, or not primarily, what the intended place of performance was, but what kind of people assembled there. By way of their original recipients, the plays are intended to be socially defined, to be given an 'owner' – and not just an early modern one. Whether Shakespeare wrote for the early modern populace or for the period's social elite decisively affects his position within the cultural framework of a given critic's own present. Obviously, however, there is no simple, historically constant mapping of the various locations in which Shakespeare's plays were performed onto a good/bad dichotomy, i.e. not every critic who assumes that Shakespeare 'really' wrote for the Globe necessarily considers this a good thing. The Globe, and with it the Globe audience, partakes of the essential ambivalence of the popular, which, as Robert Shaughnessy puts it:

> is itself hardly a singular or uncontested term or frame of reference: seen from some angles, it denotes community, shared values, democratic participation, accessibility, and fun; from others, the mass-produced commodity, the lowest common denominator, the reductive or the simplified, or the shoddy, the coarse, and the meretricious.[9]

Over the course of the centuries, criticism has produced many and often extremely controversial hypotheses about the social composition, intellectual abilities and emotional reactions of those who frequented the amphitheatres of early modern London. To some extent, the critical discourse on Elizabethan theatregoers thus reproduces the bias that characterises many contemporary accounts of them, whether the source is the London city council, to whom the theatres were a potential source of unrest, Puritan ideologues, or finally the dramatists themselves.[10] Again and again, scholars have therefore castigated what they present as the inventiveness of earlier publications in the field. Ann Jennalie Cook's 1987 *The Privileged Playgoers of Shakespeare's London*, itself highly controversial at the time of its publication, describes the situation as follows:

> [Contemporary] [r]eports of [the] nature of [the Renaissance playgoer] varied wildly. Was he ignorant or intelligent, riotous or refined, libertine or law abiding, plebeian or privileged? The answers depended always upon the nature of the report and the reporter. And so they still do. Modern accounts of the audience suffer from the bias of the writer fully as much as did the contemporary accounts. [...] As often as not, an interpretation reveals more about the interpreter's mind than it does about the mysteries of the past.[11]

The focus of this study is on the interpreter's mind. Any given period's notion about Shakespeare's first audiences is shaped by that period's needs and sensitivities at least as much as by what early modern sources tell us about the early modern theatre. This is not to say that an 'objective' account would be possible; like any aspect of history as reconstructed by later generations, any version of Renaissance theatregoers is to a greater or lesser degree a fictional construct. Accordingly, this study does not aim at separating the chaff of fictionality from the wheat of the factual. Instead, it treats the Elizabethan audience as an integral part of Shakespeare as a site of cultural meaning – a site that is permanently renegotiated and redefined, and that extends well beyond the Shakespearean text.

The discourse on Shakespeare has created an entire historical 'context' in which to embed the great dramatist, a period that is in effect evoked as an aspect of him. This is even more true of the period's theatregoers – the Renaissance become flesh, as it were. They turn abstract concepts like Tillyard's 'Elizabethan World Picture'[12] into lived historical realities. Conversely, they play an important role in determining just what kind of historical reality the Bard was faced with in the first place. Certain versions of his audience support – or preclude – certain versions of his age, as well as certain interpretations of his plays. Drawing on the principle of theatrical collusion, critics can use the audience to explain (away) virtually every feature of every play. These attempts at 'excusing' Shakespeare take on a particular urgency where the text is treated as a more or less direct reflection not only of the author's likes and dislikes, but also of his artistic integrity and general moral stamina.

Shakespeare's œuvre has been both extolled as a testimony to the unusual intellectual prowess of Elizabethan theatregoers and berated as indicative of their moral depravity and general simple-mindedness. In both cases, the aim has been not so much to establish a certain version of the early modern theatregoer as to establish a certain version of Shakespeare, who – with the help of his original clientele – can thus either bask in the glory of having successfully catered to a demanding audience or be unburdened of any responsibility for his perceived 'lapses', and sometimes both at the same time.

## Identity, alterity, authenticity

The driving force behind such manoeuvres is of course the special status of Shakespeare within British culture. As the still undisputed national poet, Shakespeare embodies literary as well as extra-literary norms and values, and has been doing so for the almost four hundred years since his rise to iconicity. He has helped define national identity as it changed over the centuries, and been a considerable asset for certain social groups in shaping (or attempting to shape) this identity according to their own preferences. Shakespeare's rise to literary stardom is therefore subject to mechanisms that govern the constitution and constant negotiation of collective identities.

As a relational term, identity cannot exist without alterity: the existence of an outside, a 'not-us', is decisive for the constitution both of the subject and of the group. The latter's set of auto-stereotypes is commonly matched by a corresponding set of hetero-stereotypes:[13] we generally know what we are as well as (sometimes more distinctly) what we are not. Regarding the Elizabethan audience's implication into the formation of a collective national identity, what is crucial is that the dividing line between us and not-us, between self and other, need not necessarily be drawn vis-à-vis another, alien culture (such as classical Greece as opposed to the 'barbarians', colonial Europe as opposed to the 'savage'). Another means of defining cultural identity is the concept of historical alterity, which permits a nation/culture to define its own present as a counter-model to, even a refutation of, its own past: 'we' are not what 'we' used to be. This logic is particularly useful where the past or certain aspects of it would suggest the historical relativism of accepted norms and values. If the past is indeed totally different from (and ideally patently inferior to) the present, its disregard for the standards of the latter poses less of a threat. A past being used in this manner must change as the culture's self-image changes, for a different identity requires a different kind of 'other', an alterity to match. In the words of Sander Gilman:

> [e]very social group has a set vocabulary of images for [its] external-ized Other. These images are the product of history and of a culture that perpetuates them. None is random; none is isolated from the historical context. From the wide range of the potential models in any society, we select a model that best reflects the common presup-positions about the Other at any given moment in history.[14]

The history of Shakespeare reception, and more particularly the discourse on his original audience, throw this into sharp relief. The meaning of Shakespeare is not conclusively defined either by his works or by the known facts of his life, but 'invented' to suit the cultural needs that are brought to him. It is only because Shakespeare is treated as to some extent conceptually separate from the actualities of his text that his – or, rather, his critics' – claims to timelessness and universality become viable. This, however, cannot be openly acknowledged. The national poet must seem stable and unchanging, despite the fact that he is continually being refashioned. In creating this semblance of stability, of 'timelessness', the Elizabethan audience plays an important role, one based on a dichotomy established already by Ben Jonson in the First Folio: 'for an age' versus 'for all time'. There are effectively two Shakespeares: a practically meta-historical figure who wrote 'for all time' and serves as a cultural point of reference on the one hand, and 'Shakespeare the Elizabethan' on the other, a figure who wrote 'for [his] age' and whose fundamental alterity explains those features of the Shakespeare canon not compatible with current norms and values as occasioned by his historical situation. The Elizabethan audience is this historical situation become flesh, as it were, the embodiment of the historical alterity criticism ascribes to early modern England. Gilman points out that 'stereotypes can [...] be perpetuated, resurrected and shaped through texts containing the fantasy life of the culture, quite independent of the existence or absence of the group in a given society.'[15] Especially within continental European tradi-tions of literary criticism (particularly of German *Literaturwissenschaft*, the 'science' of literature), which have traditionally emphasised objectivity and analysis, it may appear like a bit of a stretch to think of Shakespeare scholarship as part of the 'fantasy life' of British, or, for that matter, of any culture. But the critical history of Shakespeare's first audience makes clear that this is not the case.

From a historical point of view, the primary aim of the audience as imagined by later-born critics has been to explain and thus defuse those elements of Shakespeare's plays perceived as incompatible with his (rise to) iconicity. In eighteenth-century England, this process operates both in the theatre and in the increasingly numerous editions of Shakespeare. In their history of English drama, Simon Shepherd and Peter Womack write:

> The Shakespeare cult [...] led to the general diffusion of a printed text which partially failed to confirm the deity of the cult's own object. SHAKESPEARE, as bardolatrous typesetters preferred to call him, was undoubtedly immortal, but somehow not everything written by Shakespeare was SHAKESPEARE. The rhetorical struggle to deal with this central instability is a rich source of eighteenth-century critical metaphor: gold and ore, flowers and weeds, jewels and rubbish, sun and cloud. Most of these images implicitly recommend a programme of purification, and this is what the theatre of Garrick did. The scripts were adapted to fit the mid-eighteenth-century theatre's production values, literary conventions and canons of decency. [...] In 1773, when the acting editions were printed, the editors made the best of it; they had, they said, preserved Shakespeare's beauties while expunging his deformities [...].[16]

This dehistoricisation of the text does not, however, quite suffice to establish why Shakespeare is 'for all time'. If his works indeed transcend history, then why do they need to be purged from the historicity they are claimed not to be subject to in the first place? What is called for is the integration of the merely 'historical' bits into a coherent whole: 'the age of Shakespeare', which effectively comes to embody the Bard's historical alterity.[17] Shakespeare's Elizabethan audience (a concept which for the overwhelming majority of critics is general enough to include Jacobean theatregoers as well) thus emerges as a site of cultural meaning along the lines of the Bard himself. Whenever Shakespeare is claimed for the norms and values of a given time and place, his original audience is used to explain those elements of his works that are incompatible with them. Where he is turned into 'self', his audience is turned into 'other'. An object of projection *par excellence*, Renaissance theatregoers throw the mechanisms of selection, appropriation and exclusion that enable Shakespeare's rise, and continuing claim, to iconicity into particularly sharp relief.

Critics have not been unaware of this fact. In an article published in the 1951/52 volume of *Modern Philology*, the most sustained treatment of the topic up to that time, Moody Prior described the Elizabeth audience as the unacknowledged *ultima ratio* of Shakespeare criticism:

> Most of those who interest themselves in the Elizabethan audience [...] are concerned not primarily [...] with restoring the theatrical life of the past but with discovering in such information support for certain conclusions about the plays. [...] The selection of the elements which in any given instance are combined to define the audience is not governed usually by the requirements of disciplined historical procedure. Rather, it seems to follow the demands of some critical end. [...] [S]ome significant characteristic of the audience [...] proves invaluable in illuminating some feature of the plays. In reality, the dramatic problem comes first, the audience is selectively created to meet the problem, and the 'explanation' follows. [...] By this means the critic can meet any difficulty.[18]

Under the influence of the critical developments of the following decades, especially of Cultural Materialism, what Prior in 1952 presents as a not particularly reputable kind of cure-all for the logical impasses of Shakespeare criticism turns into an important aid in adapting Shakespeare to the value systems of a given period – or perhaps more precisely, a given social group, for the discourse on Shakespeare's Elizabethan audience bears witness to the fact that national identity, and with it the national poet, is an object of intra-cultural contention. Cultures are never as homogeneous as the idea of a shared self-image would seem to imply. Different parts of the nation proffer competing definitions of what the nation actually is, and this struggle is reflected in varying ideas of what Shakespeare actually is – and was. Contrasting versions of the age that he lived in and the theatre that he wrote for are not simply different interpretations of the historical evidence (however much of it was actually accessible to a given critic), but rival bids for cultural power.

Many publications which study Shakespeare as an intrinsically political site of cultural meaning display an implicit knowledge of the importance of the Elizabethan audience for Shakespeare's continuing iconicity. Sustained engagements with the topic are rare, however. The German version of Robert Weimann's *Shakespeare and the Popular Tradition in the Theatre* (*Shakespeare und die Tradition des Volkstheaters*, 1967) has a short chapter on the popular stage in eighteenth-century criticism, and Simon Shepherd and Peter Womack's *English Drama: A Cultural History* features an important chapter on the nineteenth-century invention of the groundling to which this study is deeply indebted. More recently, Amy Rodgers has looked at representations of the Elizabethan audience in films and historical novels,[19] most of which draw heavily on the idea of the groundling as developed by Victorian Shakespeare critics. The mystique of the groundling is indeed alive and well: it has decisively influenced audience behaviour as displayed (some would say endorsed) at the New Globe in Bankside and other replica theatres.[20] There, the standees in particular contribute in significant ways to the bona fide early modern experience which the structure (and the institution behind it) promises its patrons.

This reflects a trend in the discourse on Shakespeare's original audience to be observed from the late nineteenth century onwards: early modern theatregoers are increasingly imagined as a repository not only of alterity, but also, and increasingly more importantly, of authenticity. The Renaissance and its 'inhabitants' turn into guarantors for the correctness of a given interpretation of Shakespeare. By claiming to approach his plays in the same way that the early modern audience did (the belief that this early modern meaning is both unambiguous and accessible to the later-born inquirer is an integral part of this line of argument), scholars legitimise their own interpretations in powerful ways, particularly where these interpretations are presented as based on seemingly objective historical givens. In an almost paradoxical manner, the concept of authenticity combines Romantic subjectivity and historicist objectivity. The quintessentially Romantic idea of the author as the ultimate authority over the meaning of his work is combined with positivist claims regarding the feasibility of objective and complete access to the past. The one meaning of the work intended by the author, it is claimed, was unvaryingly picked up by an original audience whose historical situation effectively made other, competing interpretations impossible. In somewhat less abstract terms, every early modern theatregoer adhered, and could not but adhere, to the same interpretation of, say *Hamlet*: the one (and only) intended by Shakespeare.

If the elements constitutive of English culture as embodied by Shakespeare are subject to historical change, they are essentially open to random redefinition, and both 'Shakespeare' and 'English culture' become conceptually unstable. Authenticity answers this threat by using the past in a manner completely different from the one that informs the historical apology. The 'other' against which 'self' is defined is not the supposed barbarity of early modern England, as was the case with much of seventeenth- and eighteenth-century Shakespeare criticism, but the period that lies *between* that past and the respective critic's present, more particularly, its supposedly misguided interpretations of the Bard. This essentially Protestant attitude

> privileges a return to [the] origin or source, and in practical terms it means both a revival of interest in originating texts and documents themselves (as opposed to established interpretations of those documents) and a radical repudiation of the deadening mass of accumulated interpretation, which is seen as progressively more distant from the source, and increasingly degraded by accumulated historical debris. In addition, the social agency that has claimed the role of preserving tradition is seen in this counter-movement as increasingly venal in promoting the interests of an administrative cadre to the detriment of the primary relationship between the originating source and the faithful subject.[21]

This approach becomes strategically important once a culture no longer conceives of itself as uniform: authenticity is a very effective aid in defining the *authoritative* meaning of a national icon like Shakespeare. As an extension of his creative genius, the age that he lived in is then presented 'as the moment of an original purity'[22] to which all subsequent generations should endeavour to return. Shakespeare is no longer constructed in opposition to his age, and his Elizabethan audience correspondingly turns from a counter-image to an object of identification: it embodies self rather than other.

At different stages of Shakespeare's reception history, alterity and authenticity play different roles in the discourse on his original audience. The exact nature of that role depends not least on how far advanced Shakespeare's ascent to iconicity is at a given point in time. The situation of Alexander Pope and his immediate successors, still engaged in securing a place in the canon for Shakespeare, is not comparable to that of twentieth- and twenty-first-century critics who simply perpetuate (and in some cases can even afford to question) that prestige. If virtually every generation of Shakespeare critics since the late seventeenth century refers to the Elizabethan audience, it is under widely varying auspices. The concept of historical alterity proves far more useful in the early phases of Shakespeare's afterlife, when his claim to canonicity has yet to be established, and those features of his works that are not compatible with contemporary norms and values need to be explained away. Authenticity, by contrast, is ineffective in building and expanding cultural prestige. Embodiments of cultural identity need to be firmly established before the concept of authenticity can be used in the struggle for their meaning. While the early phases of the discourse on Shakespeare's Elizabethan audience thus routinely fashion Renaissance theatregoers as other, a kind of shorthand for Shakespeare's historical alterity, it is only in later phases of Shakespeare criticism that they come to guarantee the authenticity of a given interpretation of a play, or version of the Bard. This study, despite the inconveniences and inaccuracies necessarily entailed, is therefore structured diachronically. I look at the different versions of Shakespeare's original audience as produced by subsequent phases of Shakespeare criticism and, apart from some few exceptions, I have been very conservative in my periodisation as far as the first 300 years of Shakespeare criticism are concerned. With the beginning of the twentieth century, I distinguish between different 'schools' of thinking about the Elizabethan audience. Sometimes, but not always, these overlap with more conventional critical labels. The subject of my study is Shakespeare criticism from the beginnings to the present. This means that I have not looked, or at least not extensively, at representations of Shakespeare's audience in film or in historical fiction, and neither at the idea of early modern theatregoers marketed by the Original Practices movement.[23] I have limited myself mostly to Anglophone criticism; publications in other languages are referred to only when they have made a significant impact (usually in translation) on the British and/or American discourse.

I have consciously not included an account of the current state of research on early modern theatregoers,[24] for the simple reason that I wanted to avoid writing a Whig history of Shakespeare's first audiences – from the 'errors' of older criticism to the 'truth' as uncovered by us, the living. As far as I can see, every generation of critics since Dryden has credited itself with being in possession of the truth about Elizabethan audiences, regardless of the fact that this truth, at least from the perspective of a later-born observer, has always been a truth with a purpose. While this book necessarily charts some of the more vexing rhetorical impasses and logical cul-de-sacs of almost four hundred years of Shakespeare criticism, I have tried to avoid (and I very much hope I have been successful) a kind of faults-and-beauties approach to the scholarship of earlier generations. The Elizabethan audience has been used for purposes one would be hard pressed to describe as disinterested. But in studying these purposes and the ways in which they have been pursued, one cannot help but be impressed by the resourcefulness and sheer determination that scholars over the centuries have brought to the constitution, and continuous adaptation, of Shakespeare as a site of cultural meaning.

# 1
# Shakespeare's Elizabethan Audience in Seventeenth- and Eighteenth-century Shakespeare Criticism

A bare 50 years lie between Shakespeare's death in 1616 and the re-opening of the theatres after the Civil War. Nevertheless, a feeling of dissociation and historical distance is a *leitmotif* of post-Restoration discourses on Shakespeare and his age. The Civil War marked a decisive watershed not only in political, but also in cultural terms, and Shakespeare's times were regarded as belonging to another era altogether, one which had practically no continuities with the present.[1] That this present constituted an advance over the unenlightened and uncultivated past was a view widely held. In the field of culture and the arts, this perceived progress manifested itself primarily in a new 'refinement'. Where literature, more particularly the drama was concerned, many considered refinement a matter of adherence to the neoclassicist poetics imported from France. Meeting these new, or rather re-discovered, requirements concerning content and form was taken for a sign of cultivation, a marker both of the quality of the literary text and of the education of its author. Given these parameters, Shakespeare's disregard for neoclassicist rules posed a considerable problem for, in effect, a newly refined England was in the process of elevating an often patently unrefined author to the status of a national icon.

Because of the plays' presence on the Restoration stage and their enduring popularity, Shakespeare stood not so much for a new beginning as for historical continuity. But as both the period's editions and its adaptations of Shakespeare's works make clear, this persistence came at the price of often rather substantial changes to the received text. From the turn of the seventeenth century onwards, such attempts to align Shakespeare with current moral values and standards of taste were no longer restricted to the plays, but began to extend to the author himself, the man about to become the national poet. Correcting the perceived faults in Shakespeare's works was not sufficient: the age also felt a need to explain them, and to explain them in a manner which deflected all blame from the Bard himself. For Shakespeare's apologists, the commercial nature of the early modern stage offered what seemed the best of all possible excuses: as Shakespearean drama was a literary commodity available to everyone able to pay the comparably small entrance fee to the theatres, it seemed self-evident that this forced the Bard to cater to the likes and dislikes of his paying customers. This notion is integral to the so-called 'historical apology' for Shakespeare, that is the line of reasoning which explains the 'weaknesses' of his plays as resulting from his historical situation. Shakespeare's Elizabethan audience, as imagined by eighteenth-century critics, is the incarnation of this apology. It embodies everything about his age that post-Restoration England deemed objectionable. Pope's 'Preface of the Editor to the Works of Shakespeare' is a *locus classicus* for this argument:

> It must be allowed that Stage-Poetry of all other is more particularly levell'd to please the Populace, and its success more immediately dependent upon the Common Suffrage. One cannot therefore wonder, if Shakespeare, having at his first appearance no other aim in his writings than to procure a subsistence, directed his endeavours solely to hit the taste and humour that then prevailed.[2]

Material need forces Shakespeare to cater to the 'common suffrage', a circumstance which, according to Pope, has an extremely negative impact on his work. This is not least because Shakespeare's audience was primarily composed, or so Pope claims, of 'the meaner sort of people' – 'tradesmen', 'mechanicks', in short: the Elizabethan lower classes.[3] Pope's historical apology clearly includes a sociological one. It is not only the rude, semi-civilised age that is to blame for Shakespeare's shortcomings, it is a specific stratum of the Elizabethan population that keeps him from realising his full artistic potential. Nevertheless, the Bard is not entirely determined by his audience. Almost involuntarily, his genius keeps breaking through the maze of contemporary ideas of good drama. Even in the worst parts of his plays, Pope observes:

> [...] our Author's Wit buoys up, and is borne above his subject: his genius in those low parts is like some Prince of a Romance in disguise of a Shepherd or peasant: a certain Greatness and Spirit now and then break out, which manifests his higher extraction and qualities.[4]

That the dramatist's genius (the term 'prince' is yet another emphatic reminder that Shakespeare's better authorial self has nothing to do with the lower classes which allegedly populated his theatre) flashes up in such passages, but effectively fails to prevail against his age's errors in taste, Pope considers a result of the lack of sophistication even in the age's elites: '[n]ot only the common audience had no notion of the rules of writing, but few even of the better sort piqu'd themselves upon any great degree of knowledge or nicety that way.'[5] Nevertheless, he is convinced that Shakespeare's plays improve from the moment he gains the court's protection.[6] Literary quality is hence both instrumental to and a result of social differentiation: while the Elizabethan populace is blamed for those parts of the plays that Pope deems condemnable, the elements more in keeping with Augustan standards of taste testify to the influence of early modern elites. By allotting the 'better' Shakespeare to the upper echelons of society, Pope distances the Bard from the dangerously egalitarian world of the early modern theatre. This dissociation from the stage is then cemented by first differentiating between the poet and the dramatist, then constructing a well-neigh insurmountable opposition between the two. Shakespeare's faults, Pope maintains, 'are less to be ascribed to his wrong judgment as a Poet, than to his right judgment as a player.'[7] The 'bad', 'other' Shakespeare is equated with the world of demand-driven theatre.

In the *Dunciad*, Pope presents a similarly negative view of the contemporary stage. Theobald 'and others of equal genius' are accused of having brought the entertainments of Bartholomew Fair, 'the lowest diversions of the rabble in Smithfield', to the London Theatres, 'to be the reigning Pleasures of the Court and Town.'[8] The detrimental influence of this particular subsection of the populace emerges as a historical constant: both in the theatres of Pope's own day and age and in those of Shakespeare's times, it is the lower classes who are effectively to blame for the desolate state of the stage.[9] Pope's construction of a Shakespeare whose faults can be put down to the influence of the early modern proletariat excludes the Elizabethan lower classes, just like their Augustan counterparts, from a literary culture that deserves its name.

## Faults and beauties

The list of faults for which Shakespeare's original audiences were held responsible is long, and testifies to the neoclassicist influence on the period's Shakespeare criticism. His disregard for the unities, penchant for the tragicomical, lack of familiarity with classical authors, breaches of decorum, puns and apparent belief in (or at least representation of) the supernatural were all considered incompatible with the cultural standards of post-Restoration England. Their coexistence with the 'beauties' created a major difficulty for an overall evaluation of the Bard, and for assigning him a place in the cultural hierarchy of the new era. Dryden's lamentations to this effect are representative for a whole generation of critics: 'He [Shakespeare] is the very Janus of poets; he wears almost everywhere two faces; and you have scarce begun to admire the one, e're you despise the other.'[10]

The historical apology provided a way of handling this polarity. As the embodiment of Shakespeare's barbarous age, there is no 'fault' that the Elizabethan audience is not held responsible for and, like Pope, many critics make a point of not blaming the age as a whole, but rather the particular section of society that they assumed Shakespeare was writing for. Thomas Seward, in his preface to the 1750 edition of Beaumont and Fletcher's plays, claims:

> The Taste of [the] Age called aloud for the assistance of Ghosts and Sorcery to heighten the Horror of Tragedy; this Horror Beaumont and Fletcher had never felt, never heard of but with Contempt, and consequently they had no Arche-types in their own Breasts of what they were called to describe. Whereas Shakespeare from his low education had believ'd and felt all the Horrors he painted, for tho' the Universities and Inns of Court were in some degree freed from these Dreams of Superstition, the banks of the Avon were haunted on every Side.[11]

While Beaumont's and Fletcher's education enables them to transcend their historical situation and become beacons of progress, Shakespeare shares the mind-set of the unenlightened masses, shackled by the intellectual limitations of his period. On the whole, such content-related criticism is much rarer, however, than strictures against the plays' form, with objections against the various types of verbal exuberance being particularly widespread. Rhymes and puns were the primary targets, and almost unanimously condemned. On the Duke's rhymed summary of his plot against Angelo in *Measure for Measure* (III.1.481–502), Edward Capell writes:

> Speeches, and parts of speeches, in rime (some in measures properly lyrical, like the sententious one here) are found in all parts of Shakespeare; and should be looked upon as the time's vices,

sacrifices of judgement to profit, but not always unwilling ones; for such speeches are not of ill effect in all places, of which the present is an instance. But his lovers have cause to wish, notwithstanding, that he had less consider'd his audiences and comply'd less with their taste, for it happens but too often that constraints of rime or of measure operate badly on his expression, causing breaches of grammar, strange and scarce allowable ellipsis's, and usage of terms improper.[12]

As with Pope several decades earlier, the Elizabethan audience embodies the negative influence of his age on Shakespeare, while the commercial nature of the early modern theatre is presented as the main reason why its demands held such sway over the dramatist. The same pattern can be observed, again and again, when it comes to Shakespeare's puns: in the criticisms of Dryden (1672)[13], Gould (1685)[14], Echard (1694)[15], Rowe (1709)[16], Stubbes (1736)[17] and Grey (1754)[18]. 'A quibble, poor and barren as it is, gave him such delight, that he was content to purchase it by the sacrifice of reason, propriety, and truth. A quibble was to him the fatal Cleopatra for which he lost the world, and was content to lose it'[19], sighs Johnson in 1765. Theobald, writing in 1726, holds that 'flowers of Rhetorick' were thrown in '*ad captandum populum*; or, to use the Poet's own Phrase, *to set on some Quantity of barren Spectators to laugh at.*'[20] Again, those to blame for Shakespeare's lapses are described in socially definite terms: *populus* clearly refers not to the people in the sense of the totality of the population, but to the lower classes.

On the other side of the social spectrum, James I was sometimes blamed for Shakespeare's puns and quibbles, notably by Joseph Addison in the *Spectator*, who claims that James 'made very few Bishops or Privy-Counsellors that had not some time or other signalised themselves by a Clinch, or a Conundrum.'[21] Although he is well aware that few classical writers distinguish between 'puns' and 'true wit' (only Quintilianus and Longinus are credited with doing so), Addison nevertheless tasks modern authors with drawing this fine but decisive line. Unable to point to the authority of the classics in this particular case, he offers a more contractual model of why an abstention from punning should be considered binding: '[w]hen [the differentiation between puns and true wit] was settled, it was very natural for all Men of Sense to agree to it.'[22] A manifestation of cultured taste and enlightenment values, the preference for wit over puns, arbitrary as it may seem in some cases, is both natural and sensible. An agreement on how to distinguish the one from the other, Addison suggests, is therefore easy to reach: both 'nature' and 'sense' are elevated to the status of objective categories, as the authority of natural reason supplements, and ultimately supersedes, the authority of classical writers.

Like his puns and quibbles, Shakespeare's violations of the laws of probability are derided as concessions to the demands of his unrefined Elizabethan audience. Charles Gildon, for example, puts them down to 'the Ignorant Mode of the Age in which he [Shakespeare] liv'd',[23] though he accedes that Shakespeare faced a dilemma. While he recognised that the dramatic conventions of his own day and age were inadequate (as proof, Gildon cites the respective chorus's references to the frequent changes of place in *Pericles* and the imperfect depiction of the battle scenes in *Henry V*), he was unaware of any alternative. Had he adhered to the neoclassical rules, Gildon claims, Shakespeare's plays would be 'far more noble'.[24] This verdict points towards the much-discussed question of Shakespeare's (classical) learning. If and to what extent the Bard was familiar with the authors of Ancient Greece and Rome was one of the most hotly debated issues in eighteenth-century Shakespeare criticism. His (albeit rather loose) adherence to the unities of time, place and plot in *The Tempest* and *The Merry Wives of Windsor* seemed to suggest that he was aware of Aristotle's corresponding rule. But if this was the case, the fact that he disregarded it in his other plays required an explanation – a considerable difficulty, which was usually resolved by citing the likes and dislikes of the Elizabethan audience: '[Shakespeare's] *Merry Wives of Windsor* demonstrates how much he acted against his better judgement, when he stretched his wings into the extravagance of popular prepossessions.'[25] That this argument was usually constructed with its end (to rescue Shakespeare from a possible loss of prestige) rather than with its plausibility in mind is apparent from the peculiar vagueness of the relationship between Shakespeare and his original audience. With most critics, it is never made quite clear just *how* alienated Shakespeare felt from the rabble that flocked to the Globe, and why his alleged intellectual superiority over his clientele had so little impact on his works. Elizabeth Montagu is a case in point. Writing on the last act of *3 Henry VI*, she states:

> Our author, by following minutely the chronicles of the times, has embarrassed his drama's [sic] with too great a number of persons and events. The hurley-burley of these plays recommended them to a rude illiterate audience, who, as he says, loved a noise of targets. His poverty, and the low condition of the stage (which at that time was not frequented by persons of rank) obliged him to this complaisance;

and unfortunately he had not been tutored by any rules of art, or informed by acquaintance with just and regular drama's [sic].[26]

Whether a Shakespeare more versed in the classics would have been able to transcend the 'low condition of the stage' remains unclear, especially because the word 'complaisance' implies that he was in fact aware of what would have constituted a better drama. This is a conception of Shakespeare that, on the one hand, elevates him to the status of a time-transcending genius able to envision a stage reformed according to the postulates of the ancients, while on the other hand it denies him any possibility of acting on this vision – because of material constraints. As such, it is indicative of a fundamental ambivalence towards the commodification of art, a field in which the eighteenth century saw massive change. While aristocratic patronage was increasingly on the wane, the writing and reading of literary texts was slowly turning into a market economy. A significant part of Montagu's contemporaries saw this as a regrettable deterioration of literary culture and feared that the writer's dedication to his art would be sullied by financial considerations, and irreparable damage to the aesthetic and moral authority of literature would ensue.[27] One significant factor in this anticipated loss of prestige was the newly broadened literary public. Even before the Civil War, authors obviously did not write exclusively for the one educated, aristocratic and wealthy patron to whom the work was dedicated; now, however, they had to reach comparably large parts of the population in order to make a living. For critics like Montagu, this constituted a potential threat to the quality of the literary text, as they saw a direct correspondence between the intellectual level of the work and the intellectual level of its target audience. Within this framework, the quality of drama as a 'popular' art form is directly dependent on the quality of the people's education. For Montagu, this nexus effectively explains why Shakespeare does not follow the classical model:

> Shakespeare's plays were to be acted in a paltry tavern, to an unlettered audience, just emerging from barbarity: the Greek tragedies were to be exhibited at the public charge, under the care and auspices of the magistrates of Athens; where the very populace were critics in wit, and connoisseurs in public spectacles.[28]

If Shakespeare is to be styled into a symbol of national identity, it seems fitting – as later critics indeed do – to explain the greatness of his works as a result of their expressing a national character that all Englishmen have in common, irrespective of their social standing. Montagu, by contrast, creates a national icon that is defined by his dissociation from the people. It seems impossible to think of the latter as a positive factor in the creation of literary artefacts unless distanced to the historically distant realm of classical Athens (and even there, 'the care and auspices of the magistrates' presumably played a decisive role). This has a direct impact on the debate over Shakespeare's adherence to the three unities and his classical learning. Where an assumed knowledge of Aristotelian poetics implies that Shakespeare must have made concessions to the taste of his uncouth contemporaries, such knowledge is often vehemently denied. Benjamin Heath, for one, was clearly not happy with the thought:

> [...] [W]hat does the poet get by this illjudged illiberality towards him? Only the imputation of a sneaking submission to the ignorance and unimproved taste of the age he lived in, when he himself had it in his power by the superior knowledge we would attribute to him to have instructed, and by the unrivalled ascendency [sic] of his genius, which is indisputable, to have reformed it.[29]

John Dennis minced his words even less: '[...] he who allows that *Shakespeare* had learning and a familiar Acquaintance with the Ancients, ought to be look'd upon as a Detractor from his extraordinary Merit, and from the Glory of *Great Britain*.'[30] Shakespeare's failure to conform to neoclassical rules is declared an integral part of his specifically British form of genius. This remains a minority position however. Most critics prefer the idea of a total dissociation between Shakespeare on the one hand and his lower-class audiences on the other. In the most influential of the period's historical apologies for Shakespeare, Nicholas Rowe presents an Elizabethan Age whose utter barbarity left Shakespeare without any opportunity to transcend his historical situation. At the same time, the age's very lack of culture makes it an ideal foil for the dramatist's genius. In the dark night of the Elizabethan stage, Shakespeare's star shines all the brighter, or, as Rowe puts it: '[w]hen one considers that there is not one play before him of a reputation good enough to entitle it to an appearance on the present Stage, it cannot but be a matter of great wonder that he should advance dramatick Poetry so far as he did.'[31]

By putting down Shakespeare's 'faults' to the requirements of his uncultivated lower-class audience, seventeenth- and eighteenth-century Shakespeare criticism succeeds not only in defending Shakespeare against the strictures of neoclassicism, but in claiming him for their own standards and values. Taste and politeness, disregarded by Shakespeare under what the period's leading critics saw as the pernicious influence of his original audience, were central elements in the collective identity of the new social elites. At least theoretically, attaining them was a matter of education rather than inheritance: 'Conversation with Men of Polite Genius', being familiar with 'the Writings of the most Polite Authors' and 'well versed in the Works of the best *Criticks* both Ancient and Modern'[32] were ways of cultivating refinement potentially open to everyone. This idea of self-improvement, suggests a model of both individual and social progress typical of the Whig interpretation of history. Although eighteenth-century commentators tend to downplay their political dimension, the import of taste and politeness clearly transcends the purely aesthetic; in fact, their rise can be read as a direct reaction to the experience of the Civil War. As a form of self-regulation, politeness encourages moderation on both the personal and the political level, while taste provides aesthetic and moral guidelines that further increase social cohesion.[33] The relevance of the latter thus goes far beyond the realm of sophisticated living and good manners. Situated at the intersection of the private and the public, taste is a manifestation of political responsibility.[34]

When considered against this backdrop, the view of the Elizabethan audience prevalent during the late seventeenth and early eighteenth century emerges as a way of reinforcing some core elements of a post-Civil War national identity by defining its opposite. The Elizabethan audience is everything that the England of Pope and Addison is not. Its very rudeness offers a rationale for the Civil War; its very otherness guarantees that history won't repeat itself. The nature of its alleged composition, however, the fact that it is presented as decidedly lower class by such a vast majority of critics, serves purposes that have little to do with a diachronic definition of the new society's collective identity, but instead are clearly concerned with the present. In effect, the Elizabethan audience as imagined by eighteenth-century scholars is a vehicle of internal differentiation for those critics' own day and age. While refinement and taste serve as indicators of a person's superior social standing, the period's lower classes are described as similarly uncivilised, coarse and effectively 'unrefineable' as were the (allegedly) lower-class spectators that flocked to Shakespeare's Globe. English national culture has no place for *hoi polloi* in either their Elizabethan or their Augustan incarnation. Dryden's prologue to *Cleomenes*, to give but one example, leaves little doubt about the author's intended audience:

> I Think or hope, at least, the Coast is clear,
> That none but Men of Wit and Sence are here;
> That our Bear-Garden Friends are all away
> Who bounce with Hands and Feet and cry Play, Play
> Who to save Coach-hire, trudge along the Street,
> then print our Matted Seats with dirty Feet;
> Who, while we speak, make Love to Orange Wenches,
> And between Acts stand strutting on the Benches:
> Where got a Cock-horse, making vile Grimaces,
> They to the Boxes show their Booby Faces.
> A Merry-Andrew, such a Mob will serve,
> And treat them with such Wit as they deserve:
> Let 'em go people Ireland, where there's need
> Of such new Planters to repair the Breed;
> Or to Virginia or Jamaica Steer,
> But have a care of some French Privateer;
> For if they should become the Prize of Battle,
> they'll take 'em Black and White for Irish Cattle.[35]

About to become an institution of high culture, the stage as envisaged by Dryden seeks to attract the wealthy (who need not save expenses on transport) and demands a newly controlled physicality. Dirty feet on the theatre seats, lively gesticulating, cries of 'Play, play!', animated facial expressions and (verbal) eroticism (the reference to the orange wenches is virtually *de rigeur*) are all relegated to the realm of a newly stigmatised popular culture, which Dryden even likens to the bestial ('Irish Cattle'). If the behaviour of the 'Bear-Garden Friends' is rejected as inappropriate for the English mother country, but accepted (albeit sarcastically) as fitting the conventions of colonies like Ireland, Virginia or Jamaica, this is an indicator of the intentions that underlie Dryden's polemics. Clearly, there is little interest in imparting one's own refinement to society as a whole. Instead, the speaker sets himself above large parts of the population, an attitude that is mirrored in his understanding of the colonial project. While the official version, until well into the twentieth century, stressed the civilising mission of the colonisers, Dryden's speaker unabashedly locates the benefits of colonialism on the side of the mother country: in an act of national self-cleansing, unwanted elements are conveniently disposed of in the colonies. The public sphere envisioned here is defined primarily by what it is *not*, with the Restoration theatre a prime site for the operation of such mechanisms of exclusion. Here, authors 'took up the task of transforming the mixed and unruly body inherited from the Renaissance into attentive citizens'[36] and began to propagate a binary view of cultural production and consumption in which the newly invented categories of 'high' and 'low' did not mix – at least in theory. Post-Restoration views of Shakespeare's original audience can be seen as one way of giving this theory the semblance of actual fact. By presenting Elizabethan theatregoers as uncultured and rude, the opposition between high and popular culture is projected onto the time before the Civil War. That way, the existence of two distinct cultural realms can be presented as a transhistorical given.

## Nature, the nation and the Elizabethan theatregoer

While the faults-and-beauties-approach and the neoclassicist strain in the period's discussions of Shakespeare offer a convenient explanation for the genesis of this particular stereotype of Shakespeare's Elizabethan audience, other factors complicate the period's seemingly one-dimensional idea of Renaissance theatregoers. And even though there is an obvious connection between this version of the Bard's early modern clientele and neoclassicist strictures against him, neoclassicism is inadequately described as the dominant influence on the Shakespeare criticism of the long eighteenth century. Although Shakespeare's defenders did see a need to react to continental diatribes (Voltaire being a case in point, though Voltaire's rejection of Shakespeare is not as absolute as the period's critics tend to assume[37]), as well as to the harsh criticism of a Dennis or Rymer, Shakespeare's prestige, as Brian Vickers points out, was already too great for the neoclassicists to do it significant damage.[38] Furthermore, 'the neoclassicists' were not the homogeneous school that later ages have wanted to see them as, and their championing of the rules was much more resolute when it came to modern drama than when it came to Shakespeare. For the majority of the period's critics, the Bard's 'natural genius' legitimised the liberties he took regarding the form and content of his plays.[39]

'Natural genius' – a category invented 'in order to account for what was peculiar about Shakespeare'[40] – factors significantly into the period's discourse on Shakespeare's Elizabethan audience. If Shakespeare's failure to adhere to the rules is both apostrophised as 'nature' and explained as a concession to the tastes of early modern theatregoers, the two equations behind these arguments (lack of art equals nature and lack of art equals the age and its audience) produce a potential third one in which the rude, uncultured Elizabethan age and its uncouth audience equal nature. As the defining characteristic of (Shakespeare's) genius, nature has positive connotations, giving rise to a practically irre-solvable but largely unacknowledged contradiction. If the Elizabethan audience embodies nature in the same way that Shakespeare does, it can no longer be denounced as a detrimental influence on his work. In consequence, Shakespeare can no longer be claimed for the upper echelons of society: if the Elizabethan rabble assembled at the Globe is 'nature', then Shakespeare the natural genius fundamentally belongs to that rabble. Genius, as Jonathan Bate puts it, 'is no respecter of rank'.[41]

The logical impasses inherent in using the historical apology along-side a defence of natural genius suggest two parallel and sometimes conflicting processes in the formation of an English national identity after the Civil War. On the one hand, this identity is defined against rival nations, particularly against France and 'French' neoclassicism. Here, nature stands for an intuitive concept of literature, an expression of the nation's characteristic 'love of liberty'. But on the other hand, English national identity is also defined against the nation's own past, in which an all-too natural state of society, with the accompanying lack of culture, civilisation and refinement, supposedly led to the Civil War that the nation now urgently needs to forget – a desire that is well served by turning the Renaissance into a new Dark Ages. This need for dissociation is not, however, all-encompassing. The period's elevation of Shakespeare to the status of a national icon attests to a yearning for continuity, even if the very existence of a link to the past sometimes appears to be more important than the precise nature of that link. While Shakespeare as an abstract entity comes to embody the quintessence of Englishness, his works are divided into faults and beauties, that is, into 'real' Shakespeare on the one hand and 'bad' Shakespeare on the other: an attitude towards the text which is hardly affirmative. Whether the otherness of the past or its continuity with the present is foregrounded depends on the needs of the individual critic and his argument.

Ideas of natural genius aside, neoclassicism itself, at least implicitly, offered an alternative approach to Shakespeare's Elizabethan audience. In keeping with the Horatian maxim of *prodesse et delectare*, it sees lit-erature as a means of educating the public. This turns the poet into a teacher as well as an artist: rather than blindly catering to the demands of his audience, he is to better its tastes in a manner which will make it more and more like the ideal audience in which neoclassicism sees the proper addressee of all literary endeavours. Within this didactic framework, however, the end is understood to justify the means: what ultimately legitimises neoclassicist rules is the effect that heeding them (allegedly) has on the audience. Where that effect is produced, the rules are of secondary importance – at least for the majority of British critics. Johnson writes:

> Almost all [of Shakespeare's] plays are divided between serious and ludicrous characters, and, in the successive evolutions of the design, sometimes produce seriousness and sorrow, and sometimes levity and laughter. That this is a practice contrary to the rules of criticism will be readily allowed; but there is always an appeal open to criticism from nature. The end of writing is to instruct, the end of poetry is to instruct by pleasing. That the mingled drama may convey all the instruction of a tragedy or comedy cannot be denied [...].[42]

In a sense, neoclassicism itself thus provides an excuse for ignoring neoclassicist rules, for it is not some abstract set of formal requirements, but the audience's actual reaction which is the touchstone of the poet's art. The audience is thus not limited to the subordinate role of a learner. As the ultimate authority on the success of a writer's endeavours, it occupies a far more equal position vis-à-vis the poet. Eighteenth-century critics exploited this to construe yet another apology for Shakespeare's more liberal approach to the drama, one in which his original audience plays an entirely different part than it does in the faults-and-beauties approach. Here, it provides a tangible reason why Shakespeare's breaches of the neoclassicist rules are not to be condemned: this was the best, and perhaps only way of achieving the desired effect with his contemporaries. This is an argument frequently put forward to excuse Shakespeare's disregard of the unities – an indicator both of the incomplete acceptance of neoclassicist poetics in England and of the anti-French impulse that often informed it. Already in 1694, Dryden's dedicatory letter to *Love Triumphant* describes neglect of the unities as a defining feature of English drama, because 'tis agreeable to the *English* genius. We love variety more than any other Nation; and so long as the Audience will not be pleased without it, the Poet is oblig'd to Humour them.'[43] Other neoclassicts, Charles Gildon among them, also adduce English national character as the reason why adherence to the three unities is not necessarily required in English drama, citing 'love of liberty' alongside 'love of variety' as the defining characteristics of English taste.[44] The Bard's mixing of genres is often explained in a similar manner. 'So convinced was Shakespeare', Thomas Davies claims, 'that his countrymen could not be satisfied with their dramatic exhibitions without some mixture of merriment that, in his most serious plays, he has thrown in characters of levity or oddity to enliven the scene.'[45] The ultimate justification for the legitimacy of this procedure is provided by the fact that 'these characters and scenes never fail to produce the same effect at this day [...]'.[46] Johnson's 'nature' finds its embodiment in Davies' nationalist version of Shakespeare's original audience. Not only is Shakespeare's disregard for the rules (in this case, the ban on mixed genres) vindicated by the effect his plays (supposedly) had on early modern audiences, the Bard also proves visionary in his anticipation of the fact that they will affect later – English – audiences in just the same way. By catering to the tastes of his contemporaries, Shakespeare also caters to the demands of the transhistorical ideal audience. Crucially, both audiences are characterised primarily by their nationality ('his countrymen'). No longer a hetero-stereotype, they embody the national taste in drama, serving not as a foil for the nation's new collective identity but as an object of identification.

This, however, was still a minority position. Both neoclassicism and the aesthetics of genius (*Genieästhetik*) essentially placed the writer outside or above society, albeit to varying degrees. The neoclassicist view of the poet as teacher, while integrating him into the community, presupposes superior insight on his part – to be imparted to his less enlightened contemporaries. Genius, by contrast, is characterised by its ability to create from within itself. Strictly speaking, neither permits an apology for the author on the basis of his historical situation, as transcending the latter is seen as either his central task or as what defines his genius in the first place. The poet-teacher's first obligation is to his superior judgment, the poetical genius's to his quintessential autonomy, which is why a majority of critics defines Shakespeare in opposition to his contemporaries. Some, however, claim he made efforts to educate the latter – probably not least out of a desire to strengthen the Bard's moral credentials. Guthrie proposes:

> While the stage was thus over-run with ignorance, impertinence and the lowest quibble, our immortal Shakespear arose. But supposing him to have produced a commission from that heaven whence he derived his genius, for the reformation of the stage, what could he do in the circumstances he was under? He did all that man, and more than any man but himself could do. He was obliged, indeed, to strike in with the peoples [sic] favourite passion for the clangor of arms,

and the MARVELLOUS of exhibition, but he improved, he embellished, he ennobled it. [...] But are we to imagine that Shakespear could reform the taste of the people into chastity? No; they had the full, the wanton, enjoyment of his genius, when irregular; and they were both too uninformed, and too incontinent, to exchange LUXURY for ELEGANCE. This would, undoubtedly, have been the case, even supposing Shakespear to have attempted a reformation of the drama. But I believe he attempted none.[47]

Several of the unresolved contradictions that riddle the period's notion of the relationship between Shakespeare and his Elizabethan audience are apparent here. Shakespeare's genius is clearly conceived as metaphysical in nature; nevertheless, he fails at instigating even a half-hearted reform of the stage. This is slightly embarrassing given the almost heroic rhetoric Guthrie uses in describing his endeavours: 'he improved, he embellished, he ennobled it' – *veni, vidi, vici*? No wonder Guthrie eventually prefers the idea of the Bard not even having attempted a reform, even though this entails viewing the relationship between him and his audience in commercial rather than in didactic terms. That this has ethical implications, rather than solely aesthetic ones, is never openly acknowledged, but is obvious from Guthrie's wording: 'chastity', 'luxury' and 'wanton[ness]' are terms reminiscent of Puritan rhetoric. For Guthrie, as for a majority of his contemporaries, thinking of Shakespeare as a literary entrepreneur was patently unacceptable. [48]

In fact, the Bard's alleged readiness to cater to the demands of an audience essentially unworthy of him poses a considerable threat to his new status as a national culture hero, and critics attempted to deflect it in various ways. Some declared Shakespeare's ability to comply with the tastes of his audience an integral part of his genius. Discussing the supernatural elements in *Macbeth*, Arthur Murphy (perhaps best known for his 1801 *Life of David Garrick*) maintains that Shakespeare 'has selected his infernal Ceremonies with the utmost Judgment. He artfully conforms to vulgar Opinions and Traditions [...].'[49] Though Murphy is following Johnson's note XXXV on *Macbeth* IV, 1 almost verbatim, the notion of 'artful conformity' is new, particularly the sense of accomplishment that it conveys. Shakespeare is familiar with the superstitions of his audience and consciously includes them in his work, but not completely determined by his historical situation: his superior insight or education (Murphy does not specify which) takes him one step above his 'vulgar' audience. Like many others, Murphy has little doubt about the social standing of spectators at the Globe, but that does not keep him from envisioning a more or less harmonious relationship between Shakespeare and his clientele. This makes him an exception among eighteenth-century critics, the majority of whom prefer to dissociate the Bard, at least emotionally and cognitively, from a theatre more or less tacitly acknowledged as being governed by the rules of the marketplace. Rowe, for example, sees 'a disgust he had taken at the then ill taste of the Town, and the mean condition of the Stage'[50] as the reason behind Shakespeare's retreat to Stratford at the end of his career. Montagu diagnoses a similar revulsion on the part of each and every Renaissance dramatist.[51]

Only a small handful of critics do not see the reason for Shakespeare's weaknesses in his dependence on the Elizabethan audience, and those that put the blame elsewhere generally diagnose a different set of 'faults' than most of their contemporaries. John Upton's *Critical Observations on Shakespeare* has no objections to Shakespeare's neglect of the neoclassical rules, yet laments the effects of his dependence on patronage: 'One could wish that Shakespeare was as free from flattery as Sophocles and Euripides. But our liberty was then in its dawn, so that some pieces of flattery which we find in Shakespeare must be ascribed to the times.'[52] In a manner that was to become seminal for later writers, Upton's wish for a more independent Shakespeare is conjoined with a strong anti-French impulse which manifests itself in an attack on both the neoclassicist rules and the alleged effeminateness of French culture in general. Unlike many of his contemporaries, Upton subscribed to a regressive view of history. Combined with his particular brand of nationalism, this entailed an exceedingly positive view of the Elizabethan age and its theatregoers: while the people as assembled at the public theatres are presented as a stronghold of English values, the decadent court of James I is blamed for Shakespeare's lapses, as well as for the eventual decline of a genuinely English literary culture. Other critics share this view of the age as representing a still unsullied state of 'pure' Englishness.[53] But while they concur with Upton in presenting Shakespeare as a representative of national character 'before the fall', as it were, most are socially restrictive in a manner that Upton is not: described as mixed or unambiguously lower-class, the Elizabethan audience is clearly meant to evoke negative associations. Shakespeare's tribute to the tastes of his contemporaries is seen as a 'sacrifice of virtue to convenience'[54] or a 'sacrifice of judgement to profit'[55] by the vast majority of Upton's coevals. Montagu's lack of forbearance regarding these concessions is entirely representative:

Shakespeare is never more worthy of the true critic's censure, than in those instances, in which he complies with false pomp of manners. It was pardonably in a man of his rank, not to be more polite and delicate than his contemporaries; but we cannot so easily excuse such superiority of talents for stooping to any affectation.[56]

Obviously, attesting Shakespeare, this not inconsiderable weakness of character was vastly preferable to thinking of him as sharing the aesthetic and moral standards of his audience. To a modern observer, this can seem puzzling, though perhaps less so when one considers this bias as part of a basic mechanism of cultural appropriation in which Shakespeare's judgment is implicitly equated with the respective writer's own. That way, the Bard vouches for the transhistorical rightness of current values, in this case, those of post-Civil War and later Enlightenment England. Individual as well as collective identity is thus secured against the challenges of historical relativism, for, if Shakespeare acts against his own better knowledge rather than simply according to his own – yet different – standards, then this better knowledge, even if it is never put into practice, is valorised as an apt foundation for current processes of identity formation.

Significantly, Shakespeares's elevation to the status of a national icon goes hand in hand with an increasing monopolisation of authority over the meaning of his texts: more and more, interpretation of the Bard is shifted from the theatre (where the audience's collusion is indispensable) to the realm of critical analysis and exegesis. In the period's editions, Shakespeare increasingly comes to stand 'for the values of the printed book as against oral tradition and the spoken word [...]: a poet whom critics and scholars wished to see as an embodiment of natural genius, a brilliant individual, rather than as a social function.'[57] This brilliant individual was much easier to appropriate for the social elites than the man of the theatre would have been. But at the same time as it fashions Shakespeare into an author-god accessible only to the initiated, eighteenth-century criticism also constructs a dramatist forced to supply what the Elizabethan audience demands of him, a writer deprived of authority over his own texts. Shakespeare's text is truly his only where he conforms to eighteenth-century aesthetic standards. Where he fails to do so, his ownership is insistently denied. On the surface, it may seem to pass into the hands of the Elizabethan audience; in reality, however, it is claimed for the period's newly-formed intellectual elites.

## The audience as *topos*

By the beginning of the eighteenth century, neoclassicist poetics began to lose what clout they had had among English Shakespeare critics, as did the historical apology. In Theobald's preface to his 1733 edition, the usual comment on the 'barbarity' of Shakespeare's age is already presented in a much attenuated form. Though he cites deference to the reigning taste as a possible reason for the plays' perceived weaknesses, he also points out that '[t]he Genius that gives us the greatest Pleasure, sometimes stands in Need of our Indulgence'.[58] Theobald does not fail to mention his *own* age's lapses in taste, a fact which somewhat vitiates his negative view of the time when Shakespeare was writing. Unlike Dryden, who had proclaimed a total dissociation between his own age and the one preceding it, Theobald adopts a more gradual view of the historical progress made by the nation since Shakespeare's death. A similar tendency can be observed in Johnson, who blames Shakespeare's penchant for the marvellous on the demands of the 'rude people' assembled at the Globe, but also claims that by writing in this manner, the Bard has 'perhaps excelled all but *Homer* in securing the first purpose of a writer, by exciting restless and unquenchable curiosity and compelling him that reads [!] his work to read it through'.[59] At a first glance, Johnson retains the conventional view both of Shakespeare's 'faults' and of the early modern audience. By mentioning Homer, and by giving Shakespeare credit for having served 'the first purpose of a writer', however, the Bard and his plays are granted intrinsic value, regardless of their failure to conform to the demands of neoclassicism. The Elizabethan audience is similarly rehabilitated. Since reactions to Shakespearean drama have hardly changed since the Bard's lifetimes, Renaissance theatregoers approximate the transhistorical, ideal audience envisaged by neoclassicism. Whereas the majority of Shakespeare's apologists start with Shakespeare's breaches of neoclassicist rule, then invents an audience to account for these breaches, Johnson proceeds the other way round. His starting point is Shakespeare's enduring success with audiences over time. As Shakespeare's disregard for the rules has not affected his efficacy as a dramatist, the universal validity of the rules is called into question. The (transhistorical) audience, rather than the neoclassicist critic, makes or breaks Shakespeare's reputation. While Johnson still uses the past for apologetic purposes, he does not use it exclusively for that end:

> When a writer outlives his contemporaries, and remains almost the only unforgotten name of a distant time, he is necessarily obscure. [...] [Shakespeare] copied the manners of the world then passing before him, and has more allusions than other poets to the traditions and superstitions of the vulgar; which must therefore be traced before he can be understood.[60]

The fact that knowledge of Shakespeare's historical circumstances considerably contributes to an understanding of his work is accepted: the 'traditions and superstitions' of Elizabethan theatregoers must be 'traced before he can be understood'. This does not entail any recognition of their intrinsic validity though. Like the majority of his contemporaries, Johnson considers Shakespeare's original audience to have been lower class and therefore necessarily uncultivated ('the vulgar'). That these people need to be understood in order to understand Shakespeare does not mean that Johnson cannot continue to deplore them. This attitude foreshadows Malone, who, as Margareta de Grazia has shown, approaches Shakespeare's text as a historical document, a witness to the aesthetic standards of its *own* times. Instead of treating the past as an amorphous mass, Malone isolates a distinct 'age of Shakespeare' with its own standards and conventions. But while historical relativism governs his explanation of Shakespeare, essentialism continues to rule supreme when it comes to judging him.[61] For Malone, as for Johnson, Shakespeare's concessions to an uncultivated lower-class audience remain a historical fact, even though their rejection of neoclassicism renders the historical apology redundant.[62]

# 2
## 'No man of genius ever wrote for the mob': Shakespeare's Elizabethan Audience and Romantic Shakespeare Criticism

With the inception of the Romantic movement, the factors that governed the discourse on Shakespeare's Elizabethan audience changed fundamentally. Romanticism redefined concepts like authorship and, even more basically, literature as such, and it did so using Shakespeare as its prime example. Unlike with the neoclassicists, Shakespeare was not criticised from a pre-existing concept of literature, but was himself a key influence in the development of the Romantics' literary program: 'the great exception' became 'the great exemplum'.[1] The extent to which this great exemplum stood in need of apology decreased significantly, and so did the frequency with which critics referred to the Elizabethan audience in order to account for any perceived 'faults' in Shakespeare. But the transition of Shakespeare from an exception to an exemplar was not the only reason his original auditors played a more marginal role during this period: another was the changed attitude towards the place where he earned his living. Where the previous generation of critics had shown a marked distaste for the *Elizabethan* stage (and its audiences), the Romantics in general had little time for the stage as such. Notwithstanding the fact that their predecessors had habitually excused what they saw as the Bard's blemishes as concessions to the requirements of Renaissance theatregoers, many opined that Shakespeare had not written for the stage in the first place.[2] An institution governed by the rules of the marketplace and actually dependent on the approval of its paying customers could only appear hostile to the expression of poetic genius, which the Romantics worshipped with quasi-religious fervour.[3] The much-quoted 'turn from stage to page' is part of a larger development that redefines Shakespeare as a poet to be read rather than a playwright to be produced. It was a long-term process of canon-formation in the vernacular languages in which:

> [...] a select group of honoured works in the modern literatures played an increasing role as alternatives to commercialized mass culture. [...] Samuel Johnson had defined his high evaluation of Shakespeare in response to the question of what 'can please many, and please long'. Shakespeare, it began to seem, offered a 'higher', 'deeper', overall more challenging and difficult experience than the term pleasure conveys.[4]

The terms 'challenging' and 'difficult' are highly significant, for they point towards a third factor in the Romantic discourse on Shakespeare's early modern audiences: the fact that the Romantics, or at least a considerable proportion of them, did not think of Shakespeare as belonging to the general public, regardless of how much the movement prided itself on its rediscovery, and revaluation, of 'the people' and their culture. That some of the leading Romantics (continue to) see the Bard as part of a socially exclusive high culture explains why references to his original audience, when they actually occur, do so in a virtually unchanged form. Charles Lamb writes on *Richard III*: 'Shakespeare has not made Richard so black a Monster, as is supposed. Wherever he is monstrous, it was to conform to vulgar opinion. But he is generally a man.'[5] Similarly, William Wordsworth contends:

> A dramatic Author, if he writes for the stage, must adapt himself to the taste of the audience, or they will not endure him [.] [...] At all events, that Shakespeare stooped to accommodate himself to the People, is sufficiently apparent; and one of the most striking proofs of his almost omnipotent genius is, that he could turn to such glorious purpose those materials which the preposessions of the age compelled him to make use of. Yet even this marvellous skill appears not to have been enough to prevent his rivals from having some advantage over him in public estimation; else how can we account for passages and scenes that exist in his works; unless upon a supposition that some of the grossest of them, a fact which in my own mind I have no doubt of, were foisted in by the Players, for the gratification of the many?[6]

The affinity with the people proclaimed in the *Preface to Lyrical Ballads* apparently does not rule out a traditionally negative view of 'the people' as assembled in Shakespeare's theatre. The *Preface* itself is ambiguous towards those echelons of society from which Wordsworth and Samuel Taylor Coleridge profess to have taken their inspiration. Not only does it mention the 'real defects' and 'lasting and rational causes of dislike and disgust'[7] in the language of the simple folk, it also states quite clearly that 'the people' is not automatically to be equalled with the lower classes. Its view of the urban working classes is hardly complimentary.[8] While, on the one hand, Wordsworth sides with simple country folk, he explicitly turns against urban massification and the city proletariat. The *Preface*'s identification with the people is not a partisanship with the lower classes in general, but an often rather nostalgic espousal of certain pre-industrial lifestyles that were already beginning to disappear. The Romantics' attitude towards 'the people' is deeply ambivalent, a fact that their comments on the popular theatre of Shakespeare's day and age amply bear out. Two of the most influential Romantic Shakespeare critics write extensively on the Bard's contemporaries: Hazlitt and Coleridge. Even more markedly than with the neoclassicists, their – widely discrepant – conceptions of Shakespeare's Elizabethan audience are informed by their political allegiances.

## Coleridge and Shakespeare's Elizabethan audience

Coleridge's role as regards the discourse on Renaissance theatregoers is perhaps best described as that of a conservative innovator. In opposition to the vast majority of eighteenth-century critics, he sees Shakespeare neither as subject to the demands of the marketplace nor as 'pure nature'. Instead he focuses on his exceptional poetical judgment, on his intentional artistry – a view of the Bard which is incompatible with excusing isolated elements of his plays as concessions to his original audience as this would imply that the 'faults' were intentionally integrated into the text. A Shakespeare prepared to degrade his works in this way could not easily be styled as the author-god which many Romantics wished to see in him. In his integrated view of Shakespearean drama, Coleridge therefore does not categorically distinguish between 'faults' and 'beauties', but attempts to place the elements formerly criticised within an all-encompassing authorial intention. His organic vision of the Shakespeare canon explicitly includes those elements of the plays which the neoclassicists had criticised with particular vigour, such as Shakespeare's clowns and fools. In one of his lectures, Coleridge states: 'Shakespeare at the same time that he accommodated himself to the taste of the times employed [the comic figure] to a most terrible effect in heightening the mysery [sic] of the most distressing scenes.'[9] While admitting that Shakespeare attempted to meet the demands of his audience ('the taste of the times'), Coleridge immediately puts these concessions into perspective by pointing out their dramatic effectiveness and their artistic quality. Shakespeare yields to the demands of early modern theatregoers only where they can be integrated into his overall conception of a given play. Effectively, these concessions are thus not concessions at all: Shakespeare is emphatically *not* writing down to his audiences. Accordingly, Coleridge makes a strong case against earlier attempts to 'excuse' Shakespeare on such grounds:

> Coleridge went on to ridicule the modern commentators still further asserting that they only exercised the most vulgar of all feelings – that of wonderment – They had maintained that Shakespeare was an irregular poet that he was now above all praise and now if possible below contempt & they reconciled it by saying that he wrote for the mob. – No man of genius ever wrote for the mob – he never would consciously write that which was below himself. Careless he might be or he might write at a time when his better genius did not attend him but he never wrote anything that he knew would degrade him. Were it so, as well might a man pride himself on acting the beast [...].[10]

Coleridge rejects the traditional association between Shakespeare's perceived faults and the assumed demands of his Elizabethan audience, not only because it is incompatible with his idea of genius, but also because it situates Shakespeare in a social context in which he does not wish to see him. That he speaks of Elizabethan theatregoers as a 'mob' is unsurprising given that by this point, Coleridge had turned his back on the French revolution. Under the impression of the events in Paris, any crowd, particularly an allegedly lower-class one, could appear a potential source of trouble, 'the dire murmuring and strange consternation which precedes the storm or earthquake of national discord.'[11]

Coleridge clearly recognises the sociological dimension of the historical apology established by the previous generation of critics. Although his views of Shakespeare and of literature in general differ fundamentally from those of the neoclassicists – Coleridge sees few 'faults' that need accounting for – he continues to dissociate Shakespeare from the popular theatre of his age, albeit, as we shall see, in a modified manner. This is a seminal move in the ongoing appropriation of Shakespeare for 'high culture', and for those echelons of society who claimed 'high culture' as their own – precisely the people to whom Coleridge's lectures were addressed.[12] To these audiences, as well as to the poet himself, the Elizabethan age as presented by Coleridge offered a blueprint on which to model the intellectual life of the present:

> There was, in truth, an energy in the age, an energy of thinking, which gave writers of the reigns of Elizabeth & James, the same energy. At present, the chief object of an author [is] to be intelligible at the first view; then, it was to make the reader [!] think – not to make him understand at once, but to show him rather that he did not understand, or to make him to review, & re-meditate till he had placed himself upon a par with the writer.[13]

The idea of Shakespeare as 'difficult', a writer demanding a constant intellectual effort on the part of his recipients (which Coleridge, tellingly, imagines as readers rather than theatregoers) necessitates a modification of the way communication between that author and his first audiences is conceived of. If those audiences indeed deserve to be called a 'mob', one cannot think of Shakespeare's literary efforts as anything but permanent theatrical failures, for a 'mob' would hardly be able to keep up with this challenging dramatist. Coleridge, however, does not want to believe in a Shakespeare underestimated and unrecognised during his own lifetime. He therefore introduces the concept of a split audience, composed of two separate segments which explain, respectively, both the plays' weaknesses and their extraordinary qualities: 'The author [Shakespeare] had to deal with a learned public; & he had no idea of a mixed public – it was divided, in truth, between those who had no taste at all & who went merely to amuse themselves – and those who were deeply versed in the literature to which they gave encouragement.'[14]

In addition to the mob that earlier critics imagined to have populated the Globe, Coleridge assumes the existence of a second segment of spectators, consisting of the highly educated *cognoscenti* and patrons who incited early modern dramatists to their outstanding literary achievements. While the elite part of Shakespeare's original audience, just like Coleridge and *his* audiences roughly 200 years later, can consider themselves the true addressee of Shakespeare's works, the mob, desiring nothing but amusement, is denied any real understanding of the plays. Coleridge's notion of Shakespeare as an intellectually superior author-genius is corroborated by the presence of spectators actually able to fully appreciate him. In fact, the Shakespearean stage as he imagines it not really a theatre in the first place:

> The circumstances of acting were altogether different from ours – it was much more of [a] recitation, or rather, a medium between recitation & what we now call recitation – The idea of the poet was always present, not of the actors, not of the thing to be represented. It was [...] more a delight & employment for the intellect, than [an] amusement for the senses.[15]

Given the conditions under which Shakespeare was originally working, it is hence well-neigh impossible to produce his plays 'authentically' or 'correctly' on the nineteenth-century stage. Instead, he is to be read. The nature and composition of Elizabethan theatregoers as presented by Coleridge helps legitimise his approach to Shakespearean drama, or, more precisely, the elite part of the split audience does. What brought the mob to the Globe remains unclear. Coleridge has the following to offer:

> One man would carry away nothing but the jokes and what was externally ludicrous, while the other would be pleased that his fellow-citizens had received an innocent enjoyment, which had to him been a profitable employment. He saw that which gave him a deeper knowledge of his own heart, & of the actions of his fellow-creatures, and he wonders that this great man could at the same time excite the admiration of the most profound metaphysician & draw tears or awake laughter from the most ignorant.[16]

The fundamental divide running not only through Shakespeare's original audience, but apparently also through his works stands in considerable contrast to the rhetoric of organisicism that Coleridge cultivates elsewhere. If 'homogeneity, proportionateness and totality of Interest'[17] indeed characterise Shakespearean drama, then explaining why this kind of drama elicits such divergent reactions among the different parts of the audience is not without its challenges. Coleridge seems to assume that the mob-pleasing surface ('what was externally ludicrous') and the 'real' play that lies below it are intimately bound up with and in fact inseparable from one another, but in what way is never quite spelled out. What is more than obvious, however, is that the organic unity of Shakespeare's drama does not create a comparable social unity among his spectators, and, arguably, is not meant to. It is no coincidence that Coleridge speaks of 'classes' of spectators: his version of Shakespearean drama sustains and deepens social difference. In contrasting two classes of Elizabethan theatregoers, Coleridge reveals a paternalistic view of society in which the socially 'lower' part of the audience can be sure of the elites' benevolence as long as it limits itself to 'innocent enjoyment', the harmless distractions of the young and/or uneducated. In Coleridge's view, this kind of patronising benevolence also characterised Shakespeare's stance towards the lower classes. With this 'mob', Coleridge maintains, the Bard is never 'angry [...], but hugely content with holding up its absurdities to its face; and sometimes you trace a tone of almost affectionate superiority, something like that in which a father speaks of the rogueries of a child.'[18] In a manner typical of the later Coleridge, this kind of paternalism is then presented as thoroughly apolitical. Shakespeare, he claims, 'never promulgates any party tenets', he is 'always the philosopher and the moralist.'[19] While Coleridge himself may indeed have believed that 'affectionate superiority' towards the 'mob' qualified as a neutral political stance, his contemporaries may not necessarily have agreed. His strong emphasis on the intrinsic value of tradition and continuity, his endorsement of a society structured on the model of the family (with the lower classes as the child in need of parental supervision) are more than a distant echo of Burke. 'Coleridge's Shakespeare criticism is political in its essence, not merely in certain superficial details'[20] – this certainly holds true for his idea of the Bard's Elizabethan audience.

In Coleridge's Shakespeare criticism, the role of Renaissance theatregoers changes in essential ways. Leaving aside some isolated eighteenth-century voices, this is the first time that Shakespeare's Elizabethan audience (also) functions as an object of identification, and not just as a hetero-stereotype. While the cultured elite that makes up one half of Shakespeare's newly 'split' audience is clearly a backward projection of Coleridge himself, and of the intellectual bourgeoisie which made up his audiences, the early modern 'mob' continues to stand for everything banned from the cultured refinement which these audiences claimed for themselves. Its at best rudimentary understanding of what was being offered at the Globe confirms a point which earlier critics had already made quite clear: Shakespeare is emphatically not of, or for, the lower classes. Coleridge also highlights that there is no middle ground: it is either the elite or the mob. This assumed internal order of the Elizabethan audience, itself a miniature model of Elizabethan society as a whole, provides a counter-model to his own times, where formerly impenetrable social barriers were becoming more and more permeable. Coleridge's Shakespeare is a socially conservative bulwark against this development.

## Jacobin Jacobeans: Hazlitt

When Coleridge produced his Shakespeare criticism, the revolutionary fervour of his early years had passed. With Hazlitt, the case is different. That a poet as established as Shakespeare should appeal to a self-declared radical like him is not as self-evident as scholars have sometimes assumed. '[I]nertial motion'[21] may go some way towards explaining the Bard's staying power, as may the fact that the innovative criticism of the second half of the eighteenth century, in which neoclassicism was a negligible influence, was dispersed in journals and books that looked hardly pertinent at a first glance. Many Romantics felt that Shakespeare was still in need of comprehensive rehabilitation, and prided themselves on their part in 'gaining' him the position he deserved,[22] in a manner similar to what was happening in continental Europe. There, Shakespeare's disregard for the international system of aesthetic norms that was neoclassicism was often perceived as a manifestation of English liberty, the kind of aesthetic as well as political freedom continental Romantics desired – and which the English mostly already enjoyed. The opposition between Shakespeare and neoclassicism which eighteenth-century criticism had been so preoccupied with thus became one of the main reasons why Shakespeare was enthusiastically embraced by continental Romantics and became one of the figureheads of the movement. Hazlitt's Shakespeare criticism reconceptualises the Bard on continental terms, as it were, despite the fact that regarding his prestige within Britain, Shakespeare not necessarily needed a revolution on his behalf.

While Coleridge claims Shakespeare for paternalism, Hazlitt situates him on the opposite side of the political spectrum. As with Coleridge, his starting point is a radical rethinking of the Elizabethan age as a whole. In a manner typical of Romantic nationalism, he links the concept of national particularity to the idea of natural purity and immediacy:

> [In the Elizabethan age,] our writers and great men had something in them that savoured of the soil from which they grew: they were not French, they were not Dutch, or German, or Greek, or Latin, they were truly English. They did not look out of themselves to see what they should be; they sought for truth and nature, and found it in themselves. [...] The mind of their country was great in them, and it prevailed. With their learning and unexampled acquirement, they did not forget that they were men: with all their endeavours after excellence they did not lay aside the strong and original bent and character of their minds.[23]

The 'artlessness' which eighteenth-century critics like Guthrie or Upton had lauded as one of the most distinguishing features of Shakespeare's oeuvre is declared a manifestation of English national character: it is not only typical of Shakespeare, but typical of the nation as a whole. The period that gave rise to such unadulterated expressions of Englishness no longer stands in need of apology. Using the past as a foil for the supposed progress and refinement of the present is hence condemned in no uncertain terms. 'There is not a lower ambition, a poorer way of thought', Hazlitt writes, 'than that which would confine all excellence, or arrogate its final accomplishment to the present, or modern times.' Doing so is declared the diachronic version of misled nationalist pride:

> If we have pretty well got rid of the narrow bigotry that would limit all sense of virtue to our own country, and have fraternized, like true cosmopolites, with our neighbours and contemporaries, we have made our self-love amends by letting the generation we live in engross nearly all our admiration and by pronouncing a sweeping sentence of barbarism and ignorance on our ancestry backwards [...].[24]

Just like, in Hazlitt's view, equality and fraternity are to rule relations with foreign countries, they are to rule attitudes towards the nation's own past. Ultimately, what he demands is for historical relativism to include the present, whose standards are no longer automatically to be considered superior to those of Shakespeare's times. If the nation's past is indeed a foreign country, as it were, then the present is to fraternise with it.[25]

With Hazlitt's strong emphasis on the fundamental equality of men, the notion of a fundamental dissociation between Shakespeare and his original audience necessarily disappears. Moreover, there is no quasi-metaphysical idolisation of Shakespeare himself. Hazlitt's view of the Bard's position within the Elizabethan age therefore differs decisively from that of the neoclassicists. If we perceive Shakespeare as a solitary genius in a wasteland of barbarity, he argues, then this is due to our lack of knowledge of the Elizabethan age and its cultural achievements. While Shakespeare did surpass most or all of his contemporaries, they are to be taken seriously as artists in their own right, artists from whom he differed in degree but not in kind: '[Shakespeare] did not form a class or species by himself, but belonged to a class or species.'[26] Instead of being an absolute, transhistorical and hence effectively extra-societal author figure Hazlitt presents Shakespeare as embedded in his age, and especially in the society that he lived in. The poet speaks not for himself, but for the community that he is part of: for the people. Similarly, the bearers of political and cultural progress do not belong to a separate, especially elevated class but are 'representative men' in the sense that they focus the intellectual energies of the people as a whole: 'All the greatest poets, sages, heroes, are ours [the people's] originally, and by right.'[27] It is not possible to think of them as in any way isolated from this collective.[28] Possible weaknesses of a poet's work therefore cannot be blamed on the influence of his (popular) audience. This is for two reasons: first because the influence of the people is seen as fundamentally positive, second, because there is no artistic inspiration in which the people do not have a share. To speak of its influence is hence not only understated, but illogical. As a popular poet, Shakespeare can no longer be excused by citing his original audience. It is indeed open to question whether a popular poet in Hazlitt's sense is not always already excused, given that he represents the tastes and views of the community as a whole: to criticise the people's poet would mean to criticise the people themselves.

Hazlitt's radical reinterpretation of Shakespeare's rootedness in popular traditions, formulated in conscious opposition to the neoclassicist stance, provides a pattern for future 'alternative' Shakespeares to model themselves upon. A cultural movement that thinks of itself as a countermovement does not propagate its own cultural icons, but makes use of an already iconic figure whose prestige it tries to enlist for its own purposes. In doing so, the 'counter'-movement in a sense remains inherent to the system which it officially opposes: it does not attempt a complete overthrow of existing icons, but contents itself with disputing their meanings.

## The Elizabethan audience in nineteenth-century American Shakespeare criticism

Given that the post-revolutionary United States put into practice many of the ideals that European radicals like Hazlitt were trying to propagate in their own countries, it would be reasonable to expect American critics to follow in Hazlitt's footsteps as far as Shakespeare's Elizabethan audience is concerned – where indeed they accept the Bard as a desirable part of the nation's cultural heritage. But though this is often the case, American views on early modern theatregoers are far from uniform, and testify to the contentious nature of what, from a European perspective, constitutes the radical experiment of American democracy.

One form in which this radicalism manifests itself, though only rarely, is in a total rejection of Shakespeare. One of the period's most notable detractors is Walt Whitman. Almost predictably, his rejection of the Bard is based, among other things, on what Whitman thinks the Bard's original audience was like, though curiously, his vision of it seems most closely related to the elite part of Coleridge's split audience – a rare conjunction of two otherwise rather dissimilar minds. Whitman's starting points are the 'low characters', which (so he claims) 'all in themselves nothing – serve as capital foils to aristocracy. The comedies [...] have the unmistakable hue of plays [...] made for the divertisement only of the élite of the castle, and from its point of view.'[29] '[P]oisonous to the idea of the pride and the dignity of the common people, the life-blood of democracy',[30] Shakespeare's dramas are incompatible with the democratic credo of the United States. Whitman thus takes precisely the step that Hazlitt avoids: the self-proclaimed vanguard of a new era, he topples the idols of the past. In effect, he does so by affirming the (implicit) claims of earlier critics: Shakespeare does indeed truly 'belong' to the cultural elites of the ages succeeding him, for the reason that (and here Whitman is far more radical than most of his European predecessors) he originally wrote for the elites of his own lifetime, catering to their tastes and political leanings – which is precisely why he has no place in the democratic culture of the United States.

But Whitman's rejection of Shakespeare remains a largely isolated phenomenon. While his vision of the Bard's original target audience would certainly justify denying him a place in American culture, this is not what actually happens. Shakespeare's staying power, it seems, is too great. Instead, views of said audience are adjusted. If art that addresses itself to an exclusive elite is unsuited to American democracy, then plays that cater to the common people and their tastes are as proper as can be. And it is this that makes American Shakespeare reception in the nineteenth century so interesting from the point of view of this study. In the period under consideration (and arguably in all subsequent ones), 'democracy' is the constitutive factor in American national identity, earlier and more distinctively so than in England, where – unlike the 'English liberty' that was traditionally seen as more or less compatible with constitutional monarchy – it never developed comparable ideological clout. Concerning the relation between the one and the many, between the genius and the broad masses, American critics therefore face challenges that are different from those of their transatlantic counterparts.

The ways in which Shakespeare and his original audience are adapted to American requirements are various, and not always obvious.

A recurring feature is an increasing equanimity towards the dramatist's financial dependence on Elizabethan theatregoers. Richard Grant
White declares: '[The fact] that Shakespeare did his work with no
other purpose whatever; moral, philosophical, artistic, literary, than
to make an attractive play which would bring him money, should be
constantly borne in mind by the critical and reflective reader of his
plays.'[31] Similarly unemotional statements on this matter by British
critics are virtually nonexistent, at least in the period under discussion,
even though the cash nexus is behind every apology of Shakespeare
that utilises his Elizabethan audience. This notwithstanding, the exact
nature of the relationship between the demands of the marketplace
on the one hand and individual genius on the other often remains
ambivalent. Most critics prefer to think of Shakespeare as cultivating an
actual relationship with his audiences, one that is characterised – and
this is a specifically American innovation – by more than just business
considerations. Brander Matthews opines: 'That Shakespeare believed
in the good feeling and the intelligent receptivity of the average man
is shown by his freely putting the best of himself into his plays, meant
for the plain people.'[32] He can thus be credited with 'intense human
sympathy, the noblest quality of our modern democratic movement.'[33]
Alongside this more equitable relationship between Shakespeare and
his Elizabethan audience, critics take up the idea of 'folk literature'
(Herder's *Volkspoesie*) to align both the dramatist and his audience with
constitutive elements of American identity. The origins of poetic inspiration are presented as identical with those of democratic sovereignty:
they are located in the people. The statesman and historian, George
Bancroft, who held a doctorate from the University of Göttingen and
was deeply imbued in German Romanticism, wrote:

> [...] [W]ho are the best judges in matters of taste? Do you think the
> cultivated individual? Undoubtedly not, but the collective mind.
> The public is wiser than the wisest critic. [...] [I]f with us the arts are
> destined to be awakened into a brilliant career, the inspiration must
> spring from the triumphs of democracy. [...] Who are by way of emi-
> nence the poets of all mankind? Surely Homer and Shakespeare. Now
> Homer formed his taste, as he wandered from door to door, a vagrant
> minstrel, paying hospitality by a song; and Shakespeare wrote for an
> audience, wholly composed of the common people.[34]

In a manner directly opposed to the way British critics had tended
to look at the Elizabethan audience, the socially 'low' or at least not

particularly elevated provenance of Renaissance theatregoers ('common', the term Bancroft employs, is used far more frequently by American critics than by their British counterparts) vouches for the outstanding quality of the works of art produced for them. The poet who knows no class differences but addresses himself equally to everyone becomes the voice of a collective mind whose judgment can lay claim to universal validity. It is only this kind of artist who is capable of creating exceptional art. Shakespeare's original audience thus plays a seminal role in the creation of his works.

When Emerson describes the poet as 'a heart in unison with his time and country',[35] this sounds a similar note: '[W]hat is best written or done by genius [...] came by wide social labour, when a thousand wrought like one, sharing the same impulse.'[36] Emerson claims that this is especially true of the drama, where collective and popular traditions play a particularly important role.[37] There is also, however, and perhaps unsurprisingly, given Emerson's focus on concepts like individualism and self-reliance, a certain ambivalence towards the influence of the Elizabethan audience, which he decries as being 'uncritical'.[38] In catering to this audience, Shakespeare cheapens himself, in a now notorious phrase, to a 'master of the revels to mankind':

> [T]his man of men, he who gave to the science of the mind a new and larger subject than had ever existed, and planted the standard of humanity some furlongs into Chaos – that he should not be wise for himself – it must even go into the world's history, that the best poet led an obscure and profane life, using his genius for the public amusement.[39]

Shakespeare's failure consists in being too much in tune with the collective mind, thereby neglecting his true responsibility towards his audience and towards the people as a whole, to whom he is bound by a double obligation: in that his artistic endeavours are not creations *ex nihilo*, but ultimately the results of a collective effort, and in that his particular talents compel him to educate and guide his audience,[40] a task which Shakespeare, according to Emerson, carelessly neglects. In this tradition, the perceived weaknesses of the plays are more likely to be read as failures on the part of the Bard than as indicators of the depraved taste of his audience – which in any case he would have been called upon to improve.

George Wilkes' discussion of the mutilated Lavinia in *Titus Andronicus* illustrates this idea of a failed educational mission. Instead of making

the usual references to the early modern thirst for blood, Wilkes enter-
tains the proposition of a morally less than flawless Shakespeare, who
'may be acquitted of the barbarity of this device, but [...] cannot be
excused the error of adopting it. [...] [A]n author who takes advantage
of the trust reposed in him by his audience, to wound their best feelings with unnecessary horrors, is nearly as bad as the characters who
perpetrate them.'[41] The connection between Shakespeare's reputation
and the reputation of his Elizabethan audience is particularly obvious
here. As soon as early modern theatregoers are styled into representatives of the people as a whole, Shakespeare himself has to bear the
responsibility for those passages in his plays which are perceived as
objectionable, at least where the idea of the people, as is officially
the case in democratic America, has positive rather than negative
connotations. In Wilkes's eyes, Shakespeare is at best an amoral artist, and measures up to the 'instinctive goodness of the big-hearted
multitude',[42] the 'tender and generous nature of the people'[43] only
where he provides them with the happy endings they desire. Like
other American critics,[44] Wilkes blames Shakespeare for what he perceives as a lack of respect for the common man, and a concomitant
'servility to royalty and rank.'[45] The Bard's essentially anti-democratic
attitude, he predicts, will inevitably cause his prestige to decline: '[...]
the spell has lost a great deal of its force, and can no longer prevent
the condemnation of the poet's principles by the English-speaking and
liberty-loving people of America. And, as much may be said for the
rugged intelligence and resolute progress of the present liberty-loving
English masses.'[46]

   Staunchly democratic though it may seem, this way of looking at
Shakespeare does not become widely accepted in the United States.
To a surprisingly large extent, American views on early modern audiences are identical with British ones. The majority of writers assume
that Shakespeare wrote for a popular audience, and the uses to which
they put this notion are often those established by eighteenth-century
British criticism. In nineteenth-century America, the historical apology
is far from obsolete, despite the fact that neoclassicism played no role
to speak of and that American Shakespeare criticism only came into
its own when the age of Shakespeare, at least in Britain, was no longer
considered uncultivated and rude. The Reverend Henry N. Hudson,
one of the earliest American editors of Shakespeare, thus opines:
'[Shakespeare], struggling through manifold and manifest obstruc-
tions of ignorance and depravity, [...] gave to a clapping and shouting
mob-audience a chaos utterly incapable of catastrophe.'[47] Even with an

avowed democrat like Wilkes, there is the occasional glimpse of decidedly anti-democratic feeling. On the extremely one-sided depiction of
the English victory over the French in *Henry V* (29 English deaths as
opposed to 10 000 on the French side), he writes:

> A result manufactured for the play-house by a playwright who
> was catering to audiences, as the playwrights of to-day cater for
> the uproarious swarms of the Surrey Theatre in London, the Porte
> St Martin in Paris, or the Bowery Theatre in New York; catering, how-
> ever, only for their shouts and shillings – which Shakespeare knew
> how to do – and not for their sensible and historical appreciation, as
> would have been the aim of a rigid philosopher like Bacon.[48]

The term 'uproarious' evokes a less than distant memory of the spectre
of anarchy and mob rule. Tellingly, these unwanted forms of government by the people are once more linked to the commercial nature of
the Shakespearean stage, conceptually as well as alliteratively ('shouts
and shillings'). Even where the Elizabethan audience is idealised as
representing a miniature version of the people, what is actually being
glorified is frequently an abstract idea rather than a cross-section of the
population as it actually exists. Writing in 1908, the American critic
Brander Matthews could still describe Fletcher as trying to appeal to
'the lewd fellows of the baser sort', whereas Shakespeare 'does not so
much write down to the mob as write broad for the crowd.'[49] The most
undiluted forms of the received, derogatory *topos* of the Elizabethan
audience are to be found in the nascent Anti-Stratfordian movement.
Here is Delia Bacon:

> Compelled to refer the origin of ['Shakespeare's'] works to the sordid
> play-house, who could teach us to distinguish between the ranting,
> unnatural stuff and bombast which its genuine competitions elicited,
> in their mercenary appeals to the passions of their audience, minis-
> tering to the most vicious tastes, depraving the public conscience,
> and lowering the common standard of decency [...], who could teach
> us to distinguish between the tone of the original, genuine, play-
> house fustian, and that of the 'dozen or sixteen lines' which Hamlet
> will at first, with the consent and privity of one of the players, cause
> to be inserted in it?[50]

Similarly, Joseph C. Hart in *The Romance of Yachting* takes a stage
thoroughly corrupted by the principles of market economy as the

starting point for his deliberations concerning the true or false author of 'Shakespeare's' plays:

> [...] Shakespeare's obscenity exceeds that of all the dramatists writing before him, and contemporaneously with him [...]. This was the secret of his success with the play-goers. The plays he purchased or obtained surreptitiously, which became his 'property' and which are now called his, were never set upon the stage in their original state. They were first spiced with obscenity, blackguardism and improprieties, before they were produced; and this business he voluntarily assumed, and faithfully did he perform his share of the management in that respect. It brought money to the house.[51]

'To revise, to strike out, to refit, to revamp, interpolate, disfigure, to do anything to please the vulgar and vicious taste of the multitude'[52] – this, according to Hart, is what the 'factotum' Shakespeare was tasked with. The 'man from Stratford' is thus put on a level with his age's depraved theatregoers, while the 'true' author of the morally and intellectually flawless parts of the plays is freed from any responsibility for the passages Hart perceives as offensive. With their penchant for the aristocratic, these early anti-Stratfordians pursue much the same aim as those who blame a popular Elizabethan audience for Shakespeare's perceived faults: the aim of dissociating Shakespeare from the lower classes. Both in their exotic theories concerning 'true' authorship and in their much more conventional denunciation of the Elizabethan audience, Hart and Bacon display a bias against the common people that is shared by many altogether more reputable American Shakespeareans of the period.

Just like its transatlantic counterpart, nineteenth-century American discourse on Shakespeare's original audience frequently reflects a negative attitude towards the lower classes, even if it became increasingly problematic to refer to them by that name. To at least some extent, this may simply be a *topos* adopted, more or less uncritically, from earlier British traditions. However, 'dissing' Shakespeare's Elizabethan audience also fulfils a function that is specific to the American context. It offers the possibility of voicing doubts and reservations concerning the United States' experiment in democracy without immediately attracting accusations of false consciousness. While Hazlitt and Coleridge pave the way for thinking of the Elizabethan audience as an object of identification rather than as a hetero-stereotype, American Shakespeare criticism of the nineteenth century makes clear that these two functions are not mutually exclusive, and that Renaissance theatregoers may in fact serve as both at the same time. While audiences in early modern London are frequently presented as – albeit temporary – democracies *avant la lettre*, embodiments of the people in the most politically loaded sense of the term, American critics also vividly remind their readers that *demos* is an exclusive rather than inclusive term.

# 3
# Enter the Groundlings

[...] I believe that species come to be tolerably well-defined objects, and do not at any one period present an inextricable chaos of varying and intermediate links: firstly, because new varieties are very slowly formed, for variation is a very slow process, and natural selection can do nothing until favourable variations chance to occur, and until a place in the natural polity of the country can be better filled by some modification of some one or more of its inhabitants. And such new places will depend on slow changes of climate, or on the occasional immigration of new inhabitants, and, probably, in a still more important degree, on some of the old inhabitants becoming slowly modified, with the new forms thus produced and the old ones acting and reacting on each other. So that, in any one region and at any one time, we ought only to see a few species presenting slight modifications of structure in some degree permanent; and this assuredly we do see.[1]

The nineteenth and early twentieth centuries witness a decisive development in the discourse on Shakespeare's Elizabethan audience: the appearance of a new species of Renaissance theatregoers, the groundlings. To this species, Darwin's theories fully apply. Its appearance, or rather, its invention, is not the result of 'an inextricable chaos of varying and intermediate links', no isolated or autonomous development, but a reaction to changes in the cultural framework in which discussions about Shakespeare's original audiences, and more generally about the national dramatist himself, take place.

That the term for this subsection of Shakespeare's Elizabethan audience was actually coined by Shakespeare is symptomatic of the circular reasoning that often underlies notions about those present in the early modern theatres. Hamlet's complaints about the inaptitude of actors and the inanity of audiences are the earliest instances of the term being used for a specific part of the theatre audience instead of for a species of fish dwelling on the bottom of ponds or lakes.

> *Hamlet*: [...] O! it offends me to the soul to hear a robustious periwig-pated fellow tear a passion to tatters, to very rags, to split the ears of the groundlings, who, for the most part, are capable of nothing but inexplicable dumb-shows and noise.[2]

Of the meanings of the term as listed in the *Oxford English Dictionary*, two are relevant here: 'a frequenter of the ground or "pit" of a theatre; hence, a spectator of low or inferior tastes; an uncritical or unrefined person' and 'one of humble rank; one of base breeding or sentiments'.[3] The new coinage was already taken up during Shakespeare's lifetime. Dekker mocks in 1609: '[Y]our Groundling and gallery-Commoner buyes his sport by the penny.'[4] In Fletchers *Prophetess* (I, iii), Geta, the fool, proclaims: 'We Tilers may deserve to be Senators, [...] For we are born three Stories high; no base ones, / None of your groundlings, master.'[5] The OED cites several instances of the word from the seventeenth and eighteenth centuries; these, however, are almost all from literary texts rather than literary criticism. With the exception of Maurice Morgann's 'Essay on the Dramatic Character of Sir John Falstaff' (discussed later on), it plays no role to speak of in the discourse on Shakespeare.

In many cases, the distinction between the two meanings given by the OED is a matter of theory more than of practical usage. Dekker refers to 'Groundling and Gallery-*Commoner*' [my emphasis] in one breath: the place a person occupies in the theatre is obviously taken as indicative of their place on the social ladder. Renaissance dramatists already use the term to describe a social reality outside the theatre: 'one of humble rank; one of base breeding or sentiments'. Notions about what groundlings are like are first and foremost notions about their social position.

Coleridge and Hazlitt's revaluation of the Renaissance had rendered it impossible to blame Elizabethans wholesale for Shakespeare's 'faults', and Coleridge had replaced the old historical apology with a newly explicit sociological one. The groundling is the lexical manifestation of this development: he is by, definition, lower class. That this apparently predisposes him to the role of a scapegoat is already obvious from the OED entry and its use of the word *hence* ('a frequenter of the ground or "pit" of a theatre; *hence* [my emphasis], a spectator of low or inferior tastes').

The nexus between a spectator's location in the theatre and his or her 'bad' taste is by no means evident. In defining the term, the OED reproduces precisely the sort of class prejudice that motivates the groundlings' appearance in Shakespeare criticism.

Although Renaissance theatregoers are usually characterised in a more than derogatory manner by eighteenth-century critics, the term *groundling* is hardly ever used. At the beginning of the nineteenth century, it still occurs mostly in the form of more or less direct quotations from *Hamlet*,[6] but as the century progresses, the groundling begins to appear in contexts less directly related to the Bard's great tragedy. One of the most significant early occurrences is in a piece of writing concerned not with Shakespearean drama, but with the merits and demerits of Shakespearean criticism. In 'Shakespeare's Critics: English and Foreign', G.H. Lewes writes:

> [Even in the eighteenth century,] [n]o system of criticism could obscure the splendour of [Shakespeare's] genius. It was necessary, therefore, that an attempt of some kind should be made to reconcile the contradiction presented by a great poet, acknowledged to surpass the most finished artists in his effects, yet supposed all the time 'totally ignorant of art'. The reconciliation was brought about by means of the word 'inspiration'. In this attempt we read the idolatry of Shakespeare's admirers. Homer, indeed, might occasionally nod; Aeschylus be obscure; Euripides prosaic, and Virgil verbose and tautologous; for they were men. – But Shakespeare could have made mistakes only because he had not read certain classic authors: a tincture of learning would have infallibly guarded him from every error! *If he wrote trash sometimes, it was to please the groundlings* [my emphasis]; while his false metaphors, disgusting images, and tedious speeches must have been 'foisted in by the players.' Thus Pope, in his celebrated Preface, attributes the bombast and triviality to be found in Shakespeare, wholly to the necessity of addressing a vulgar audience. And with this judgment Warburton agrees [...].[7]

Lewes points out what has since become a truism: that every period fashions Shakespeare in its own image. He himself is of course implicated in this process, albeit on a largely subconscious level. 'If Shakespeare wrote trash sometimes, it was to please the groundlings' is an adequate summary of the way Pope, Warburton and many others utilise the Elizabethan audience – but Lewes refers to a category unknown to these earlier critics. His own refashioning of Shakespeare and his original audience takes the form of a statement on *past* criticism. By implying that eighteenth-century Shakespeareans blamed the groundlings for Shakespeare's faults when in reality they thought of the Elizabethan audience as an amorphous mass of hooligans (Hazlitt and Coleridge being notable exceptions), Lewes bestows historical credentials on a concept newly discovered by him and his Victorian contemporaries. If nineteenth-century critics talk about groundlings and if eighteenth-century critics did likewise, then their actual existence during Shakespeare's lifetime cannot seriously be called into doubt.

Eighteenth-century Shakespeareans refer to early modern audiences frequently and with great aplomb, but they rarely or never cite actual source material to corroborate their claims. In the few cases where the Elizabethans' alleged lack of refinement is considered in need of proof and not simply taken for granted as one among many manifestations of the period's general barbarity, critics tend to rely on the invectives of Renaissance dramatists, whose railings are never presented as anything less than justified. The nineteenth century's idea of what a groundling was like is even further removed from the historical reality of Shakespeare's day and age. As the example of G. H. Lewes makes clear, critical assumptions about this subsection of Elizabethan theatregoers are derived not from historical source material of whatever kind, but from an already established discourse on the information supposedly contained in this source material – in which, on the whole, the eighteenth century had not been very interested in the first place. 'A whole class of Elizabethan spectators [the groundlings] [comes] into existence on the basis of a couple of contemporary references',[8] Simon Shepherd and Peter Womack conclude. When scrutinised more closely, the situation turns out to be even more complicated: A whole class of Elizabethan spectators seems to have come into existence on the basis of a host of diffuse eighteenth-century references to a couple of questionable early modern references. That this complex process advances as smoothly as it does testifies to the usefulness of, perhaps even need for, the new concept and the newly differentiated view of Shakespeare's first auditors that comes with it. Victorian critics have little difficulty in defining the groundling above and beyond his place in the early modern theatre; in fact so successful has their installation of this new 'species' been that to this day, '[e]ducated people [...] apparently know intuitively what these spectators were like, how they behaved and – despite the fact that, being *ex hypothesi* illiterate, they left no records of themselves – exactly which scenes they enjoyed.'[9]

Just how useful – and elastic – the concept was (and is) for all manner of literary critics can be gauged from the fact that it leaves the more or less narrow confines of Shakespeare criticism not long after its original gestation. In 1873, the groundlings appear in John Addington Symonds' musings on the literary public of classical Greece: 'Had the Greek race perceptions infinitely finer than ours? Or did the classic harmonies of Pindar sweep over their souls, ruffling the surface merely, but leaving the deeps untouched, as the soliloquies of *Hamlet* or the profound philosophy of *Troilus and Cressida* must have been lost upon the groundlings of Elizabeth's days, who caught with eagerness at the queen's poisoned goblet or the byplay of Sir Pandarus?'[10] In 1903, Herbert Weir Smyth transfers them directly into ancient Greek theatres: 'The dithyramb was a meretricious art and appealed to the taste of the groundlings.'[11] That the groundling should find a new habitat in classical Athens further corroborates that the concept has little if any relation with the material reality of Elizabethan theatres – not least because of the architectural dissimilarities between them and the theatres of classical Greece. The graecised groundling, though a patron of the theatre, is obviously not defined by it. Conversely, the easiness with which he migrates between early modern England and pre-modern Greece allows the conclusion that the original British groundling is not only, and perhaps not even primarily defined by the theatre either, for if he were, the blatant anachronism of transferring him into the world of classical antiquity would hardly be possible. The concept is best looked at as a blank space, to be filled by the imagination of nineteenth-century critics. That this process is at least partly determined by earlier traditions of looking at Shakespeare's original audience is obvious. Nevertheless, the groundling begins his life very much a stranger, a phantom. The genre particularly apposite to Victorian sensibilities, the detective novel, would have started the search for this phantom in the place it was last seen: the theatre. As it turns out, the Victorian theatre indeed provides important clues as to why the groundlings appeared when they did, and why they were imagined the way many still think of them today.

## Groundlings, pit and carnival

Depending on whether the search took place nearer the beginning or the end of the nineteenth century, spotting the Victorian equivalent of the groundlings was a potentially difficult task. A groundling is by definition to be found in the theatre pit – an architectural feature that British theatres had abolished by the turn of the century. This was not only the end of a theatrical tradition that had spanned several centuries, it also meant that an essential physical link to the theatre of the Elizabethan age had been lost. In a sense, the groundlings can be seen as a replacement for this physical link: a collective memory of an older theatre. As this older theatre waxed increasingly distant and alien, the figure of the groundling gained in prominence, and many of its supposed characteristics were taken directly from what contemporaries knew, or thought they knew, about audiences in the eighteenth- and nineteenth-century pit.

One defining feature of these audiences was their ambivalent position within the theatre. The pit was:

> privileged, because it had the most immediate relationship with the stage, and because it could be seen from many of the other seats; but also *low*, not only literally, but also in its traditions of exhibitionism, jostling and noise. A box *contains* its occupants – that is, both affords them a protected space and prevents them from invading other people's space; in the pit, on the other hand, you are out in the open, at once less protected and less constrained.[12]

Besides the pittites' non-containment, their privileged visibility and their awareness of it ('exhibitionism'), there is yet another factor which shapes their relationship with the rest of the audience. The pit is located between the stage and those on the more expensive seats, which enables pittites to influence relations between the two: the pit is a potential source of disruption both for the actors and for the other spectators. This constitutes a threat to the theatre's social order in that those in the cheaper parts of the house, despite their 'low' position, have the power to ruin the theatrical experience of those 'higher up' – always assuming that unbroken theatrical illusion is what the latter actually came for. Contemporary records suggest that this was not necessarily the case, and that watching the pit may have been as much part of the entertainment as watching the actual play on stage. This notwithstanding, the pit's disruptive power is a distortion of the situation *outside* the theatre, where more money usually equals more power. Its disappearance can therefore be seen as an adjustment of the theatre to social reality: 'It is no coincidence that the final triumph of the changes in theatre seating occurred in the same era that saw three classes of railway carriages and even separate lifts in blocks of flats.'[13] Architectural changes to theatres reflect the needs of a society heavily invested in the policing of social status. The invention of the groundlings also caters to this need:

'their appearance in the accepted picture of Elizabethan audiences is an ideological reflex of [the pittites'] expulsion from the Victorian ones.'[14] Unbeknownst to them, what theatres got rid of when they abolished the pit was not necessarily the lower classes however. As research especially on the Old Price Riots has shown, pittites came from all social classes – if anything, they were 'popular' in the most comprehensive sense of the term. Nevertheless, contemporary observers tended to *assume* that pittites were mostly lower class.[15] Together with the discursive traditions of the seventeenth and eighteenth centuries this could not but affect their idea of the early modern groundlings' social standing. Just like the *imagined* Victorian pittite, the groundlings are a 'class myth'.[16]

Class is, however, not the only defining characteristic of this newly invented subsection of the Elizabethan audience. A second, equally important one is the kind of audience participation no longer deemed compatible with the sort of theatrical illusions increasingly privileged by the Victorians. Describing ritualised forms of protest during the 1809 Old Price riots, such as noise, counter-monologues or the famous OP-Dance, Baer remarks: 'What should be evident [...] is that for most theatre disturbances and certainly for the OP riots, "disorder" was only a variation of normal patterns of audience participation in or reaction to the theatre.'[17] These patterns live on in Victorian notions of the Elizabethan audience. Paradoxically, the text in which this becomes most obvious was written by a Frenchman, Hippolyte Taine. His *Histoire de la litterature anglaise*, though not written in England, was widely read there, not least because it preceded similar English endeavours by more than a decade.[18] Taine's influence on conceptions of early modern audiences can hardly be overestimated. His views of 'the Elizabethans' remain formative far into the twentieth century – particularly what Taine presents as the innate theatricality of an entire age:

> There was no model imposed on them [the Elizabethans], as nowadays; instead of affecting imitation, they affected originality. Each strove to be himself, with his own oaths, fashions, costumes, his specialities of conduct and humour, and to be unlike every one else. They said not, 'So and so is done,' but 'I do so and so.' [...] Their inborn instincts have not been tamed, nor muzzled, nor diminished. [...] They were carmen in body and gentlemen in sentiment, with the dress of actors and the tastes of artists.[19]

No wonder Elizabethans wear 'the dress of actors'. Taine describes them as stage-managers of their own individuality, albeit an individuality that seems consciously created rather than constitutional: 'Each *strove* to be himself.' Their originality is the result of artistic ambition; Taine clearly anticipates Greenblatt's self-fashioning.[20] His version of the Renaissance is, however, concerned less with containment and more with anarchy, particularly when it comes to Renaissance theatre audiences. Unruly behaviour takes different forms with the two groups of spectators that Taine distinguishes: 'the people in the pit, butchers, mercers, bakers, sailors, apprentices' on the one hand and '[a]bove them, on the stage, [...] the spectators able to pay a shilling, the elegant people, the gentlefolk' on the other.[21] Despite the great differences between these two classes of theatregoers, they share an attitude towards the stage that is defined by various forms of trangression. The pittites,

> [w]hile waiting for the piece, [...] amuse themselves after their fashion, drink beer, crack nuts, eat fruits, howl, and now and then resort to their fists; they have been known to fall upon the actors, and turn the theatre upside down. At other times they have gone in disgust to the tavern to give the poet a hiding, or toss him in a blanket; they were rude jokers, and there was no month when the cry of 'Clubs' did not call them out of their shops to exercise their brawny arms.[22]

The subversiveness of Taine's groundlings (though he does not call them that) takes the rather straightforward form of physical aggression. Both the structural integrity of the playhouse and the physical integrity of the actors may be affected by the standees' displeasure if expressed in this manner. And yet this is more than mere rioting: by claiming the privilege of action, of *acting*, early modern pittites breach the conventions of a later period, and a different theatre.

When actors present the fictional story invented by the author on stage, they relocate this fiction from the realm of the purely imaginary to that of visual and auditory perception. In this sense they 'act', albeit not according to their own intentions, but within the more or less narrow parameters set by the dramatist. The stage thus occupies an intermediate position between play, mere pretence, and 'actual', fully intentional action – a precarious position that begs to be regulated, not least with regard to the *audience's* freedom of action. The eighteenth and nineteenth century saw a marked increase in such regulation. Increasingly, the only permissible action on the part of the audience was that of applauding the performance. By thus limiting the scope of licit reactions to the action on stage, the fact/fiction divide is rendered more stable. It is this divide that Taine's rowdy butchers, bakers and apprentices call into question. The privileged spectators on stage, in turn, whose physical location already entails a special proximity to the fiction there enacted, are involved in a similar blurring of categories. Taine writes:

> [The gentlefolk] gesticulate, swear in Italian, French, English; crack aloud jokes in dainty, composite, high-coloured words: in short, they have the energetic, original, gay manners of artists, the same humour, the same absence of constraint, and, to complete the resemblance, the same desire to make themselves singular, the same imaginative cravings, the same absurd and picturesque devices, beards cut to a point, into the shape of a fan, a spade, the letter T, gaudy and expensive dresses, copied from five or six neighbouring nations, embroidered, laced with gold, motley, continually heightened in effect or changed for others: there was, as it were, a carnival in their brains as well as on their backs.[23]

'All the world's a stage, and all the men and women merely players' – this is the essence of Taine's Renaissance theatre. The elegant world on stage is involved in a performance that competes with the 'real' play. As much as the show delivered by the players, the persona the aristocratic spectators present on stage is a work of art. Just like the pittites, the on-stage gallants hence embody the permeability of the fact/fiction divide. The destabilising effects of this are obvious from Taine's wording. Clothing is 'motley', 'continually heightened or changed', a patchwork of fashions from five or six different countries, hence refusing to be tied to a predefined identity, semantically fluctuating and vague and thus difficult to control – just like Taine's sentence, which continually eludes the reader waiting for a full stop.

This staging of the aristocratic subject in the Elizabethan theatre partakes in the ontological vagueness that is characteristic of all drama. The nineteenth-century playhouse attempts to contain this ambiguity and distinguish between play and non-play with a set of structural oppositions: the auditorium is dark while the stage is illuminated, the curtain marks the beginning and the end of the theatrical fiction as well as any interruptions to it. Performance is limited to a stage open exclusively to the actors. The Shakespearean stage, by contrast, foregrounds the drama's ontological vagueness and inclines to play with the border between fiction and reality. For Taine, the essential alterity of this theatre manifests itself not only in an undisciplined appetite for (self-) performance, but also in similarly unbridled forms of corporeality:

> When the beer took effect, there was a great upturned barrel in the pit, a peculiar receptacle for general use. The smell rises, and then comes the cry, 'Burn the juniper!' They burn some in a plate on the stage, and the heavy smoke fills the air. Certainly the folks there assembled could scarcely get disgusted at anything, and cannot have had sensitive noses. In the time of Rabelais there was not much cleanness to speak of. Remember that they were hardly out of the middle age, and that in the middle age man lived on a dunghill.[24]

The name Rabelais, at the very latest, cannot but evoke Bakhtin's idea of the carnivalesque. Different aspects of carnival ('there was, as it were, a carnival in their brains as well as on their backs') are allocated to different segments of the Elizabethan audience. The groundlings' eating and drinking is a crucial function of the grotesque body, while the gallants on stage point towards the participatory nature of carnival, its instability and essential openness.[25] The eighteenth- and nineteenth-century pit unites all of these aspects. It is an atavism, saturated with that 'undestroyable nonofficial nature'[26] to be banned from a theatre whose aim is shifting from entertainment to education and moral improvement, at least when it comes to Shakespeare. Its gradual disappearance from nineteenth-century theatres can indeed be read as 'a slow but steady replacement of carnivalesque with bourgeois in the ordering of theatre audiences'.[27]

Although the concept was not a part of their intellectual repertoire, Victorian commentators frequently describe their working-class contemporaries in terms of a carnivalesque *avant la lettre*, as it were. Taine, for one, sees a historical continuity between the manners of nineteenth-century lower classes and those of Elizabethan England more generally:

> [Henry VIII] is so fond of combat, that publicly, on the field of the Cloth of Gold, he seized Francis I. in his arms to throw him. This is how a soldier or a bricklayer nowadays tries a new comrade. In fact, they regarded as amusements, like soldiers and bricklayers, gross jests and brutal buffooneries. [...] The great lords, the well-dressed ladies, spoke Billingsgate slang. When Henry V paid his court to Catherine

of France, it is with the coarse bearing of a sailor who might have taken a fancy to a sutler; and like the tars who tattoo a heart on their arms to prove their love for the girls they left behind them, you find men who 'devoured sulphur and drank urine' to win their mistress by a proof of affection.[28]

The carnivalesque survives in the lower classes of Taine's own present, who are thus marked as latecomers in the history of civilisation, relics of an older state which nineteenth-century elites have long left behind. The carnivalesque has moved down the social ladder: expelling it from the theatre therefore implies a social rise for the stage.

If carnivalesque passages in Shakespeare's plays are attributed to the demands of the Elizabethan audience, and more specifically to those of the groundlings, then this is an attempt to adjust the Bard to the newly respectable, anxiously non-carnivalesque stage. The first glimpses of this are already apparent in a critical tradition established during the eighteenth century, that of ascribing 'improper' appearances of the fool in a tragedy to the demands of Shakespeare's original audience. These include the old countryman in the last scene of *Antony and Cleopatra*, the fool in *King Lear* (especially III, ii), the gravediggers in *Hamlet* (V, i) and the Porter scene in *Macbeth* (II, iii).[29] A quasi-institutionalised manifestation of the carnivalesque, the fool threatens the solemnity of tragedy and its traditionally high social prestige. Attempts to contain this subversive potential are triggered not only by the intrusion of the comic figure into a tragic space reserved for his social betters, but also in cases where these social betters are overpowered by the comic in a manner deemed inappropriate to their position – especially when that position is of historical significance. In those cases, the levelling power of laughter is particularly heavily policed. F. S. Boas, for one, permits himself a nexus between Shakespeare and subversive laughter only in the form of a question. Concerning Caesar's ostentatious disregard of all warnings, natural and supernatural, about a potential attempt on his life, his 'pretensions of superiority to human weakness', he speculates timidly: 'What is the meaning of all this? Are we to conclude that Shakespeare deliberately intended to turn Caesar into a laughing-stock for the benefit of the groundlings in the Globe, or that he had radically misconceived his true character?'[30] While the answer to both of these questions, at least for Boas, is obviously 'no', it is clear that such a debunking, if it indeed had been Shakespeare's intention, would exactly have suited the groundlings and their (assumed) preference for the topsy-turvydom of carnival. A. C. Swinburne, in his discussion of Henry V's wooing of Catherine of France, proceeds from the same assumption:

> [Henry's] rough and ready courtship of the French princess is a good deal expanded as to length, but (if I dare say so) less improved and heightened in tone than we might well have wished and it might well have borne; in either text [the 'bad' Quarto as well as the First Folio] the hero's addresses savour rather of a ploughman than a prince, and his finest courtesies are clownish though not churlish. We may probably see in this rather a concession to the appetite of the groundlings than an evasion of the difficulties inherent in the subject-matter of the scene; too heavy as these might have been for another, we can conceive of none too hard for the magnetic tact and intuitive delicacy of Shakespeare's judgment and instinct. But it must fairly and honestly be admitted that in this scene we find as little of the charm and humour inseparable from the prince as of the courtesy and dignity to be expected from the king.[31]

The English model king, of all people, is behaving in an unkingly manner – it can only be because the groundlings wanted it that way. That his acting 'like a ploughman' has implications beyond mere decorum is implied in Swinburne's peculiarly inapt use of the word 'inseparable': if anything, the scene demonstrates how very separable from the king these qualities actually are. Henry not only disappoints expectations tied to his position as a nobleman and a head of state, he also, and perhaps more fundamentally, disappoints expectations of fictional consistency – in this case, consistency of character, an important precondition for an undisturbed unfolding of the theatrical illusion. If the king steps out of character, the audience may step out of the illusion. That a 'dangerous' scene like this is attributed to the groundlings indicates they are associated with a certain tolerance for disturbances or interruptions of this kind. In the collective imagination of the Victorians, the groundlings are more interested in performance *per se* than in the undisturbed continuity of performance – one more reason why the open, participatory nature of carnival is perfectly suited to their tastes.

The problem of the comic figure turns out to be the problem of the comic as such, for its effectiveness on stage frequently depends of performative elements which cannot or can only partly be put down in writing. This close interdependence between the comic, the carnivalesque and the improvised plays a seminal role in filling the term groundling with (new) meaning. This is already obvious from one of the earliest occurrences of the term within Shakespeare criticism, Maurice Morgann's 1777 'Essay on the Dramatic Character of Sir John Falstaff'. Attempting to defend Falstaff against accusations of cowardice, Morgann differentiates between the Falstaff of the actors and the Falstaff of the text. How Falstaff (and, implicitly, Shakespeare) benefit from this can be seen in Morgann's remarks on Falstaff's feigned death in the battle of Shrewsbury:

> This incident is generally construed to the disadvantage of Falstaff: It is a transaction which bears the external marks of Cowardice: It is also aggravated to the spectators by the idle tricks of the Player, who practises on this occasion all the attitudes and wild apprehensions of fear; more ambitious, as it should seem, of representing a Caliban than a Falstaff; or indeed rather a poor unwieldy miserable Tortoise than either. – The painful Comedian lies spread out on his belly, and not only covers himself all over with his robe as with a shell, but forms a kind of round Tortoise-back by I know not what stuffing or contrivance; in addition to which, he alternately lifts up, and depresses, and dodges his head, and looks to the one side and to the other, so much with the piteous aspect of that animal, that one would not be sorry to see the ambitious imitator calipashed in his robe, and served up for the entertainment of the gallery. – There is no hint of this mummery in the Play: Whatever there may be of dishonour in Falstaff's conduct, he neither does or says any thing on this occasion which indicates terror or disorder of mind [...].[32]

'Wrong' views of Falstaff's character, Morgann claims, are triggered by the actor's comic improvisation, not by the actual text or stage directions. The improvised, body-centred art of the 'painful Comedian' is thus excluded from the 'correct' Falstaff. A later version of the same essay indicates that Morgann was at least partly aware of the vulnerability of this line of reasoning. Falstaff's impious handling of the body of Hotspur, for example, is an indisputable part of Shakespeare's text. In the 1777 version, Morgann seems unbothered by this: 'I have nothing to do with Shakespeare's indecorums in general. That there are indecorums in the Play I have no doubt: The indecent treatment of Percy's dead body is the greatest [...].'[33] In a later version, however, this broad-mindedness gives way to a certain indignation:

> [The scene] was a Sacrifice to the Barbarity of the Age and He [Shakespeare] left the Players & the groundlings to make the most of it. Thus circumstanced the Manner of representing it does not come

Within the Line of my Censure. To the Player & the gallery Where the groundlings are now seated it belongs in full Property and I will not disturb their possession.[34]

The groundlings come in where blaming actorial improvisation is not an option, that is, where offensive elements cannot be explained away as not a part of the text. Just like Morgann's argument concerning Falstaff at Shrewsbury, however, they serve to construct an opposition between 'stage Shakespeare' and 'real Shakespeare'. They are 'a function of the process of literarization: preparing the play for consumption as literature, the critic needs this waste bin to contain its indigestible scraps of theatricality.'[35] As the pit was ousted from Victorian theatres, that with which it was most strongly associated – the comic, the improvised, the carnivalesque – was ousted from the official version of the Bard.

Against the backdrop of the class society that was Victorian Britain, the carnivalesque – and with it the pit – indeed offered 'the chance [...] to enter a completely new order of things'.[36] In a culture as invested in social distinction as Victorian Britain, its anarchic potential turned it into an anachronism – and, once it had been abolished, into a collective fantasy. The groundlings are a projection of that fantasy on the nation's own past. At the same time, of course, they are a result of the period's need to distinguish and separate, a need which, despite its alleged sacrosanctity, does not stop before the Shakespearean text. George Saintsbury is entirely representative of his generation when he claims that '[...] it can escape no careful student that the merely playwright part of Shakspere's [sic] work is (as is the case with no other dramatic author whatever) singularly separable.'[37]

## Dumb shows and noise

The components of the 'playwright part' which nineteenth-century critics relegated to the groundlings are not exactly new. Certain forms of verbal exuberance and playfulness continue to offend long after neoclassicism has fallen out of fashion. The traditional explanation for these 'faults' is only slightly modified: instead of the Elizabethan audience as a whole, it is now the groundlings who are to blame. Almost 150 years after Pope, Shakespeare's puns still need to be excused, and integrated into the prevailing image of the Bard. F. A. Bather writes:

Broadly speaking plays in which the puns are subordinated to dramatic effect of the highest kind, in which they are pointed and artistically worked up to, are presumed to be of later date than those in which the puns are merely to raise a laugh from the groundlings, and are introduced without literary or dramatic skill.[38]

Following Coleridge, Bather does not condemn puns on principle: when properly integrated they are an integral part of the organic work of art. But where this is not the case, they are treated as typical of an early, immature stage of Shakespeare's career, overcome and made obsolete by later stages. A perceived blemish on Shakespeare's reputation, they are incorporated into the established version of his private and professional life which fashions Shakespeare into the protagonist of a Victorian *Bildungsroman*. In Bather's version of this development, Shakespeare frees himself not only from the depths of unmotivated punning, but also from the pernicious influence of the groundlings who demand it. Whether this implies an increase in dramatic skill, as Bather seems to claim, is at least debatable: getting the audience to laugh is, after all, no mean feat in itself.

Continuities between eighteenth- and nineteenth-century Shakespeare criticism (and Shakespeare is being criticised rather than critiqued in this context) go well beyond the puns. Passages which the Augustan Age routinely blamed on the Elizabethan audience are often precisely those which are now presented as concessions to the groundlings. A. C. Bradley's disquisition on Shakespeare's original spectators aptly summarises – at the same time as it subtly censures – more than two centuries of critical discourse on Renaissance theatregoers:

We are not to imagine that the audience at a private theatre (say the Blackfriars) accepted Jonson's dramatic theories, while the audience at the Globe rejected them; or that one was composed chiefly of cultured and 'judicious' gentlemen, and the other of riotous and malodorous plebeians; and still less that Shakespeare tried to please the latter section in preference to the former, and was beloved by the one more than by the other. The two audiences must have had the same general character, differing only in degree. [...] The tastes to which objection was taken [by contemporary dramatists] cannot have been confined to the mob. [...] Neither can these groundlings have formed the majority of the 'public' audience or have been omnipotent in their theatre, when it was possible for dramatists (Shakespeare included) to say such rude things of them to their faces. We must not delude ourselves as to these matters; and in particular we must realise that the mass of the audience in both kinds of theatre must have been indifferent to the unities of time and place, and more or less so to improbabilities and to decorum (at least as we conceive it) both in manners and in speech; and that it must have liked excitement, the open exhibition of violent and bloody deeds, and the intermixture of seriousness and mirth.[39]

But despite this no-nonsense approach to the Golden Age of Elizabeth and an unusually nuanced take on the period's theatre audiences, Bradley promotes a rather conventional view of the groundlings' characteristics and tastes:

What distinguished the more popular audience, and the more popular section in it, was a higher degree of this indifference and this liking, and in addition a special fondness for certain sources of inartistic joy. The most prominent of these, perhaps, were noise; rant; mere bawdry; 'shews'; irrelevant songs, ballads, jokes, dances, and clownage in general; and, lastly, target-fighting and battles. [...] It [the audience] liked tragedy to be relieved by rough mirth, and it got the Grave-diggers in *Hamlet* and the old countryman in *Antony and Cleopatra*. It liked a 'drum and trumpet' history, and it got *Henry V*. It liked clowns or fools, and it got Feste and the Fool in *King Lear*.[40]

This is a comprehensive summary of the critical uses of Shakespeare's original audience from the late seventeenth century onwards. But in addition to such neoclassicist watchwords as 'improbability' and 'decorum', Bradley introduces a significant new term, 'inartistic joy' – the enjoyment of which supposedly distinguished the groundlings from the rest of the audience. What exactly it is that the groundlings allegedly have a penchant for remains rather vague in Bradley's treatise. The precise nature of 'inartistic joy' does, however, become more tangible when looking for the place in which its constituents could be found in Victorian England. Sound effects, verbal exuberance, songs, ballads, jokes, dances and clownery were all staples of the music hall and of melodrama, forms of stage entertainment that before the repeal of the Patent Act had been firmly banished to the realm of non-licensed theatre. And if early modern groundlings could be presented as aficionados of the music hall *avant la lettre*, there was little if any doubt where their Victorian counterparts were to be found. In 1859, G. A. Sala beckoned:

Come with me and sit on the coarse deal benches in the coarsely and tawdrily decorated theatre, and listen to the sorrily-dressed actors and actresses – periwigged-pated fellows and slatternly wenches, if you like – tearing their passion to tatters, mouthing and ranting, and splitting the ears of the groundlings.[41]

Associating the groundlings with formerly non-licensed forms and institutions of stage entertainment was facilitated by the fact that the most popular offering, the melodrama, featured some of those traits that critics had traditionally objected to in *Shakespeare's* works, and put down to the influence of his early modern audiences: mixing of genres and lack of psychological motivation and/or probability. The former was a popular target for satire:

> The only points of Stage 'law' on which we are at all clear, are as follows:–
> That if a man dies, without leaving a will, then all his property goes to the nearest villain.
> But that if a man dies, and leaves a will, then all his property goes to whoever can get possession of that will.
> That the accidental loss of the three and sixpenny copy of a marriage certificate annuls that marriage.
> That the evidence of one prejudiced witness, of shady antecedents, is quite sufficient to convict the most stainless and irreproachable gentleman of crimes for the committal of which he could have no possible motive.
> But that this evidence may be rebutted, years afterwards, and the conviction quashed without further trial by the unsupported statement of the comic man.[42]

Such improbabilities reminded critics of some of Shakespeare's more laboured plots – the jealousy of Leontes or Othello are cases in point. Seemingly written to 'excit[e] his audience to the limit of their endurance',[43] they brought Shakespeare perilously close to the melodrama and its lack of social prestige. The alleged demands of early modern theatregoers provided an easy and by now more than well-established way of avoiding any association between the Bard and this popular form of entertainment.

At the beginning of the nineteenth century, the traditional division of the canon into 'real Shakespeare' on the one hand and 'audience parts' on the other had found an equivalent of sorts in a similar division of the London theatre world, where Drury Lane and Covent Garden, the only two theatres licensed for 'serious', spoken drama, towered over the non-licensed, hence intrinsically (far) less respectable establishments. As has often been noted, the Patent Act constituted not only a form of state censorship, but also an institutional consolidation of two different cultural spheres. In theory, serious, respectable spoken drama could be differentiated from popular entertainment solely on the basis of its place of performance. Even before the repeal of the Patent Act, this opposition was less than stable however. More or less random musical interludes were used to escape state control over the spoken drama. That way, the melodrama claimed a larger and larger share of the market originally monopolised by the licensed theatres. After the repeal, the situation of 'serious' drama could thus seem precarious – not only economically, but also because the differentiation between high art and light entertainment seemed in danger of collapse. When the actor Charles Kean, whose family name was so strongly associated with Shakespeare and high culture, strayed into the realm of melodrama (1852 in *The Corsican Brothers*), this left a critic like G. H. Lewes highly indignant. Commenting on a stage duel in which the original sword fight turned into a knifing when the swords broke, he writes:

> This does not read as horrible, perhaps; but to see it on the stage, represented with minute ferocity of detail, and with a truth on the part of the actors, which enhances the terror, the effect is so intense, so horrible, so startling, that one gentleman indignantly exclaimed *un-English*! It was, indeed, gratuitously shocking, and Charles Kean will damage himself in public estimation by such moral mistakes, showing a vulgar lust for the lowest sources of excitement – the tragedy of the shambles! But it is the fatality of melodrama to know no limit.[44]

Non-adherence to certain aesthetic standards seamlessly turns into a moral failure and, even worse, a national disgrace ('un-English!'). Just as seamlessly, this disgrace is then associated with the commonality ('vulgar', 'low'). By implicitly likening (a specific segment of) the early modern audience to the clientele of contemporary melodrama, critics implicitly define the groundlings' class affiliation. By asserting that melodramatic, hence popular elements of his plays are not part of his 'real' artistic intentions, Shakespeare is then – once more – claimed as the cultural property of a social elite – and used to help 'prove' that the increased presence of melodrama on the contemporary stage constitutes an undesirable deviation from established traditions of serious drama, not least because it grants the patrons of melodrama (or whom critics imagined those patrons to be) an undue influence. Dickens' Joe Whelks is a case in point:

> Heavily taxed, wholly unassisted by the state, deserted by the gentry, and quite unrecognised as a means of public instruction, the higher English Drama has declined. Those who would live to please Mr Whelks, must please Mr Whelks to live. It is not the Manager's province to hold the Mirror up to Nature, but to Mr Whelks – the only person who acknowledges him.[45]

By characterising the upside-down world of a theatre dominated by Mr Whelks and his likes with a distorted quotation from Shakespeare, Dickens implies that the right sort of theatre (to be described by the quote in its rectified form) would put Mr Whelks in the right sort of place: certainly not the one he occupies now. A stage ruled by Mr Whelks can never be an appropriate stage for Shakespeare. In those cases where the Bard seemed to be writing *for* (an early modern) Mr Whelks, he, at least in the eyes of A. C. Bradley, 'knew clearly what he was doing, did it deliberately, and, when he gave the audience poor stuff, would not seriously have defended himself.'[46] While it does little for Shakespeare's artistic integrity, this deliberate catering to the uneducated parts of the audience further cements the opposition between elite culture on the one hand and popular culture on the other: melodrama has always belonged to the lower classes, whether Elizabethan or Victorian, while the 'real' Shakespeare has always belonged to their betters. The historical constancy of this distribution was confirmed by empirical studies of the Victorian present, Mayhew's *London Labour and the London Poor* being most prominent among them:

> [Among the main] amusements of [the costermongers] are the theatre and the penny concert, and their visits are almost entirely confined to the galleries of the theatres on the Surrey-side – the Surrey, the Victoria, the Bower Saloon and (but less frequently) Astley's. Three times a week is an average attendance at theatres and dances by the more prosperous costermongers. The most intelligent man I met with among them gave me the following account. He classes himself with the many, but his tastes are really those of an educated man. – 'Love and murder suits us best, sir; but within these few years I think there's a great deal more liking for deep tragedies among us. They set men a thinking; but then we all consider them too long. Of *Hamlet* we can make neither end nor side; and nine out of ten of us – ay, far more than that – would like it

to be confined to the ghost scenes, and the funeral, and the killing off at the last. *Macbeth* would be better liked, if it was only the witches and the fighting. The high words in a tragedy we call jaw-breakers, and say we can't tumble to that barnikin. We always stay to the last, because we've paid for it all, or very few costers would see a tragedy out if any money was returned to those leaving after two or three acts.'[47]

The tastes of Mayhew's costers are clearly very similar to the ground-lings': they like the supernatural, the violent and the sensational, and it is clear that their expectations, only partially satisfied by Shakespeare, are shaped by the conventions of melodrama. This is obvious not only from a certain indifference towards the plot (most costermongers find the tragedies too long), but also from their 'sensationalist' preference for strong visual and emotional stimuli.

By presenting melodramatic passages in Shakespeare as concessions to a certain subsection of the Elizabethan audience, critics like Bradley[48] and Bridges distance Shakespeare and serious drama from mere enter-tainment. They also reaffirm an already well-established claim to the Bard as part of elite or high culture: linking the groundlings with melodrama fulfils essentially the same functions as linking them with the carnivalesque. That both should converge in the groundlings is not surprising given that melodrama preserved important elements of the carnivalesque culture of the pit, above all 'the importance of the specta-tors, not only as observers of the action but, perhaps most significantly, as participants in the plot.'[49] This included the traditional right to pass judgment. Early (though not necessarily later) nineteenth-century melodrama consciously united these responses into a collective – and not apolitical – 'voice of truth and justice'.[50] Exactly how just and truthful this voice was constituted a matter of debate, however. While some commentators saw the melodrama's clear differentiation between good and bad as a sign of its inherent morality, others perceived a cor-respondence between the ubiquity of the villain in melodrama and the alleged presence of criminal elements in its lower-class audiences. In both cases, the underlying assumption is that like attracts like.

## 'Wretched beings': The Elizabethan audience and Victorian morality

As in every part of Victorian cultural life, morality played a, perhaps the, decisive role in the period's approach to Shakespeare. Unavoidably, it also shaped its view of the Bard's original audience, for if contemporary melodrama offered cause for moral indignation, so – at least sometimes – did the Bard. As the former was seen as popular entertainment and hence *a priori* in need of social control, its offences did not destabilise existing cultural hierarchies. Shakespeare's 'lapses', however, did, and hence needed to be explained away.

Robert Bridges' 1907 essay on 'The Influence of the Audience on Shakespeare's Drama' is a prime example of the way that early modern theatregoers were used in the 'moral' approach to Shakespeare that begins with Thomas Bowdler's 1807 *Family Shakespeare* – and which, one hundred years later, was still far from obsolete. Whatever offends Bridges' moral sensibilities (and there are a lot of them) is explained as the result of an Elizabethan lack of ethics and finer feelings. Bridges uses an explicitly intuitive approach in diagnosing the obnoxious passages:

> The appeal of poetry [!] is primarily to the emotions and feelings: and since one can, without fear of intellectual disqualification, separate what one dislikes from what one likes, this first step may, even with Shakespeare, be taken in absolute security […]. Just as a chemist, who has some complicated mixture to analyze, will begin by treating the unknown compound with a simple reagent, and thereby find a precipitate which will serve him as a basis and clue to further examination, so I would begin by separating from Shakespeare's work the matters that most offend my simple feelings, and by the examination of the nature and cause of these offences find a clue to further procedure.[51]

It is for good reasons that Bridges calls the feelings that guide his analysis 'simple'. The simple is the natural, hence this particular epithet strengthens rather than weakens the claim to universal validity posed by his emphatic subjectivity – notwithstanding the fact that Bridges puts on a semblance of scientific objectivity by comparing himself to a chemist. Initially, his finer feelings are provoked by the same features of Shakespeare's work that already irritated eighteenth-century critics with their emphatic rationality. Regarding Shakespeare's 'foolish verbal trifling', he opines: '[I]t shows Shakespeare's desire to please a part of his audience with whom we have little sympathy, and proves that he did not aim at maintaining all parts of his work at a high level.'[52] Unlike the neoclassicists, however, he assumes that it is not the Elizabethan audience in its entirety that is to blame, but only its most uncultivated part. Although Bridges does not give a name to this particular subsection, the majority of his contemporary readers is bound to have thought of it as the groundlings.

Much worse than offensive form, however, is offensive content. Here as well, the idea of a subgroup of theatregoers specifically responsible for such lapses is retained: 'In Shakespeare's work we cannot wholly account for [obscenity] by any theory that does not embrace the supposition that he was making concession [sic] to the most vulgar stratum of his audience [...].'[53] What seems especially lamentable is that even female figures are subject to this flaw – with Bridges' definition of obscenity being a very wide one. Even Miranda's veiled allusion to adultery ('I should sin/To think but nobly of my grandmother/Good wombs have borne bad sons', *The Tempest* I, ii, 117–19) falls under it, despite the fact that the statement is purely hypothetical and brandished as a breach of propriety by Miranda herself. An 'Angel in the House', even as late as 1907, apparently could not be allowed to think such thoughts. From their surfacing in Shakespeare's plays Bridges deduces that part of Shakespeare's audience was defined by 'brutality' and 'coarseness', and that parts of the plays (though small ones) were written specifically for them. Passages explained in this manner include those that are particularly violent – 'the murder of Macduff's child, the blinding of Gloster, "the pittious moane that Rutland made"'[54] – but also verbal derailments such as Valentine's towards Thurio in *The Two Gentlemen of Verona* or Leontes' treatment of Hermione in the first two acts of *The Winter's Tale*. Constellations in which close personal bonds are violated draw particularly harsh censure. Claudio's cruelty towards Hero 'enfeeble[s] the plot of *Much Ado*', and Capulet's haranguing of his daughter justifies her disobedience.[55] That such exemplars of Shakespearean bawdy as Gonzalo's 'I'll warrant him for drowning, though the ship were no stronger than a nutshell and as leaky as an unstanched wench' (*The Tempest* I, i, 41–43) or instances of undisciplined, carnivalesque corporeality like *The Tempest* IV, i, 181–84 ('At last I left them/I' the filthy-mantled pool beyond your cell, There dancing up to th' chins, and that the foul lake/O'er-stunk their feet.') attract Bridges' criticism goes without saying.

The presence of such passages in Shakespeare's plays leads Bridges to construct the Elizabethan audience as fundamentally other. While the Bard's obscenities offend his own sensibilities, they did not clash with those of early modern theatregoers: '[...] Shakespeare had to reckon with an audience far blunter in feeling than he would find today.'[56] This audience is the reason not only why these reprehensible scenes make it onto the stage in the first place, but also why, in many cases, they are so promptly forgiven by Bridges.[57] For importantly if not exactly surprisingly, Shakespeare remains aloof from his auditors' coarseness:

> [...] [O]ne [should not] say that it was an advantage to have to write for a public of 'iron nerves'. These iron nerves were no part of Shakespeare's constitution; and to welcome thus the brutality in his work implies the belief that if his audience had been more like himself, and more capable of understanding his best, he would not have written so well. Insensibility is not incompatible with bravery, and in semi-barbarous natures may even be part of it, but it is as cognate with fear and cowardice. To order a fellow-creature to be burnt alive in one's presence argues iron nerves, and the people of the sixteenth century being possessed of this sort of stupidity, Shakespeare knew that he must reckon with it.[58]

Although it remains alien to the common Elizabethan (interestingly, the more differentiated view of the early modern audience is given up here), the moral sensibility so important for the Victorians' collective identity is shared by Shakespeare, who once more turns out to be far ahead of his age. The Bard's emotional dissociation from his unfeeling contemporaries is a recurring theme in this strand of Victorian Shakespeare reception. Although its logical pattern is obviously adopted from older criticism, the strategies used to substantiate it are more complex and go beyond the assumption of a direct relation between the taste of the audience (or a subsection of it) and allegedly immoral passages in the plays.

The porter scene in *Macbeth* is a favourite trigger of such rhetorical manoeuvres, not only because of its 'melodramatic' mixing of tragic and comic, but also for its violation of religious as well as sexual taboos. Among the critics who see this scene as an instance of Shakespeare catering to the demands of the 'lower' parts of his audience is A. C. Bradley. But while he cites the *topos* of the comprehensively guilty groundling, he modifies it in subtle, though important ways:

> The Porter does not make me [Bradley] smile: the moment is too terrific. He is grotesque; no doubt the contrast he affords is humorous as well as ghastly; I dare say the groundlings roared with laughter at his coarsest remarks. But they are not comic enough to allow one to forget for a moment what has preceded and what must follow. And I am far from complaining of this. I believe that is what Shakespeare intended, and that he despised the groundlings if they laughed.

Of course he would have written without the least difficulty speeches five times as humorous, but he knew better.[59]

The potentially subversive humour of the Porter scene, which is perceived as threatening the august seriousness of tragedy is contained by two coupled logical operations. Traditionally, of course, the scene was ascribed to the presence of groundlings in Shakespeare's theatre. While Bradley perpetuates this belief (the groundlings *did* actually exist), and describes their (of course entirely hypothetical) reactions in the conventional manner, he also denounces this alleged reaction as wrong: it is not what Shakespeare hoped to elicit. That way, Shakespeare is safeguarded against the moral and/or artistic blemish which the historical apology in its conventional form puts upon him: he did not in fact make concessions to the vulgar barbarians who populated the Globe. Bradley's argument thus almost reverses the logical operations of eighteenth-century criticism. While these were aimed at preventing a loss of status on Shakespeare's side by attributing the 'vulgar' scene to the tastes of a similarly vulgar audience, Bradley in effect achieves an increase in Shakespeare's artistic and moral credentials through his discussion of exactly the same scene. In his view, its high degree of complexity permits it to elicit the coarse laughter appropriate to its surface structure from the groundlings – even though this laughter is contrary to the real artistic aims Shakespeare pursues in this scene. *Honni soit qui mal y pense*: the Porter scene is turned into an indicator of the individual spectator's moral constitution. The groundlings' roaring laughter (*if* they laughed – Bradley does not take this for granted) points towards their own depravity, not to the intrinsic immorality of the scene as such. Bradley's own reaction is far superior to the largely irrational[60] response of the mob. Not only does the porter fail to make him laugh, he does not even make him smile, for as a professor of literature, he recognises Shakespeare's real intentions behind the mob-pleasing surface. The complex structure of this seemingly simple scene not only increases Shakespeare's already considerable prestige by protecting him against allegations of immorality, it also legitimates the existence of him (and a male it certainly is at this point) who is capable of recognising this complexity: the literature specialist as produced by university departments of English.

Regarding the groundlings' alleged immorality, Bradley remains conventional. What is new however is that Shakespeare is no longer imagined as consciously writing down to them – Coleridge's 'No man of genius ever wrote for the mob' is more than a distant echo. As a matter of fact, the newly discovered groundlings (just like Coleridge's idea of a split audience) make the idea of Shakespeare selling out to his audience even more problematic than it already was. By focussing on this specific segment of early modern theatregoers, the historical apology in its traditional form is basically rendered invalid since Shakespeare's 'lapses' can no longer be explained as due to the circumstances. Instead, they appear as a selective reaction to very specific givens of his professional surroundings – a reaction which seems more and more like a matter of free choice rather than an unavoidable necessity. This, in turn, can elicit rather laboured lines of argument. J. W. Hales, writing twenty years before Bradley, provides an example:

> I have not been careful to allude in this Paper to what is commonly said as to the disputed passage [the Porter scene] by those who allow it to be by Shakespeare, that it was inserted for the sake of the groundlings, or the gods, as we should say, because I am not inclined to think that Shakespeare would have made any undue sacrifice to that part of his audience. [...] Moreover, is it so certain that such an interruption of the terror would have gratified the 'groundling'? Would not the genuine animal – and individuals of his [sic] species were and are to be found in other parts of the theatre besides that from which he derives his name – have rather had 'On Horror's head horror accumulate?' – the darkness deepened, his blood yet more severely chilled [,] his every hair made to stand on end? The thorough-bred sensationalist would surely vote the Porter to be an obnoxious intrusion. He would long for a draught of raw terror, and it is from such a potation that the Porter debars him.[61]

On the one hand, Hales explicitly refers to an existing tradition ('what is commonly said') of explaining passages like the Porter scene as concessions to a specific part of the audience. On the other hand, he attacks the idea of a Shakespeare willing to sacrifice moral integrity to audience demands that is constituent in this tradition. He does so by questioning the nexus between inferiority and (in-) authenticity established by preceding criticism: 'The argument on which the rejectors of the passage take their stand is the intrinsic inferiority of it. An unsatisfactory argument. It involves two questions: First, is the inferiority of it so signal and admitted? and, secondly, if it is so, yet is the passage therefore not by Shakespeare?'[62] Like Bradley, Hales rejects conventional views of the passage as 'bad'. Unlike him, however, he concedes that even the Bard may have had weaker moments: 'Interdum dormitat Homerus.' Homer is sometimes caught napping. But Shakespeare never? No one would deliberately say so; and yet perpetually critics argue on this presumption.[63] The passage's perceived inferiority hence does not imply that it is inauthentic. A Shakespeare capable of producing the occasional blunder replaces the idea of an unvaryingly brilliant genius prepared to compromise his artistic integrity. Hales' matter-of-factness should not obscure the fact that the concomitant loss of prestige on Shakespeare's part is ever so slight though, and that no revaluation of the plays' 'popular' elements is intended. Quite to the contrary: Hales' most significant innovation is that those passages from which the existence of the groundlings had been deduced in the first place no longer need be seen as concessions to their tastes. The 'real' groundling – even when situated outside the pit – is a 'genuine animal', a 'thorough-bred sensationalist'. Shakespeare's 'bad' bits are simply not bad enough to appeal to these semi-barbarians, hence cannot have been put in in an attempt to meet their tastes.

Both Hales and Bradley deny a direct relationship between a scene that is perceived as obscene and impious on the one hand and the groundlings' demands on the other. This is an important step in the discourse on Shakespeare's Elizabethan audience in that it effectively separates the groundlings from the text to which they owe their existence. They have become a historical 'fact' independent of the Shakespeare canon. This has distinct advantages. By cleansing the text of the groundlings it is cleansed of the negative characteristics associated with them. Shakespeare can then join the great integrators of art and morality. Matthew Arnold pronounces contentedly:

> The motive of Shakspeare, the master-thought at the bottom of Shakspeare's production, is the same as the master-thought at the bottom of the production of Homer and Sophocles, Dante and Molière, Rousseau and George Sand. With all the differences of manner, power and performance between these makers, the governing thought and motive is the same. It is the motive enunciated in the burden to the famous chorus in *Agamemnon* – [...] 'Let the good prevail.' Until this is recognised, Shakspeare's work is not understood. We connect the word morality with preachers and bores, and no one is so little of a preacher and bore as Shakspeare; but yet to understand Shakspeare aright, the clue to seize is the morality of Shakspeare. The same with the work of the older French writers, Molière, Montaigne, Rabelais.[64]

Because not all Victorians equally subscribed to 'Victorian morality', turning Shakespeare into a paragon of this ethical code is an act of appropriation in more than one sense. Various social studies, the government's Blue Books among them, attested the contemporary lower classes the same degree of brutalisation that Bridges, Bradley, Hales and others present as the defining characteristic of the groundlings. The depravity of the lower classes is in fact a recurring theme in a wide variety of publications, ranging from Matthew Arnold's *Culture and Anarchy*[65] to the novels of George Gissing[66] and, of course, the proto- (or perhaps pseudo-) sociological studies of Henry Mayhew. The latter's description of the audience at a penny gaff foregrounds carnivalesque unruliness as well as moral indifference:

> The 'comic singer', in a battered hat and the huge bow to his cravat, was received with deafening shouts. Several songs were named by the costers, but the 'funny gentleman' merely requested them 'to hold their jaws', and putting on a 'knowing' look, sang a song, the whole point of which consisted in the mere utterance of some filthy word at the end of each stanza. Nothing, however, could have been more successful. The lads stamped their feet with delight; the girls screamed with enjoyment. Once or twice a young shrill laugh would anticipate the fun – as if the words were well known – or the boys would forestall the point by shouting it out before the proper time. When the song was ended the house was in a delirium of applause. The canvas front to the gallery was beaten with sticks, drum-like, and sent down showers of white powder on the heads in the pit. [...] [The performance forced] into the brains of the childish audience before them thoughts that must embitter a lifetime, and descend from father to child like some bodily infirmity.[67]

With some slight modifications, this passage might pass for a description of groundling behaviour at the Globe. That penny gaff culture went against everything that the Victorian middle class believed in is evident (the discrepancy between the morally sick children described by Mayhew and the child martyrs and child saints of a Dickens could hardly be greater). At the same time, Mayhew's account features many of the elements usually associated with the groundlings: music, physical clowning and above all, obscenity. Mayhew's costers live in a realm of libidinous anarchy, an exotically foreign world that exists in the midst of Victorian respectability.[68] As a bourgeois projection,[69] they fulfil functions similar to those of the groundlings.[70]

Habitually presented as a means of social integration, Victorian morality was in fact class-specific. In the eyes of their 'betters', the lower classes had little if any moral integrity. If Shakespeare's moral lapses are blamed on a segment of the Elizabethan audience whose moral depravity resembles that of contemporary lower classes, this implies that just as the groundlings have no part in 'real' Shakespeare, their Victorian equivalents are excluded from participation in the national culture represented by the Bard. Disreali's much-quoted 'two nations' not only adhere to two different moral codes, they also have two different Shakespeares at their disposal: melodramatic interludes, razzle-dazzle, coarseness and obscenity for the groundling, whether Elizabethan or Victorian, the aesthetically valuable rest for the higher classes. What one likes about Shakespeare ultimately defines who one is:

> [...] Shakespeare should not be put into the hands of the young without the warning that the foolish things in his plays were written to please the foolish, the filthy for the filthy, and the brutal for the brutal; and that, if out of veneration for his genius we are led to admire or even tolerate such things, we may be thereby not conforming ourselves to him, but only degrading ourselves to the level of his audience, and learning contamination from those wretched beings who can never be forgiven their share in preventing the greatest poet and dramatist of the world from being the best artist.[71]

Given the predilections of the 'wretched beings' at the Globe and the apparently inevitable need to cater to them, it is rather remarkable that Shakespeare also managed to include the soaring flights of intellect and the moments of unparalleled poetic beauty that turn him into the world's 'greatest dramatist' (if not artist). Victorian critics can explain this too, however. Bradley concedes: 'Ignorant, noisy, malodorous, too fond of dances and songs and dirty jokes, of soldiers and trumpets and cannon, the groundling might be: but he liked poetry. If he had not liked it, he, with his brutal manners, would have silenced it, and the Elizabethan drama could never have been the thing it was.'[72] The national poet, it seems, depended on the boisterous scallywags in his audience in more ways than one.

## A nation of groundlings?

Within the contexts analysed so far, Victorian notions of the Elizabethan audience and more especially of the groundlings have proven to be thoroughly negative. Early modern theatregoers, particularly those in the pit, are a counter-model to the collective identity of those who claim Shakespeare for hegemonial culture. Against this backdrop it appears more than a little incongruous that one of the foremost Victorian Shakespeare critics, Edward Dowden, should have written the following: 'The [Elizabethan] drama was not the creation of a few eminent individuals, but rather a product of the national mind distinguished by the features of the national character.'[73] For him, just as for Hazlitt before him, the excellence of Elizabethan drama is the manifestation of a collective sensibility rather than the result of individual talent. Romantic notions of genius and *Volkspoesie* (folk poetry) are clearly far from obsolete.

Viewing the English Renaissance as a period of national greatness, as Dowden does, is of course diametrically opposed to the way the traditional historical apology uses the period. As the *topos* of the Elizabethan audience is an integral part of that apology, one would expect critical conceptions of it to change radically as soon as the early modern age itself is revaluated. We see this happen with Hazlitt and, to a somewhat lesser extent, with Coleridge. The majority of Victorian critics, however, do not take this step – with one notable exception: historians, particularly historians of English literature. Well before Dowden, well before Bradley and his poetry-loving ruffians, J. A. Froude presents a version of the Elizabethans that is a de facto refutation of the accepted picture of Elizabethan theatregoers. His idea of the period is a backward-looking utopia of sorts:

> No great general ever arose out of a nation of cowards; no great statesman or philosopher out of a nation of fools; no great artist out of a nation of materialists; no great dramatist except when the drama was the passion of the people. Acting was the especial amusement of the English, from the palace to the village green. It was the result and expression of their strong tranquil possession of their lives, of their thorough power over themselves, and power over circumstances. They were troubled with no subjective speculations; no social problems vexed them with which they were unable to deal; and in the exuberance of vigour and spirits they were able, in the strict and literal sense of the word, to play with the materials of life.[74]

Similar concepts appear in the new genre of literary history, particularly relevant to public discourse because of its focus on the national. Ideas of Shakespeare's popular theatre and his popular audience as presented in these histories differ considerably from those discussed so far. Ward's

*History of English Dramatic Literature to the Death of Queen Anne* is a *locus classicus* of the new paradigm:

> Before the Elisabethan [sic] period, there existed no higher secular literature which was, properly speaking, the possession of the nation. It was unacquainted with what it possessed, and therefore did not possess it. [...] The stage had at last furnished a field for the growth of a literature which was *of its nature essentially popular* [my emphasis]. Men of talent, quite recently even men of genius, had begun to awake to so magnificent an opportunity. [...] When, therefore, Shakspere came up to London as a youth ambitious of trying his fortune, he had before him the choice of entering the old or the new sphere of literary life. [...] Shakspere, without wholly abandoning the intent to please by literary offerings of the other kind, chose the stage. The motives which determined the choice it is impossible to estimate; the result was that he at once and for ever associated his genius with the tendency which popularised and nationalised poetic literature.[75]

Because of the collective nature of theatre, the drama more than other literary genres offers an opportunity to represent, and thus pass on, a spirit of national unity. A genuinely 'popular' theatre, uniting all social classes in a shared theatrical experience, is a miniature model of the nation as such. In the context of cultural nationalism conceptions of the 'mixed' Elizabethan audience are therefore necessarily positive. Social or intellectual elites and the 'coterie theatre' produced for them are demoted to a negative foil against which the star of the truly national drama shines all the brighter. Boas remarks:

> [...] [T]he growth of permanent theatres guaranteed that the drama should have as its patrons and inspirers, not a clique or a coterie, but the nation at large. Sidney and his school might sigh after an ideal of classical perfection, and ridicule the conventionalities of popular drama, rendered so transparent by the simplicity of Elizabethan mise-en-scène. But the people, with its eager, straining life, was careless of perfection. What it wanted was vigour and movement, and these it found in the plays which were the product of untutored instinct, not of formal rule. Thus a mighty impulse was given to the native species of dramatic art, and that in more ways than one.[76]

Boas's phrasing is unambiguous: 'clique' and 'coterie' are the antipole to the people with its natural, instinctive desires. The animal crudeness that characterises the groundlings in their negative incarnation is here presented as a manifestation of unbridled vigour – the people's 'eager, straining life' is an unmistakeable sign of the nation's vitality. Such accounts coexist with the thoroughly negative ones outlined earlier; in fact, one and the same critic's views of audiences at the Globe can vary widely, depending on whether early modern theatregoers are meant to represent the English nation as a whole or to explain the perceived weaknesses of Shakespeare's plays. Although he presented the groundlings as primitive sensationalists when discussing the Porter scene in *Macbeth*, J. W. Hales proposes an exceedingly positive view of the Elizabethans elsewhere, attesting them 'active intellectuality', 'keen intellectual impulses', 'readiness and facility of their imaginations': 'Was there ever in England such an age of movement? – an age so eager, so fearless, so sanguine, so exultant in its liberty, so swift to do or die? Never, perhaps, was the national imagination so quickened and so vigorous.'[77]

'Vigour', 'movement', 'eagerness' – Boas and Hales even use the same words in their respective descriptions of Elizabethan England.[78] Hardiness, vitality and intellectual agility become increasingly popular attributes to bestow on the Elizabethans from the late nineteenth century onwards as a certain picturesqueness begins to dominate critical accounts of Shakespeare's first audiences. Often, this goes hand in hand with a tendency to mystify those who flocked to the Globe, the Merry Englanders whom critics more and more come to see not as 'wretched beings' but as appealingly exotic not-quite aliens.

> His quick-pulsed audience! Yes, we must take that into account. Athenian audiences are a mystery; Elizabethan audiences more mysterious still. Was it the grandeur of the age in which they lived? Or the might of the ale which they quaffed? Or the 'merrie heart', which has long ceased to be a symbol of England? What was it which fired their brains with intelligence and made them appreciate drama, whose power is, after all, literary, though human, not conveyed through incident or 'situations'; the most exacting drama which the world has seen; of which, indeed, Shakspere is but as a 'Jupiter' in a sphere of planets; drama appealing to intellect and not to curiosity.[79]

Mysterious and inscrutable (the contrast between grandeur and strong ale – *coincidentia oppositorum* – heightens rather than curtails their allure), the Elizabethans become a quasi-metaphysical phenomenon. This does not necessarily imply a lowering of the status of Shakespeare himself. It rather seems that his prestige has reached such dimensions as to rub off on his fellow playwrights and the period's theatre-going public. (Re-) uniting him with the theatre does not downgrade the Bard, but upgrade the stage and its patrons. As Shakespeare is styled into a symbol of national greatness, the old historical apology is turned on its head. The Renaissance is increasingly viewed as a period of national greatness, a prime example of what Englishness is and what it is capable of. The theatre, in turn, is seen as the main voice of the period, a place where the essence of Renaissance England finds 'a habitation and a name'. In this process, early modern audiences and their national pride play a decisive role:

> But if the national mind had become more wide and diversified in its sympathies, yet there had never been, and never could have been, a time in which those sympathies were more generally and intensely directed towards the nation's own history. The greatness of England was now no phrase, no dream: it was a reality. [...] Let any period of contagious and active patriotism be taken in the history of any nation, and in the popular literature of that period will be found the inevitable reflex of that spirit – sympathy with the national history. [...] And so the great national age of the latter half of Elizabeth's reign was in truth a golden time for the most directly popular expression of the nation's historic sense – the English historical drama.[80]

In its own age, the Elizabethan audience appreciated history in the form of the history play to establish a national identity. By the Victorian period, it has itself become a symbol of this identity, not least because of its pioneering role in creating a national consciousness. Its 'sympathy with the national history' is certainly something Victorians are to emulate: early modern theatregoers have turned into a role model for later generations. That this notion is incompatible with received notions of the audience as rowdy and uneducated goes without saying. Given that nationalism relies on a fundamentally positive concept of the people, singling out the groundlings as responsible for Shakespeare's moral and artistic lapses presents a considerable argumentative difficulty. The problem is, of course, not exactly new: eighteenth-century notions of the 'age of Shakespeare' as a time of unaffected, genuinely English simplicity also relied on a thoroughly positive image of the time's theatre-going public. Deriving from an anti-French impetus, this idea exists simultaneously with the conventional historical apology. In effect, nineteenth-century critics, even and especially where they present the Elizabethan audience as a model of Englishness and national pride, are no more consistent than their predecessors. Hales rhapsodises about the vitality and cleverness of Elizabethan audiences, but reduces the groundlings to a level even below that of the already 'low' Porter scene. Thomas Seccombe and J. W. Allen declare popularity with the people the defining characteristic of a truly national literature, yet explain Tamburlaine's 'rhodomontade' as a concession to the groundlings.[81] Even Ward is ambivalent. Concerning the authorship of *The Birth of Merlin*, he argues: '[...] [T]he possibility of Shakspere's participation in the piece is out of the question. [...] [H]ad Shakespeare addressed himself to this part of the Arthurian legend, he would hardly have contented himself with dressing it up in this way for the gratification of the groundlings.'[82]

These incongruities are inadequately explained as the idiosyncrasies of individual authors – they are symptomatic of the problems inherent in turning the Bard and his age into a symbol of English national greatness while continuing to use his audience, albeit only a specific part of it, to excuse passages incompatible with Victorian middle- and upper-class sensibilities. A period that wanted to see Shakespeare as an 'angel messenger of the Almighty God'[83] somehow had to deal with the fact that he was perhaps not the most suited preacher of the period's master narratives. Its solution was to add to, or perhaps rather narrow down the old historical apology and invent the groundling, a creature whose amorality, alleged penchant for melodrama and generally riotous behaviour likened him to the contemporary lower classes. By constructing their Shakespeare in opposition to the groundlings, Victorians placed him in opposition to the lower strata of their own society. There is of course a glaring opposition between this class-bound Shakespeare and the rhetoric of national unity for which he is enlisted. The Bard provides both a means of national self-definition and an instrument of inner-English social differentiation, a class marker: hence the numerous ambiguities and inconsistencies in the period's concept(s) of Shakespeare's Elizabethan audience. Where Victorian criticism arrives at something like a solution to this dilemma, this solution involves the groundlings. The new species permits critics to define Shakespeare's greatness as resulting from the exemplary Englishness of a socially undefined Renaissance audience. At the same time, elements of the plays that are seen as incompatible with a quasi-religious veneration of the Bard are blamed on the groundlings, who are thus not only excluded from the 'official' Shakespeare, but also from the nation which he officially represents.

# 4
## Childish and Primitive: Shakespeare's Elizabethan Audience and the Turn-of-the-century Theatrical Avant-garde

Between 1890 and 1940, the national poet is refashioned in ways that affect conceptions of his Elizabethan audience in a particularly tangible manner. Shakespeare is now increasingly, and with increasing explicitness, claimed by groups that think of themselves as an avant-garde, or, alternatively, as the last stronghold of high culture, but in any case, as a minority. The discourse on his original audience reflects this process in at least three different (not always neatly separable) ways. It positions the Bard vis-à-vis the theatrical avant-garde of the turn of the century, it identifies (or rather, re-discovers) the early modern addressees for Shakespeare's newly foregrounded complexity, and it uses his original audience to historicise him – and thus turns the serious study of Shakespeare into a prerogative for the specialist, that is, the professional, university-tenured Shakespearean. The most prominent change during these decades is hence that early modern theatregoers are imagined with increasing variety. Only rarely do established traditions become obsolete, thus old and new ideas about Shakespeare's first audiences, even when they directly contradict each other, can be found side by side, with already existing strands of the discourse being subtly modified to accommodate new 'discoveries' about Shakespeare's original clientele. The groundlings lose some (if certainly not all) of their pre-eminence. To many a critic, the role they played in nineteenth-century criticism begins to seem quintessentially Victorian, and therefore outmoded. In the British Academy's Shakespeare Lecture of 1929, John Dover Wilson advocated a new start:

> The Victorian Shakespeare [...] condescends to lay aside the philosopher, but not for the purpose of devotion and instruction. No: he stoops from the heights of his serene omniscience to tickle the palate

of a degraded audience, to pander to the taste of Caliban himself with dish after dish made savoury with the spice of 'the foolish, the filthy and the brutal'. And if we ask why, the answer must be, to get his living, to make money, to purchase New Place, a coat of arms and other trappings of gentility, since if we are to believe Sidney Lee – 'his literary attainments and successes were chiefly valued as serving the prosaic end of making a permanent provision for himself and his daughters'. [...] [This idea] represents a hybrid monster begotten of an honest though ill-considered attempt to reconcile the Victorian conception of Shakespeare with certain facts which the Victorians overlooked or found it convenient to ignore. [...] To attack the 'wretched' Elizabethans for degrading Shakespeare is to attack the Elizabethan Shakespeare for not living up to Victorian standards.[1]

By pointing out how the preceding generation of critics and their Shakespeare profited from what they accepted as the 'correct' version of his original audience, Wilson (in a manner not dissimilar to G. H. Lewes in 1849) attempts to put an end to such critical manoeuvres. And indeed the groundlings fall somewhat out of fashion, though this does not result in the disinterested view of Elizabethan theatregoers that he seems to have in mind. Instead, the Elizabethan audience is simply imagined in different ways, which in turn serve their own explanatory purposes. While the nineteenth century had primarily focused on their alleged immorality and lack of propriety, many critics now advocate a seemingly more benevolent view: the Elizabethans were not depraved so much as childish and naive. Muriel St Clare Byrne's 1927 'Shakespeare's Audience' is exemplary for this shift in perspective. Unlike Wilson, she at least initially moves within the parameters of older criticism, for her disquisition on Renaissance theatregoers is spurred by what she feels is the excessive violence of some plays:

> For a point of attack [...] it will probably be simplest to regard first that aspect of Shakespeare's plays and those of his contemporaries with which the modern reader is least in sympathy. I mean, of course, those horrors and sensationalism designed to curdle the blood, which represented on the stage to-day, disgust in Shakespeare, and are usually absurd in others.[2]

For the Victorians, 'sensationalism' evoked contemporary melodrama. Byrne is aware of this frame of reference, but in contrast to the Victorians, what interests her about the genre are the imaginative – rather than moral – capacities it presupposes in its patrons. Her 'attack' is directed against A. C. Bradley, who, sometimes remarkably un-Victorian in his views of Shakespeare's audience, had credited it with a rather exceptional sensibility for the lyric, and with a distinctive power of imagination.[3] This eulogy introduces Bradley's final remarks on the Elizabethan audience, almost making the reader forget the preceding 30 pages of rather less flattering remarks in which Bradley mostly perpetuates the stereotype of the uncultured ruffian. Byrne, in any case, does not touch upon the latter – her focus is on the last few pages. The kind of imagination attributed to the Elizabethans by Bradley, she states, is incompatible with the 'horrors' in Shakespearean drama, on whose evidence the former's sensibility and imaginative powers must be rated as rather low:

> Accustomed to a very considerable degree of cruelty in real life they needed something as violent as the blinding of Gloster if their sensibilities were to be penetrated at all, and an emotional reaction aroused. [...] They had the same interest in blood and slaughter that a robust-minded undeveloped child has, and what is more they were familiar with both.[4]

While this is not really '[a] challenge [to] the most venerable and acceptable of myths'[5] – in the Victorian imagination, the groundling is certainly not so much a hyper-imaginative enthusiast as a rowdy barbarian – Byrne does however introduce a concept that becomes increasingly important in the period's reconfiguration of the groundlings: child-likeness. What Bradley had lauded as real imagination, Byrne, to use Coleridge's terminology, sees as mere fancy:

> [...] [I]t would be wiser, I think, to credit the Elizabethan audience not with an imaginative capacity distinctly superior to that possessed by the modern audience, but with an immense capacity for make-believe. By make-believe I mean the childish faculty of overlooking without effort any discrepancies which shatter the illusion of reality. [...] Pretence and make-believe are not the same thing as imagination.[6]

This somewhat overdeveloped readiness to suspend disbelief becomes one of the most commented-on traits of Elizabethan audiences in the decades up to around 1940, inside as well as outside Britain. In 1907, G. P. Baker characterises early modern theatregoers as 'delightfully childlike'.[7] The Danish critic, Georg Brandes, uses similar terms:

Audiences felt no need for [...] aids to illusion; their imagination instantly supplied the want. They saw whatever the poet required them to see – as a child sees whatever is suggested to its fancy, as little girls see real-life dramas in their games with their dolls. For the spectators were children alike in the freshness and in the force of their imagination.[8]

The French critic, Charles Sisson, presents an almost identical scenario:

The other day I saw a little girl hiding herself behind a paravent, and sitting down on the floor. 'What are you doing?' said her mother. 'Come and knock on my door', she answered, 'I'm at home and receiving visitors today.' This childish, naïve kind of imagination provides us with the key to the imagination of the Elizabethan populace.[9]

In German-speaking countries the idea of a naive audience is quite common as well. Already in 1903, Wolff describes Elizabethan theatregoers as naive ('naiv') and easily excited ('begeisterungsfähig').[10] Levin Schücking's influential *Character Problems in Shakespeare's Plays* (*Die Charakterprobleme bei Shakespeare*, 1919) subscribes to similar views. Schücking sees a relationship between the child-likeness of early modern audiences and the 'popular' nature of the early modern stage:

In attempting to interpret Shakespeare rightly, we must make it clear to ourselves that his art, unlike Goethe's or Ibsen's, does not follow a course prescribed by its own limits, but is merely one mighty wave forming part of a great river. The popular theatre, for which he wrote, arises out of anonymous obscurity, like the cinematograph of our days. It is born of the people and suffers from the want of curiosity on the part of the uneducated and the children as to the question of authorship.[11]

The idea of innocence (*Unbekümmertheit*) is reminiscent of Coleridge and his split audience, where the 'lower' part derives 'innocent enjoyment' from Shakespeare's plays, while the elite part appreciates Shakespeare's philosophical achievements. Schücking, however, assumes that the audience is homogenous – although of 'limited intellectual capacity',[12] it was 'an influential factor' in Shakespearean drama.[13] His indecisiveness about whether the Elizabethans' childlikeness is a good or a bad thing is shared by many critics of this period. It suggests a basic ambivalence of the concept of childhood as such, which has its roots in differing views of human development and/or human progress. Locke's idea of the child as *tabula rasa*, to be formed into a civilised adult only through education, has its counterpoint in the Rousseauvian notion of the child as endowed with an innocence which makes it all but superior to an adult, and which must therefore be cultivated and preserved. While Locke sees the child as in need of education at the hands of adults, there is a sense in which Rousseau sees adults as in need of the child – if not as an actual teacher, then certainly as a moral exemplar, the embodiment of an ideal state of nature. The Victorians' sentimentalisation of childhood is obviously indebted to him, but on the whole, this was a period which both in the ways it interpreted its own history and in how it envisaged its future was altogether more interested in progress than in a return to some vague state of original innocence. Broadly speaking, this was a mind-set to which Locke was more congenial than Rousseau, and it is the Lockean tradition which shapes the discourse on Renaissance theatregoers at the turn of the twentieth century.

To contemporaries, the link between the child-like on the one hand and the primitive on the other would have been familiar from another discourse which used the figure of the child for apologetic and legitimatory purposes, that of colonialism. There, it embodied the 'common and growing assumption [...] that the races existed on a hierarchy of evolutionary stages.'[14] An adult *in nuce*, the child needs a period of nurture and guidance in order to reach full adulthood and the rights and obligations that come with it. This made it ideally suited to legitimise the colonial endeavor, which could be presented as a kind of pedagogical mission to be terminated as soon as the colonised population had reached maturity. Until then, they had to be kept in child-like dependency – for their own good.[15] Like the colonised subjects (or at least the official version of them – the rhetoric of childishness conveniently masks the racist and exploitatory roots of colonialism), Renaissance theatregoers are both 'us' and 'not us'. Undeniably, they populated the period that produced the, by now, undethronable national poet. At the same time, they are sufficiently unlike 'us' to explain his occasional, sometimes fundamental, alterity. A kind of native informant, the 'child-like' Elizabethan theatregoer explains the otherness of Renaissance drama. At the same time, the figure of the child with its colonial connotations expands the discourse on Shakespeare, and on his original audience, to include the concept of exoticism: the historically distant becomes as strange and foreign, and therefore as engrossing, as the geographically remote. This lays important groundwork for many of the uses to which Shakespeare's original audience is put as the century progresses.

## Making pictures

The primitiveness of Shakespeare's age appeared to manifest itself with particular clarity in the bareness of the Elizabethan stage, which could not but appear utterly alien to a period that witnessed the apex of pictorial realism in the theatre. The stark contrast between contemporary staging practices and the Elizabethan conventions historical research was unearthing created a crisis of legitimation, at least for the more conservative of the era's theatre practitioners. Directors like Beerbohm Tree or Henry Irving believed in illusion,[16] and they had the technical means to render it as 'complete' as possible. But in order to do so, the on-stage world needed to be kept not only 'crucially separate and apart from the world of spectators in the auditorium', but also and above all 'complete, internally consistent and conventionally "real" [...], obeying historical, environmental, behavioural and dramatic laws bound together according to the principles of "unity"'.[17] Shakespeare, as had escaped no generation of critics thus far, did not always provide this kind of unity, in fact, he usually did not. This of course raised the question of whether or not his plays were actually being adequately represented by the lavish scenery of contemporary theatres, which were quite obviously far more invested in providing visual stimulation than Shakespeare's stage ever had been. Whether this constituted a form of 'progress' was hotly debated by the period's critics. Those who thought that it did, generally cited the childish Elizabethan audience as the reason why Shakespeare had not bothered to be more precise about his settings:

> To an Elizabethan audience time and place meant almost as little as they do to a child: one place was as good as another, and Verona conveyed, like the sea-coast of Bohemia, at most a vague atmosphere of strangeness but certainly nothing pictorial in the way of background. [...] For a child who possesses the [...] capacity [of make-believe and pretence] a simple statement suffices. The scene is Rome because I say it is, not because the child can imagine the appearance of Rome or does imagine an appearance for Rome. The nursery cupboard is a bear's den because architecturally it is a suitable structure, and because the child says it is a den, not because he has either seen a bear's den or imagines what it would look like. The bear is the thing, the den is so secondary as to be almost negligible. In just the same way I think the Elizabethans accept willingly the constant changes of scene upon their stage simply because there is no scene at all either in their imagination or before their eyes.[18]

'Real' imagination, according to Byrne, is essentially visual. The Elizabethans' lack of it conveniently explains, as well as legitimises, the discrepancy between early modern and contemporary ways of staging Shakespeare's plays. The lack of props and a stage design that deserved the name, which Bradley had interpreted as indicative of the Elizabethans' special power of imagination, is read in quite the opposite way, as suggesting something like imaginative sloth on their part.[19] Shakespeare, in this version of things, did not remedy this situation because of the limited technical possibilities of his stage,[20] however much he wished that he could. 'Proof' was provided by such passages as the apology of the Chorus in *Henry V*, which famously gave Beerbohm Tree reason enough to proclaim that '[Shakespeare himself] not only foresaw, but desired, the system of production that is now most in the public favour.'[21] The childish Elizabethan audience with its lack of interest in visualization is an imagined other to contemporary theatregoers with their taste for the visually lavish. These spectators (who actually went to 'hear' rather than to 'see' a play) help explain why a theatre in many ways totally different from Shakespeare's early modern one can still stage legitimate, authentic Shakespeare productions. Incidentally, they also boost the Bard's upward mobility. The audiences of 'spectacular' Shakespeare were predominantly middle-class.[22] To claim that Shakespeare 'actually' wanted to see his plays produced in a manner which suited their taste is to cement his position as minstrel to the middle classes.

Pictorial realism, however, faced major challenges as avant-garde directors began to question its aptness for Shakespearean drama. Just like the more conservative directors, they fashioned an Elizabethan audience to support their cause, and the Elizabethans' alleged mental inertness was questioned with gusto. Granville-Barker proposes:

> The 'visual law' of drama was, to the Elizabethans, a very different, and an arbitrary and inconstant thing besides. [...] We are now so used to seeing [the background] pictured, be it as *A drawing room in Mayfair*, or as *Piccadilly Circus*, or *The Forest of Arden*, or *A street in Venice*, or *Verona*, or *Rome*, that if it is not set before us we set ourselves to imagine it there; and we assume that the Elizabethans did the same – for, after all, the characters in a play must be somewhere. Yes, they must be, if we push the enquiry. But the Elizabethan dramatist seldom encourages us to push it; and his first audiences assuredly, as a rule, did not do so in despite of him.[23]

As regards the lack of visualisation, Granville-Barker's views do not differ fundamentally from Byrne's: the frequent changes of place in Shakespearean drama are no indicator of equally frequent changes of the mental picture evoked by Renaissance theatregoers. The two critics disagree about the relative importance they place on the visual in the first place, however.[24] For Granville-Barker, props are of secondary importance, for the actor's stagecraft can and will eclipse them anyway.[25]

The director to pioneer this kind of 'bare' production was of course William Poel with his Elizabethan Stage Society. Poel, like Beerbohm Tree or Irving, maintained that what he was producing on stage was a kind of realism. For him, that realism did not, however, take the form of an 'animated painting'[26] for the spectator to look at, but was conceived in far more participatory terms. It is 'the realism of an actual event at which the audience assisted, not the realism of a scene, to which the audience is transported by the painter's skill, and in which the actor plays a somewhat subordinate part.'[27] Involvement is what Poel expected from contemporary audiences, and what he believed Elizabethan theatregoers had provided as well. Needless to say, this ruled out thinking of the latter in any but the highest of terms (at least theoretically). As far as his contemporary clientele was concerned, Poel was faced with the problem that even his rather select spectators had been socialised into conventional customs of behaviour at the theatre and were therefore hard to involve in the ways he envisioned. This was a problem difficult to solve, and approached only indirectly. Unable to turn his audiences into latter-day Elizabethans, Poel provided the required audience himself, in the form of latter-day on-stage Elizabethans, pipe-smoking 'gallants' placed on convincingly 'Elizabethan' stools.[28] Their presence visually compensated for the virtual absence of any stage design and marked the production as 'authentic'. But at the same time, the mock Elizabethans flaunt the failure of theatrical collusion: so alien is the 'higher realism' of Elizabethan Stage Society Shakespeare to contemporary theatregoers that the production itself needs to supply an audience capable of appreciating it. The gallants embody the almost exotic otherness of the Renaissance and its theatre, suggesting precisely the gap between past and present that they are supposed to close. In effect, the on-stage world remains as 'closed' as it does with pictorial realism.

Arguably, Poel and the Elizabethan Stage Society mark the point where the value of Shakespeare is no longer defined by his success with audiences. What legitimises Poel's productions, in his own eyes and those of his supporters, is not their albeit moderate success with the theatregoing public, but the authenticity to which they lay claim. The latter, however, can only be appreciated by an audience capable of recognising that authenticity: a highly educated intellectual elite or, somewhat more poignantly, 'a club of cognoscenti congratulating themselves on their historical insight'.[29] The gallants on Poel's stage, in turn, are the (mock-) Renaissance version of the cognoscenti who make up the intended audience of the Elizabethan Stage Society, and who are invited to identify with this stage version of early modern elites. That this amounts to more than just a comment on the historical circumstances of Shakespeare's literary production, and in fact constitutes a kind of proprietary claim to the Bard, can be seen from Poel's reaction to the 1912 *Shakespeare's England* exhibition. This Tudor theme park *avant la lettre*, a decidedly more popular undertaking than the Elizabethan Stage Society, featured a reconstructed Globe, in which a 30-minute 'Best of Renaissance Drama' was staged. Such compilations were a staple of music hall and variety programs,[30] and the mock Elizabethans at Earl's Court were much less demure than Poel's gallants. The *Pall Mall Gazette* reports:

> In the unroofed pit of the Globe Theatre, 'prentices in quaint flat 'prentice caps and vari-coloured fustian suits settle themselves on three-legged stools, or lounge on the ground smoking old white pipes, which somewhat resemble modern cigarette holders. They [...] while away the waiting time by playing leap-frog, etc., and listening to the thin sweet strains of the viola da gamba, the viola d'amore, the oboe, and the lute, etc.[31]

Poel was not amused by the idea of Shakespeare's having written for such an audience, for it was decidedly at odds with his version of Shakespearean drama. In *The New Age*, he complained:

> [...] [E]xception might be taken to the movement of the costumed figures who are supposed to impersonate the 'groundlings'. [...] Apparently it is forgotten that between 1590 and 1610 the finest dramatic literature which the world perhaps ever has known was being written in London, a coincidence which is inconceivable were the staging so crude and unintelligent as that which is shown us at Earl's Court. Everything there appears to have been done on the assumption that 300 years ago there was less amount of brain power existing among dramatists, actors, and audience than there is found among them today, while the reverse argument is nearer to the truth,

for a Shakespearian performance at the Globe on Bankside was then a far more stimulating and intellectual achievement than it is on the modern stage today.[32]

If what was staged at Earl's Court was obviously not the highbrow audience which Poel imagined for Shakespeare, it was also not the conventionally negative stereotype of the groundling. Rather, the frolicking 'prentices embody the idea of the lusty, energetic Elizabethan as popularised by late nineteenth-century literary histories. In a manner not entirely dissimilar to that suggested by the Elizabethan Stage Society, the Earl's Court audience was called upon to identify with these avatars of Merry England (*The Times'* coverage of the event refers to the 'merry Elizabethan populace' pouring into the tilt-yard[33]). In this case, however, the auto-stereotype on offer was not exactly self-chosen. The organiser of the exhibiton, Edwin Lutyens, otherwise famed for his country houses, was firmly middle class. His usual clientele certainly did not envision its Elizabethan pendant as playing leap-frog.

Though somewhat less ambitious than the much more intellectual Elizabethan Stage Society, *Shakespeare's England* at Earl's Court is based on similar premises. On the one hand, it is the Elizabethans' exotic alterity which makes including them in the show attractive in the first place. On the other hand, too much alterity would alienate the spectators and prevent them from identifying with their mock-Renaissance selves. The kind of faux Elizabethan staged clearly depends on the (supposed) tastes of the intended twentieth-century audience. Poel's gallants are markers of an academic, scientifically verifiable authenticity in the staging of Shakespeare; a peer-to-peer offering the highly intellectual Elizabethan Stage Society makes to its elite audience. The Earl's Court groundlings, by contrast, are meant to embody a non-cerebral, emotionally 'real' Englishness – what the exhibition's organisers thought their popular audience would appreciate. In both cases, what is offered is the exoticism of the 'historically displaced and geographically internalized'[34] – that which is self and other at the same time.

The contrast between Poel's stage gallants and those on show at the Earl's Court exhibition in 1912 strikingly illustrates the increasing diversification of conceptions of the Elizabethan audience from the late nineteenth century onwards. For the rest of this chapter, I will focus on the school that foregrounds what it takes to be the Elizabethan audience's childishness and immaturity, and continues to use it in the conventional way – as a scapegoat. The critics who focus on a target audience composed of early modern intellectuals will be the subject of my next chapter.

## Telling stories, asking questions

The temporal and logical inconsistencies in Shakespeare's plots had always been one of the main triggers for the socio-historical apology. If these 'faults' are now once more singled out for comment, it is because contemporary audiences were accustomed to the conventions of realism, particularly those of the 'well-made play'. Shakespeare's non-adherence to them presented a potential challenge to his iconic status (if also to the universal value and validity of realism), which was duly deflected. Byrne writes:

> In practice time was expansive or contractile as they pleased on the Elizabethan stage. Again, like children, the audience did not imagine such a thing as a time lapse: having embarked upon pretence it was prepared to pretend right through: time simply did not exist. [...] Given a really imaginative audience, that realized as he did himself the suggestive value of place and time, I do not think Shakespeare would have allowed himself to treat time in the cavalier fashion that he does, for example, in *Othello* and *Richard II*.[35]

Following well-established patterns, the Bard's own dramatic ideals are presented as more or less congruent with Byrne's, even if they have to take second place to the demands of the commercial Elizabethan theatre and its unsophisticated audience. This audience, while largely indifferent to temporal logic, has clear preferences when it comes to the presentation of time's duration on stage:

> That Shakespeare was fully aware of the dramatic value of time there is no manner of doubt: that he was even more aware of the dramatic value of speed is perhaps even more certain. Hence, I believe that, knowing the nature of his audience he was prepared to sacrifice the first to the second.[36]

From the vantage point of a public socialised by the conventions of nineteenth-century Shakespeare productions, speed is not objectionable per se. It becomes a matter of debate only where it leads to obvious inconsistencies in the plot – and hence interferes with theatrical illusion. The temporal structure of *Othello* or *Richard II* therefore cannot but draw comment. In 1907, Bridges had explained their notorious inconsistencies as a tribute to the sensationalism of Elizabethan audiences.[37] This is an assumption Byrnes shares, although she sees their penchant for the sensational as only one among many manifestation of the audience's general naiveté. If Shakespeare fails to conform to the demands of psychological realism, notwithstanding the fact that he secretly believes in them, this must be due to the demands of early modern theatregoers. Complicated hypotheses like the idea of a double time scheme turn out to be unnecessary, for the Elizabethan audience provides a much simpler explanation:

> [...] [S]peed is essential in a good story, and speed is one of the demands that a popular [!] audience makes, and speed is effective dramatically: hence it is possible to understand, I think how, given the Elizabethan audience, it would be possible for Shakespeare the artist to decide deliberately to exploit that audience's lack of appreciation of a lesser merit in favour of a greater. It is not a question of a lack of dramatic skill, but of acquiescence in the attitude of make-believe. The audience, as yet, had no desire to make dramatic conditions approximate to those of real life, because its eyes were not yet opened to the imaginative value of either place or time.[38]

The problem with this line of argument is that the merit which Shakespeare apparently considered the greater – in this case, speed – is not always the one that later critics think most important. In the case of *Othello*, Shakespeare's alleged choice of speed affects the feature arguably considered most important of all ever since the Romantics: characterisation. That Shakespeare should sometimes seem careless about the aspect of his art that subsequent generations valued most highly is very much of an issue for critics in this period. Could it be that one was focused on something Shakespeare himself considered less important, and did one perhaps miss his actual point? Of course not. Where Shakespeare's characters seemed sloppily conceived, that is, 'unrealistic' or 'improbable', this was due to the demands of the Elizabethan audience – or rather, their *undemanding* nature. G. P. Baker states:

> [The Elizabethan theatre-goer] came, as a child comes, saying practically, 'Tell me a story', and he cared not at all, provided the story was interestingly told, if he had heard another tell it before. It is doubtful if, even when trained by the best work of Shakespeare himself, Elizabethan playgoers rose as a group to the interest of our audiences in characterization.[39]

Given this indifference, early modern audiences must have been a hindrance to the free unfolding of Shakespeare's genius more than anything else: '[...] Had Shakespeare written for the more critical of our public today he would have had a much easier task than the Elizabethans allowed him in working out the characterization which primarily interested him.'[40]

As we have seen, dissociating Shakespeare from the historical circumstances in which he lived (and, more importantly, worked) is one of the most elementary operations of the socio-historical apology. For the school of criticism under discussion in this chapter, this notion acquires a renewed urgency. Many of the period's leading dramatists thought of themselves as avant-garde and carefully cultivated a certain *un*popularity with, and disdain for, the general public – Shaw being the most notorious example. Generally speaking, the idea that a 'good' (i.e. intellectually demanding, aesthetically complex) work of art could also be popular was quickly falling out of fashion – in fact, popularity was becoming an indicator of artistic inferiority, at least in the eyes of some. For this way of thinking, Shakespeare posed an obvious problem, since his works had been both popular and acknowledged as 'great art' for centuries. The solution was the tried-and-tested one. It lay in establishing a distinction between the merely popular bits and those that 'really' constituted Shakespeare's art, with the two increasingly being seen as incompatible. Granville-Barker offers a particularly poignant version in which even Shakespeare himself is subjected to this kind of internal division:

> [...] [T]here were two sides to Shakespeare the playwright, as there are to most artists, and to most men brought into relations with the public and its appetite (which flatterers call its taste). There was the complaisant side and the daemonic side. His audience demanded exciting stories. He was no great hand at inventing a story, but he borrowed the best. They asked for heroic verse. He could do this with any one, and he did. [...] Euphuism had its vogue still. He could play upon that pipe too very prettily; and *Love's Labour's Lost* is as much homage as satire. But from the very beginning, signs of the daemonic Shakespeare can be seen, the genius bent on having his own way; of the Shakespeare to whom the idea is more than the thing, who cares much for character and little for plot, who cannot indeed touch the stagiest figure of fun without treating it as a human being and giving it life, whether it suits Shakespeare the popular play-provider to do so or not. And sometimes it doesn't. Life in the theatre will play the devil with artifice.[41]

Despite outward conformity – the play-provider wrests from the genius passages like the ending of the *Shrew* or the last act of *Two Gentlemen of Verona*[42] – Shakespeare's demonic side eventually wins (with *Hamlet*) over the side of himself that is willing to compromise. The perceived inconsistency of the plays turns into a similar inconsistency of his character. Shakespeare's demonic side is in fact his better self – the part of him that writes for an intellectually and aesthetically demanding posterity, not his lowbrow contemporaries.

Turning Shakespeare into a fellow avant-gardist, a kind of Shaw *avant la lettre*, was significantly complicated by some of the plays he had produced. While the newly established subgenre of the problem play[43] enhanced his credentials as an intellectual and social critic, parts of the canon retained what could be seen as a lack of seriousness and political commitment. Critics were particularly vexed by a perceived similarity between Shakespeare's plays on the one hand and the kind of entertainment preferred by popular contemporary audiences on the other:

> To judge from the whole mass of the dramatic fare submitted to it, the exciting stories, the medley of incidents, the abundance of displays of physical skill, the general atmosphere of alarums and excursions, the [Elizabethan] audience went to the theatre primarily to please and amuse itself. If a modern parallel is illuminating the audience was, psychologically speaking, an amalgam of the Bulldog Drummond and the musical comedy or the variety audiences of to-day. It received its pleasure from a good story; from having its emotions thoroughly aroused; from having its senses appealed to by music, dancing, noise and spectacle; from being deliciously thrilled by exciting events and crises; and finally from observing – as the Bulldog Drummond audience does to-day – the spectacle of behaviour on the part of the characters which would arouse in it not any 'obstinate questionings' but continuous and sympathetic moral assent.[44]

If the Elizabethan audience 'went to the theatre for entertainment and not for education or tragic kathartic experience or indeed anything save pleasure in the simplest meaning of the word',[45] then this parallels the way that the turn-of-the-century theatrical avant-garde saw audiences at the established theatres, including the 'respectable' ones. Already in 1882, William Archer had complained: 'Pleasure, and that of the least elevating sort, is all the public expects or will accept at even our best theatres. [...] The British public wants sedatives and not stimulants in a theatre, and it is the essence of great and serious modern drama to be stimulant and not sedative.'[46] Archer's contrasting of 'stimulants' with 'sedatives' provides the background against which to read Byrne's juxtaposition of 'obstinate questioning' and 'continuous and sympathetic moral assent'. Both essentially describe the same problem: intrinsically valuable plays (identified as such by critics and a small group of aficionados) fail to find favour with the general public. In the eyes of the most prominent British producer of such plays, Bernard Shaw, this was because:

> at present [...] mature and cultivated people do not go to the theatre, just as they do not read penny novelets; and when an attempt is made to cater for them they do not respond to it in time, partly because they have not the habit of playgoing, and partly because it takes too long for them to find out that the new theatre is not like all the other theatres. But when they do at last find their way there, the attraction is not the firing of blank cartridges by actors, nor the pretence of falling down dead that ends the stage combat, nor the simulation of erotic thrills by a pair of stage lovers, nor any of the other tomfooleries called action, but the exhibition and discussion of the character and conduct of stage figures who are made to appear real by the art of the playwright and the performer. [47]

The intellectual maturity and sophistication which Shaw sees as characteristic of (t)his intended audience contrasts sharply not only with the mediocrity of actual contemporary theatregoers, but also, and more relevantly here, with the childish naïveté of Elizabethan audiences. Byrne's 'exciting stories, medley of incidents, abundance of displays of physical skill, general atmosphere of alarums and excursions, [...] music, dancing, noise and spectacle', the main attractions for the child-like Elizabethans, correspond to the 'firing of blank cartridges by actors, pretence of falling down dead that ends the stage combat, simulation of erotic thrills by a pair of stage lovers', the 'tomfooleries' which Shaw sees as the preferred dramatic fare of his contemporaries. Schücking strikes a similar note when he writes:

> But did Shakespeare's company act before an audience of sixth-form schoolboys? What an absurdity to imagine that Shakespeare ever would or could have desired to summon the spectators of the Globe Theatre to a critical discussion on the (supposedly) traditional conception of the ethical value of the heroes of classical antiquity! [...] To read and interpret the Shakespearean drama in the light of the same standards as we do that of Ibsen would be as wrong as tacitly to identify the mental quality of Shakespeare's audience with Ibsen's. [48]

That Ibsen should be cited as Shakespeare's antipode here is telling. The primitiveness of Shakespearean drama may be only partial: 'an inexpressible delicacy and subtlety in the portraiture of the soul' stands side by side with 'props to the understanding of the most antiquated description'.[49] The modern drama, however, no longer needs these props, and Schücking certainly reads this as progress: Ibsen is quite obviously a cut (possibly several) above Shakespeare. Shaw agrees: for him, '[...] Shakespear [sic] survives by what he has in common with Ibsen, and not by what he has in common with Webster and the rest.'[50]

Under the impression of the New Drama and social realism, one part of the Shakespeare canon is thus attacked with particular vehemence: the romantic comedies. These 'potboilers'[51] are no match for the drama of Ibsen, Shaw or even Galsworthy: '*As you Like it* [sic], *Much Ado About Nothing, What You Will*! As if they and the things they ostensibly stood for were bones thrown to the dogs of the audience, that wanted their plot and their ear-tickling jokes.'[52] When compared to the 'problem play', romantic entanglements and sophisticated wordplay appear as mere trifles. Shakespeare's women, much lauded by Victorian criticism, lose much of their appeal. Rosalind, that great Victorian favourite, is nothing but a 'fantastic sugar doll'[53] to Shaw, no match for Isabella or Helena. The marriage lottery at the end of the plays with its sometimes obvious mismatches is also perceived as objectionable. That such patched-up weddings should count as a satisfactory ending is taken as yet another indicator of the alterity (and utter conventionality) of Elizabethan England:

> The Elizabethan mind, like the grocer's, was essentially practical. Society accepted the idea, which it inherited from the middle ages, that it was a woman's only business in life to get married as soon as possible. [...] Shakespeare saw how his audience regarded matrimony: he saw what happened on all sides of him. [54]

Ultimately, Shakespeare's popularity is the result of his readiness to make his plays as conventional and escapist as desired by his audience, an audience not in the least 'social, reformative or propagandist: they could no more have endured to listen to *Getting Married* than Bernard Shaw could bring himself to write a *Spanish Tragedy*.'[55] A conformist among conformists, he thinks twice about writing anything that might offend them, though the problem plays prove that he was actually capable of producing 'real studies of life and character'[56] – the part of his works that deserves to live on. Unfortunately, this kind of artistic achievement is not appreciated by many – either at the turn of the six-teenth or at the turn of the nineteenth century:

> Set your scene in medieval France, or Illyria, or ancient Rome, or Verona, or the Forest of Arden: call your characters Joan, the Dauphin, Duke Orsino, Julius Cæsar, Romeo, the Banished Duke, and the story-element, the insulating agent, allows you full scope to criticise our common human nature and behaviour. Set your scene in seventeenth-century London and call your characters Master Stephen and Master Matthew: set it in twentieth century London, calling your characters Mrs. Warren and Sartorius, and your mixed audience relegates your work to the category of Plays Unpleasant. They are too 'near and familiarly allied to the time': it is almost impossible for the mixed audience to escape their implications. [...] The Bulldog Drummond audience which demands of its writers what it terms 'a rattling good yarn', demands, as we may see for ourselves, the excision of such social problems as stir the genius of a Galsworthy. I have hazarded the deduction that the story-loving Elizabethan audience made the same demand [...].[57]

Victorian Shakespeare criticism explicitly and implicitly characterises the part of Shakespeare's original audience responsible for his 'faults' as lower class. There is no comparable specification here; instead, the audi-ence is described as 'mixed'. Apparently, the fact that those who per-ceive social realism as 'unpleasant' come from a variety of backgrounds deserves special mention. Byrne seems to imply that a less 'mixed' audience *would* appreciate Shaw – though it remains unclear what the common attribute shared by all in this audience might be. Like others of her generation, she appears to picture drama and culture more gener-ally as fundamentally a minority affair – both in her own present and in Shakespeare's day and age. This, in turn, links her to the theatre reformers mentioned earlier in this chapter, who often hold thoroughly conventional views of Elizabethan theatregoers. Poel, for example, despite the fact that he had denounced the Earl's Court groundlings of 1912 as something akin to calumny, uses them for the traditional apolo-getic purposes elsewhere. On *Romeo and Juliet*, he writes:

> Romeo's banishment brings us to the middle and 'busy' part of the play, where the Elizabethan actors were expected to thunder their loudest to split the ears of the groundlings; and Shakespeare, not yet sufficiently independent as a dramatist to dispense with the

conventions of his stage, follows suit on the same fiddle to the same
tune; and after all the ranting eloquence on the part of Romeo and
Juliet, we are just where we were before with regard to any advance
made with the story.[58]

That Poel of all people should chide Shakespeare for keeping too close
to the stage conventions of his times is surely one of the nicer ironies
in the history of Shakespeare reception – even if he, as well as Archer
and Granville-Barker, obviously took a certain pride in largely ignoring
the tastes of their own contemporaries. Their kind of director's theatre,
a revolution from above rather than from below, was based on a
disregard for the wider public that they did not attempt to hide, and
were not shy to attribute to Shakespeare as well. Granville-Barker writes:
'Shakespeare has been accused [...] of a bias against the populace. But is
it so? He had no illusions about them. As a popular dramatist he faced
their inconstant verdict day by day, and came to write for a much better
audience than he actually had.'[59] The Bard's alleged bias is not a blemish:
basically, Shakespeare is right. Shaw describes the ideal, but often non-
existing audience of the New Drama as mature and cultivated. This is
precisely what the Elizabethan audience, in the eyes of many a critic of
this period, was not. The Bard's historical situation thus resembles that
of the new dramatists at the turn of the nineteenth century: a suitable
audience is yet to be nurtured and educated. Shakespeare, too, turns out
to be an avant-gardist, albeit in some respects a fallen one: all too often,
he sacrifices his progressive artistic ideals to the demands of an audience
whose tastes are conventional at best.

The New Drama and those who produced it presented a major challenge to Shakespeare's iconic status. That Shakespeare's perceived faults
were the result of some absolute, almost metaphysical need to please
Renaissance theatregoers was no longer tenable, for Shaw and other
avant-gardists with their readiness to accept unpopularity provided an
alternative model of artistic integrity. But although their iconoclasm
towards Shakespeare does not take hold, this phase in Shakespeare's
afterlife arguably comes closer than any other to actually toppling the
Bard from his throne. The newly childish Elizabethan audience is one
way in which this threat is deflected.

# 5
# The Rediscovery of the Judicious Few

An Elizabethan audience composed of uneducated ruffians and/or child-ish sensationalists poses a number of problems for the would-be apologist of Shakespeare. If playwright and playgoers really move in totally different intellectual and moral spheres, dramatic communication is bound to fail – aside from the Bard's grudging concessions to spectators ultimately unworthy of him. And as always, his readiness to *make* such compromises throws a rather bad light on the national dramatist. All these difficulties decrease considerably once the 'judicious few' which Coleridge had identified as Shakespeare's 'real' audience, rather than the uncultured masses, are credited with having exerted the decisive influence on Shakespeare. The early modern playhouse then changes from a place of more or less continual theatrical failure into one of successful stage communication. The logic of the relation between dramatist and audiences remains the same, but is now presented from a totally different vantage point, for the influence of elite theatregoers is represented as thoroughly beneficial. Shakespeare writes as well as he does *because of* the judicious few. In the decades before the Second World War, following alterations in staging practices which turned Shakespeare from mass entertainment into something more intellectual and exclusive, this view becomes increasingly popular.[1] Here is John Dover Wilson in his 1929 British Academy Shakespeare Lecture:

> The Elizabethan Shakespeare was not [...] an Olympian pandering to a barbarous audience; he was a light-hearted dramatic poet in his early thirties who succeeded in securing what all poets of that age strove to secure, namely the admiring patronage of a powerful circle of cultivated noblemen at Court. For them he wrote his poems, and chiefly for them, too, as I believe, he wrote his comedies and

histories. And though he wrote to please, he did so to please himself quite as much as his patrons, for he admired them as much as they admired him. Their tastes were his own, and the mutual admiration sprang from 'the marriage of true minds.'[2]

Unike the groundlings, Shakespeare's cultivated, educated – and for Wilson, titled – addressees help to explain his outstanding literary achievement, not his occasional lapses. This notion of the Elizabethan audience – or rather, the part of this audience that really mattered – styles Shakespeare into the attending dramatist of a certain social class: 'the marriage of true minds' – the Bard is wedded to the aristocracy. While the non-aristocratic majority of Renaissance theatregoers continue to be used for apologetic purposes – its childishness and naiveté is 'discovered' at more or less the same time as the importance of the cultured few – the elite segment of the audience is presented as the reason why Shakespeare wrote plays as complex and demanding as he did: the gallants understood and appreciated this sort of literary effort. Which part of the audience a given critic focuses upon depends on his or her view of Shakespearean drama. Those who foreground its 'primitiveness' aim their attention at the broad masses and their alleged childlikeness, usually not even mentioning a more mature, cultivated sector. Those who read Shakespeare as predominantly complex and difficult concentrate on the audience members considered capable of understanding this sort of text: the educated, often aristocratic few.[3] The latter school effectively relinquishes the idea of Shakespeare's original audience having been more or less homogeneous. In his 1944 British Academy Shakespeare Lecture, H. S. Bennett chides:

> [...] [Critics] have rapidly proceeded to speak of the audience as though it were an entity, experiencing much the same emotions and interested in much the same intellectual excitements, no matter in what part of the house it sat. As a result of such an attitude, the groundlings have been credited with an appreciation of the subtleties of Elizabethan dialogue and rhetoric far beyond their reach, while the *élite* of the audience has been depicted as taking an interest in matters which they probably looked on as part of the price to be paid for the undoubted merits of the play as a whole.[4]

What the groundlings appreciated is described in highly conventional terms: 'wild horse-play and "slap-stick" farce [...], the noise of trumpets, the catches, rounds, and songs which form a setting to the struggles of the crowds, the wrestlings, broad-sword fights, challenges, dances, and battles'.[5] No wonder they loved *Hamlet*.[6] But neither this play nor the rest of the Shakespeare canon are all stage fights and slap-stick. To explain the presence of the intellectually demanding, aesthetically refined, all in all rather substantial rest, critics turn to the rediscovered 'judicious few'. For Bennett as for Wilson before him, the more exclusive part of the Elizabethan audience exerts the crucial influence on Shakespeare:

> For the cultured *minority* the dramatist displayed his tricks of style, his figures, his elaborate imagery, his verbal inventiveness and dexterity. [...] Subtlety of language was a delight to them, and they listened eagerly to the dramatist's inventions, their tables in their hands, ready to take down any phrase, or image or allusion which pleased them. They were 'the judicious', whose censure Shakespeare tells us 'must [...] overweigh a whole theatre of others'.[7]

This emphasis on the importance of the cultivated elite is a continuation of a tendency already latent in eighteenth- and nineteenth-century criticism. If it is argued that the 'lapses' in Shakespeare's plays must be put down to the influence of an audience implicitly and explicitly imagined as lower class, then this implies that the 'real', blemish-free Shakespeare addresses himself to the higher echelons of society. What is new is that the Bard's actual addressees are now named – and located in what are often rather exclusive social circles. The comedies, the 'potboilers' so despised by Shaw, are the first plays to be connected to aristocratic audiences. In their 1923 introduction to *Love's Labour's Lost*, Quiller-Couch and Dover Wilson voice a 'belief' that the play was written in 1593 for private performance in an aristocratic household.[8] In 1925, Campbell discovers evidence of a connection to the court in the same play.[9] In the introduction to his 1930 edition of *Twelfth Night*, Quiller-Couch hypothesises that the play was written for a 'polite audience',[10] narrowed down to a court audience by Leslie Hotson (*The First Night of* Twelfth Night) in 1954.[11] But it is not just the comedies which are thus gentrified: Alexander (1929),[12] Lawrence (1931)[13] and Campbell (1938)[14] concur that *Troilus and Cressida* was written specifically for performance at the Inns of Court; Paul (1950) hypothesises that *Macbeth* was contract work for James I, and in 1948, Bentley postulates that from 1608 onwards Shakespeare no longer wrote primarily for the Globe, but for 'the sophisticated and courtly audience in the private theatre at Blackfriars' which preferred romance over everything else.[15] Many of these hypotheses have now been superseded, but some have not. However they score regarding relative historical accuracy, there is a point to be made about the sudden interest in, and hence (re-)discovery of Coleridge's 'judicious few'.

The rise of literary modernism created a critical climate which privileged complexity and difficulty to an unprecedented degree. Shakespeare's plays had much to offer to the scholar in search of verbal and conceptual intricacy, but in order to make this approach seem historically plausible, critics needed to revise traditional notions of the Bard's original audience. In *The Essential Shakespeare* (1932), John Dover Wilson suggests:

> [...] [T]o understand Shakespeare, to follow the swiftness of his thought, the delicacy of his poetic workmanship, the cunning of his dramatic effects, the intricacy of his quibbles, to appraise in short the infinite riches of his art, we must think ourselves back into the little room at the Globe or its predecessors, in which his dramas were first given by a team of players, moving and speaking on a bare platform surrounded by a ring of faces only a few yards away, faces in front, to right, to left, above, faces tense with interest at the new miracle that awaited them, the faces of the brightest spirits and keenest intelligences of his time.[16]

'Swiftness of thought', 'delicacy', 'cunning', 'intricacy': the Shakespeare presented here is anything but simple. This, in turn, is made possible by the fact that his 'real' audience, the people he consciously writes for, is definitely not simple either, neither in the intellectual nor in the social sense. Patronage explains the outstanding achievements of an entire generation of dramatists, with royal patronage being an especially important factor: '[Under James I.], [d]ramatists were encouraged [...] to touch loftier and supremer heights, irrespective of puzzled and unappreciative audiences.'[17] Poetry, as Hazlitt had claimed, indeed becomes right-royal: the notion that Shakespeare's verbal artistry and intellectual complexity must have been incomprehensible to the majority of his original audience can be traced in virtually every publication from the period that focuses on the Bard's aristocratic patrons or the elite theatregoers he was 'really' writing for. But although the judicious few are conceived of as a kind of counter-audience to the groundlings, they fulfil precisely the same function. Just like them, they explain why the 'real' Bard is exactly what this particular critical school needs him to be – and why sometimes he isn't. Henry N. Paul's *The Royal Play of Macbeth* (1950) will provide an example of how the old apologetic patterns were transferred to a new part of the Renaissance audience. Like numerous critics before him, Paul attempts to provide an explanation for the inconsistencies in the play's plot. While the traditional solution was to blame the groundlings and their general lack of interest in the niceties of psychological motivation and temporal consistency, Paul offers a different way out: as it was written specifically for performance at the court of James I, he claims, *Macbeth* is tailored to the needs of the King, particularly to his dislike of long performances. Shakespeare accordingly compressed his subject matter – something he could be sure would not cause problems for a highly educated, astute court audience. '[*Macbeth*] contains as much dramatic material as the average play, but a much shorter time of performance is achieved by studied compression of speech. [Shakespeare] relied upon the superior perspicacity of the king and his court to catch his meaning.'[18] The players, otherwise popular scapegoats for Shakespeare's 'lapses', here become his accomplices in ingratiating himself with an elite audience – a clientele that incites both them and the playwright to prove themselves true masters of their profession. 'The royal presence gave the performance a due decorum often lacking in the public theatres, and this in turn was a stimulus to the actors. They could resort to refinements of delivery and of stage business which in the Globe Theater would have passed unnoticed [...].'[19] Unlike at the public theatres, theatrical collusion can take place in its ideal form, with playwright, actors and audience contributing in equal parts. The players in particular profit from the refined court atmosphere: it enables them to present the dramatist's intentions more fully and clearly than they could at the Globe. Paul can thus summarise contentedly (and already on page 2): '[...] [M]any difficult problems concerning [*Macbeth*] are solved when it is restored to its rightful position as one of the three or four plays which Shakespeare wrote, not for an audience such as that of the Globe Theater, but for the more highly intelligent audience of the English court.'[20]

While the judicious few are the period's favoured solution for bestowing historical credibility on its construction of a 'difficult' Shakespeare, they constitute not the only means of doing so. In a 1932 contribution to Eliot's *Criterion*, L. C. Knights presents an alternative view, though one whose tenor is very much compatible with other scholars' focus on early modern elites. Like Wilson and Bennett before him, Knights outright rejects the myth of the boorish groundling who populated the Globe and forced Shakespeare into making the concessions so much regretted by later critics. Instead of spotlighting the 'better' part of the Bard's audience, Knights, as it were, betters the audience as a whole:

> The point which I wish to establish is that of any typical audience at, say, the Globe, the majority were likely to have received an education of the grammar school type. [...] It is as false to regard the great majority of Shakespeare's audience as crude and unlettered, gifted by a happy providence with the capacity to endure as much poetry as the dramatist could give them, as to see Shakespeare himself as an unlettered genius who 'warbled his native wood notes wild' unconscious of the bonds of art. Behind the national drama of the age of Elizabeth and James I, stands the school curriculum and that method of approaching literature which was inculcated by masters in private and grammar schools and by private tutors. With that curriculum and that method the playwrights almost without exception, and the greater part of their audience, were familiar.[21]

There is no dissociation between playwright and audience here. English Renaissance drama is the product of a community similar to that described by the late nineteenth-century literary histories with their nationalist bias. Unlike the latter, however, community is a matter not so much of nationality as of educational standards shared by dramatists and theatregoers alike. Latin in particular is a decisive influence on the way audiences approach the drama:

> [...] [T]he standards applied to Latin literature were in some measure applied also to the words spoken on the contemporary stage, and [...] the attitude of the late Elizabethan audience to the words used by the dramatists was not so different from the critical attitude adopted towards Latin literature.[22]

The phrase 'critical attitude' confirms a supposition already suggested by Knights's mentioning a 'curriculum' and a '*method* [my emphasis] of approaching literature'. While the Elizabethan drama is not primarily meant to entertain, it is also not art for art's sake. Rather, it is a highly intellectual, not to say academic affair. Considering this, it is only logical for Knights to claim (and certainly not incorrectly) that the educational program of late sixteenth-century English schools had a direct influence on its development.[23] His version of the Elizabethan audience is deduced from this version of the period's drama, which, in turn, is informed by his understanding of literature more generally.

What interests him is 'the abundant use made of figures of speech by the Elizabethan dramatists, their brilliant and daring metaphors, their allusions, juxtapositions, and comparisons'.[24] This kind of 'intellectual athleticism', Knights surmises, must have been intended for an audience capable of appreciating it: spectators with 'a detached and at the same time vivid interest in words and the kind of pattern into which the dramatist might arrange them'.[25] This 'detached interest in words', in 'pattern' and 'metaphors' is of course the defining feature of New Criticism, and more generally what distinguishes the professional critics and/or academics of the first half of the twentieth century from their predecessors' often rather unabashed subjectivity. To focus on the judicious few is thus not only to put the seal of historical authenticity on a certain view of Shakespeare's plays, it is also to justify the existence of a new caste of professional literature specialists. For the latter, presenting Shakespearean drama as complex and difficult – seven types of ambiguity rarely suffice for the Bard – has clear advantages. A difficult dramatist quite obviously requires a specialist to comprehend, as well as expound upon, the many different layers of meaning present in his oeuvre. The fact that it produces (as well as hires) specialists of this kind can then, in turn, help explain the necessity of English as a university subject.[26] In what is really a revolution in the discourse on Shakespeare's Elizabethan audience, Renaissance theatregoers are presented in the scholar's own image. The Elizabethan audience as envisioned by Knights is an assembly of New Critics *avant la lettre*, the ideal audience for a drama that exemplifies T. S. Eliot's 'impersonal' theory of literature. Knights himself is clearly aware of this:

> If Mr. T. S. Eliot and Mr. Wilson Knight are correct in assuming the existence of a certain dramatic 'pattern' in the work of Shakespeare and his contemporaries – a pattern which has been unduly neglected by critics in their insistence on 'plot' and 'character' – it becomes important to know whether Shakespeare's audience were also aware of it or not. I believe that they were. The pattern is, of course, ultimately intellectual and emotional, but the approach to it is through the written or spoken word. That is to say an Elizabethan play must be regarded as a 'poem' rather than a 'slice of life' of the kind to which we have been accustomed since Ibsen, and only by bringing to it a keen susceptibility to language in its most complex forms can we gain from it all that its author intended to be gained, and that was manifest to large numbers of its first audience.[27]

This Elizabethan audience verifies the theories of certain critics, and hence is conspicuously *like* these critics in the interests that it brings to the drama. Re-imagining Shakespeare's original recipients in this manner involves a fundamental rethinking of the relationship between dramatist and spectators. The assumption is that Shakespeare's intention is usually congruent with his reception by the early modern audience: the Bard and his paying customers actually understand each other. For the rest of the twentieth century, the early modern playhouse becomes a site of successful theatrical collusion, not the place of continual failure that earlier critics had often imagined. The stage-or-study problem is neatly solved: L. C. Knights simply transfers the latter into the former. The theatre becomes if not necessarily a moral, then certainly an educational, even academic institution.

## The problem of irony

Knights's version of the Elizabethan theatre still includes groundlings, the illiterate who 'stood and enjoyed the blank verse as best as they might, and relished the horrors and the farce.'[28] They are, however, a minority – the predominant part of the audience, including the gallants, is imagined as capable of responding to Shakespearean drama in a more comprehensive manner.[29] Most critics, however, propose a more conservative view of Renaissance theatregoers, with the majority of the audience being of the groundling type and only a small proportion of gallants. This, in turn, poses considerable difficulties with regard to the intellectual demands made by Shakespeare's plays. How could they have been appreciated by an audience consisting mainly of uneducated ruffians? Many critics thought that in fact the groundlings were incapable of doing so, and in order to substantiate this claim, they introduce a concept particularly apposite to modernist sensibilities: irony. Gerald Gould's 1919 essay on *Henry V* demonstrates the uses of and difficulties inherent in this pairing in an exemplary manner. Writing in the immediate wake of the First World War, Gould proposes that the rah-rah patriotism of the play must not be taken at face value:

> None of Shakespeare's plays is so persistently and thoroughly misunderstood as *Henry V*, and one is tempted to think that there is no play which it is more important to understand. Irony is an awkward weapon. No doubt the irony of *Henry V.* was meant to 'take in' the groundlings when it was first produced: had it failed to take them in, it would have invited bitter and immediate unpopularity. But

Shakespeare can scarcely have intended that the force of preconception should, hundreds of years after his death, still be preventing the careful, the learned, and the sympathetic from seeing what he so definitely put down. *The play is ironic*: that is, I venture to think, a fact susceptible of detailed proof. [...] That Shakespeare was a patriot there is neither reason nor excuse for denying. What must be denied is that *Henry V* is patriotic. Precisely because Shakespeare *was* patriotic he must have felt revolted by Henry's brutal and degrading 'militarism'.[30]

Gould in a sense rescues Shakespeare from the moral opprobrium implicit in the traditional apology. The objectionable passages are there, but they are not really concessions to the disreputable part of his audience: they are ironic, hence do not mean what they appear to mean. As a consequence, what looks like a concession is in reality a means of exposing the moral questionability of precisely the sort of spectator that Shakespeare superficially seems to be catering to – though it remains unclear whom the latter is being exposed to in this manner. If *Henry V* is indeed a 'satire on monarchical government, on imperialism, on the baser kinds of "patriotism" and on war',[31] then who are the people capable of recognising it as such? Gould identifies them as 'the careful, the learned and the sympathetic', but the reader does not really learn whether such people existed during Shakespeare's lifetime. Instead, Gould is more interested in how to correctly understand the play 'hundreds of years after [Shakespeare's] death'. One is tempted to surmise that Shakespeare's irony is to be decoded exclusively by the twentieth-century scholar – not least because of Gould's reference to the 'learned'. This would imply that the *apparent* meaning of *Henry V*, the jingoism of the 'surface', was meant for Shakespeare's contemporaries, while its 'real' meaning, the scathing satire on militarism, was included for a latter-day audience of scholar-critics.

   Given the upsurge in historical Shakespeare scholarship in the first half of the twentieth century, this position was supremely vulnerable. As opposed to Gould, most critics who detect irony in a given Shakespearean play or passage therefore include the theatrical context, particularly the audience, in their analyses. W. W. Greg's interpretation of the ghost in *Hamlet* provides a good example of the role the 'cultured few' play in such readings. Here is a concise version:

[...] Hamlet had bestowed attention on the story [of *The Murder of Gonzago*] long before he commanded the production of the play at court. [...] *The Ghost described this particular method of poisoning because it was already present in Hamlet's mind.* In other words it was not the Ghost's story that suggested the *Murder of Gonzago*, but the *Murder of Gonzago* that supplied the details of the Ghost's story. [...] [T]he Ghost was an hallucination produced by auto-suggestion in Hamlet's brain.[32]

The full version of Greg's argument is so complex and detailed that he himself felt compelled to explain how the real nature of the ghost could have been communicated on the Elizabethan stage – and why this should be preferred over other, perhaps more obvious readings. To Greg, Shakespeare is a writer as much as a dramatist (or, to use Lukas Erne's term, a Literary Dramatist[33]), and the question of stage or study is answered with a resounding vote for the latter:

> Shakespeare, it must be supposed, expected his ghost and its story to be generally taken on the stage at their face value. [...] But may we not believe that for himself, as for other humaner minds among his contemporaries, such crude machinery would appear as a blot upon a noble piece of work? For such minds he would appear to have designed an alternative explanation, and as a warning of his real intention to have introduced the dumb-show. This piece of business does not obtrude itself on the attention when the play is acted, but in reading and upon consideration its absolute redundancy and its extraordinary results *should* immediately become apparent. It is then seen that the obvious interpretation of the action, which satisfies the generality, makes Shakespeare an astonishingly perverse bungler: while the alternative shows him not only a skilful craftsman, but likewise a considerable master of innuendo. [...] In composition Shakespeare *must* have had in mind readers as well as spectators; he must have written for the closet as well as the stage.[34]

It is only 'in reading' and 'upon consideration' that the real purpose of the dumb-show (or lack thereof) become apparent. The 'humaner minds', it seems, are generally not theatregoers. Just like Gould, Greg consciously occupies a position *not* taken by Shakespeare's early modern audience, or at least the vast majority of it – which makes him a target at times for scathing criticism. This was directed primarily against the claim that Shakespeare had intended the 'real' meaning of Hamlet not for theatregoers, but for readers (a problem which Gould circumvents by remaining rather vague about the early modern reception of

*Henry V*). Greg duly attenuated this part of his argument by attempting to explain how 'the subtler meaning' of *Hamlet* could have been conveyed in performance. According to him, two types of aid were available to the judicious few (and only them) when trying to comprehend the play. The first is an early form of peer-to-peer mentoring, a kind of seminar discussion without the seminar:

> [...] [N]eed we suppose that plays were never discussed in the taverns among the finer wits, that the latter never thought over a performance they had seen and stumbled upon points whose significance had passed unnoticed at the time or remembered difficulties that had given but a moment's pause in the excitement of representation, and that they never returned and sat through a second performance with a view to getting a clearer conception of the author's meaning?[35]

Of course not. Though the unprepared spectator may never grasp the hidden meaning of *Hamlet*, those who reflect and analyse will: effectively, the judicious few become something like close readers of *Hamlet* on stage – or rather, of the production as such, since the assumption is that they might go back to see a second (and maybe a third) performance. Greg admits, however, that even this may not suffice. He therefore recruits the actors as accomplices in this game, as the second aid to comprehension available to the elite sector of the audience. This move testifies to an esteem for the profession perhaps unprecedented in Shakespeare criticism up to this point. The early modern players envisioned by Greg are capable of conveying two contradicting meanings at the same time:

> [...] [I]t would be possible for the actors to give considerable help to the 'judicious' without running any danger of seriously confusing those who were content with the more naïve interpretation. [...] It would be quite easy to make clear to an unprejudiced and alert spectator that it was Hamlet's conduct and not the poisoner's speech that drove the King from the hall, while yet leaving the naïve groundling, who had swallowed the Ghost's revelation, to believe, like the Prince himself, in the success of Hamlet's plot. There has, for Hamlet's sake, to be a semblance of success; that would amply satisfy the uncritical generality, however clearly the acting pointed in another direction. The actors would, therefore, have plenty of scope for introducing hints for the benefit of the curious in unravelling the inner meaning of the author. Of course, many of the minor points

to which I directed attention (supposing them to be genuine points) would necessarily escape even the keenest of spectators, but once the clue was given they would serve to elucidate the interpretation, and provide critical sport, for the intelligent reader.[36]

The stage becomes, as it were, a prop to the study. The inner meaning of *Hamlet* is consciously directed at a small minority only, an in-group of intellectually superior cognoscenti. To the constitution of such a group, irony is in fact particularly conducive. According to Frye, 'sophisticated irony merely states, and lets the reader add the ironic tone himself'.[37] Sophistication, then, is at least as much a matter of readerly as of authorial competence: there are those who 'get it' and those who do not. This act of differentiation is of supreme importance for modernism as a literary movement and, by extension, for critics reared on a broadly modernist cultural agenda.[38] The cultivated minority at the Globe and the numerous aristocratic patrons which Shakespeareans (re-) discover during this phase of the Bard's afterlife are informed by an identifiably modernist literary agenda. As the Shakespeare canon turns out to be surprisingly like the works of modernist writers, critics fashion the Elizabethan audience in their own image: an assembly of would-be solvers of the 'problems' or riddles set by the author.[39]

## The cultured few and the unified public sphere

A problem that this construct raises rather than solves is that of Shakespeare's relevance to the culture as a whole – both during the early modern period and in the first decades of the twentieth century. Even more fundamentally, it raises the question of who shapes and defines 'the culture' in the first place, the 'cultured' few or the supposedly less understanding masses. The discourse on Shakespeare's Elizabethan audience offered critics a kind of testing ground on which to experiment with various models of the public sphere and the elite minority's role in it.

Ezra Pound had famously claimed that '[g]reat art is never popular to start with'.[40] Most of the period's intellectuals had not taken this to mean that the great artist was necessarily isolated;[41] instead they focused on the importance of an elite minority in defining and shaping a national cultural canon. F. R. Leavis' *Mass Civilization and Minority Culture* (1930) is both a manifesto of elitism and an elegy for its ever-diminishing social acceptability, of which Leavis is painfully (if somewhat superciliously) aware. Shakespeare and his time serve him as a counter-model to his own age and its misguided value judgments:

> 'Shakespeare,' I once heard Mr. Dover Wilson say, 'was not a high-brow.' True: there were no 'high-brows' in Shakespeare's time. It was possible for Shakespeare to write plays that were at once popular drama and poetry that could be appreciated only by an educated minority. *Hamlet* appealed at a number of levels of response, from the highest downwards. [This] is not true, Mr. George A. Birmingham [a Book Guild official] might point out, of *The Waste Land*, *Hugh Selwyn Mauberley*, *Ulysses* or *To the Lighthouse*. These works are read only by a very small specialised public and are beyond the reach of the vast majority of those who consider themselves educated. The age in which the finest creative talent tends to be employed in works of this kind is the age that has given currency to the term 'high-brow'. But it would be as true to say that the attitude implicit in 'high-brow' causes this use of talent as the converse.[42]

There used to be, Leavis claims, a consensus about what constituted a good play or a good novel, so that, from Shakespeare to Hardy, there was a direct correlation between the quality and the popularity of a given work. This correlation is about to disappear, perhaps has disappeared already, though through no fault of the authors themselves. It is the public with its dislike of everything that excels the mediocre who is to blame, forcing the more demanding authors to address themselves to a small group of educated readers. To many, Shakespeare's plays seemed to embody a period when this was not so, and offer a model of how to write for (and thus recreate) a non-fragmented literary public. T. S. Eliot is a case in point:

> I myself should like an audience which could neither read nor write. The most useful poetry, socially, would be one which could cut across all the present stratifications of public taste – stratifications which are perhaps a sign of social disintegration. The ideal medium for poetry, to my mind, and the most direct means of social 'usefulness' for poetry, is the theatre. In a play of Shakespeare you get several levels of significance. For the simplest auditors there is the plot, for the more thoughtful the character and conflict of character, for the more literary the words and phrasing, for the more musically sensitive the rhythm, and for auditors of greater sensitiveness and understanding a meaning which reveals itself gradually. And I do not believe that the classification is so clear-cut as this; but rather that the sensitiveness of every

auditor is acted upon by all these elements at once, though in different degrees of consciousness. At none of these levels is the auditor bothered by the presence of that in which he is not interested.[43]

It is open to question just how seriously Eliot wants to be taken here. 'The Waste Land' with its 'poker-faced endnotes'[44] is hardly targeted at illiterate audiences. The nexus drawn between illiteracy on the one hand and social unity on the other also seems laboured: the poet-dramatist, for one, certainly needs to be capable of reading and writing. Can he be part of a unified cultural sphere if he is so patently superior to his audience? Eliot seems to think so, for although he is certainly no blind bardolater, he presents the social effects of Elizabethan drama as thoroughly beneficial. The early modern theatre's characteristic strength lies in the fact that it is capable of reaching the groundlings alongside the more educated spectators – a task facilitated by 'a fundamental homogeneity of race, of sense of humour and sense of right or wrong.'[45] At least theoretically, the not-so-cultivated many are hence an integral part of the historical achievements of the Renaissance stage.

But despite their focus on the integrative force of early modern drama, Leavis and Eliot remain rather vague when it comes to the actual reception of Shakespeare by his contemporaries, that is, to what different groups of early modern playgoers may have taken from a given play. Both assume that there is a plurality of meanings. For Leavis, there is a clear hierarchical order to them, with the 'highest' meaning being available to the cultivated minority only. At first glance, Eliot is less exclusive, for he assumes that every spectator grasps every level of meaning, albeit to a different extent. It is relatively obvious though that the meaning which 'reveals itself gradually' is the one esteemed most highly – and available only to the select few. How such exclusiveness (particularly when irony comes into play) is to be reconciled with the idea of an essentially unified cultural sphere is a question to which critics provide different answers. D. H. Lawrence, for one, emphasises Shakespeare's appeal to the uneducated:

> In our admiration for the subtler and profounder aspects of Shakespeare's work, which set it apart so strikingly from that of his contemporaries, we must not forget that it had a strong direct appeal for simple men (which it still retains today), that it was designed to provide entertainment for the ignorant as well as the educated, and that this appeal has first to be reckoned with in any attempt to fathom his deeper meanings. His work is not like a coin, with two

separate and distinct faces, but rather like a bas-relief of intricate design, the main outlines of which are striking at a distance, but which, on closer examination, reveals new beauties of detail to the connoisseur. His plays did not have two meanings, one for the pit and the other for the gallery. He provided for the more intellectual spectators something which the groundlings, with their limited education and experience of life, could not perceive, but this was an extension of the simpler meaning of his play, and not at variance with it.[46]

A similar point is made by H. S. Bennett in the 1944 British Academy Shakespeare Lecture. Using an image that had strong emotional overtones in wartime Britain, that of the radio station, he writes:

> [...] [T]he 'judicious' no doubt got something of the subtlety and highly organized series of ideas and images which are so commonly placed in the forefront of the modern critic's discussions. [...] [But] Shakespeare, with his amazing vitality, gives prodigally, whether of incident, of character, of diction, of organized imagery. [...] He is like a broadcasting station transmitting a programme which is received well by some instruments, imperfectly by others, and scarcely at all by a few. The rich orchestration of the Shakespearian dramatic poetry was fully available, perhaps, to no one: the 'judicious' were able to get something of it, but the speed of ordinary dramatic utterance made it impossible for more than a part of what Shakespeare had to say in his more packed utterances to become available. We regret this, and we strive to put things right by a slow reading of the text in our studies.[47]

Lawrence's image of the bas-relief, and Bennett's of the radio station, are based on similar premises: Shakespeare is sending out the same message to each spectator – differences exist only with regard to how well they receive it. Bennett's commitment to the supposedly unified cultural sphere of early modernity, arguably a tribute to the sense of national community engendered by the wartime effort, does not however go very deep, as the last two sentences make clear. While the judicious – and only them – may have been capable of grasping at least a part of the semantic wealth of Shakespeare's plays, the fullness of their complexity and beauty is available only to the later-born scholar, whose training permits him to read (!) the text in a particularly close and competent manner. To this process, Bennett refers as 'putting things right'. It is only generations much later than his own who 'do right' by Shakespeare, and then only the in-group ('we') that includes Bennett himself. As the historical precursor of these particularly capable recipients, the Elizabethan 'judicious few' do occupy a special position after all, despite all claims to the contrary. The commitment to the rank and file of the audience and the unified cultural sphere is a rather rhetorical one.

While for Bennett, the elevated status of the judicious few is based mainly on their superior understanding of the text, other critics credit them with a far more comprehensive significance for the cultural life of their period. Not only are they superior recipients of Shakespeare, they are also setters of the standards which ensure that the period's artistic production satisfies sophisticated intellectual and aesthetic demands. The tastes of the average playgoer, by contrast, exercised no influence to speak of, and, according to Q. D. Leavis in *Fiction and the Reading Public*, rightly so, for the masses certainly stood to profit:

> [...] [T]o object that most of the [Elizabethan] audience could not possibly understand the play and only went to the theatre because the alternative to Hamlet was the bear-pit is beside the point for the purposes of the student of cultural history; the importance of this for him is that the masses were receiving their amusement from above (instead of being specially catered for by journalists, film-directors and popular novelists, as they are now). They had to take the same amusements as their betters, and if Hamlet was only a glorious melodrama to the groundlings, they were none the less living for the time being in Shakespeare's blank verse [...]; to argue that they would have preferred Tom Mix or Tarzan of the Apes is idle. Happily they had no choice, and education of ear and mind is none the less valuable for being acquired unconsciously.[48]

Leavis remains vague here about what it is that makes the groundlings' 'betters' so superior: social class, education or both. Several dozen pages later, however, she writes: '[...] [T]he spectator of Elizabethan drama, though he might not be able to follow the "thought" minutely in the great tragedies, was getting his amusement from the mind and sensibility that produced those passages, from an artist and not from one of his own class.'[49] Given that Elizabethan theatregoers had traditionally been seen as lower class and that 'the artist' is presented as their counterpole here, it is hard to avoid the conclusion that Leavis takes the two terms to be intrinsically incompatible. The much-lauded uniformity of

Renaissance cultural life would then result from a successful implementation of elite standards as the universally accepted ones – regardless of the fact that the non-elite majority do not understand them and see nothing but a melodrama in *Hamlet*. 'Happily they had no choice' has political as well as aesthetic implications. Leavis quotes Edmund Gosse's 1889 *Questions at Issue*, in which he warned:

> One danger which I have long foreseen from the spread of the democratic sentiment, is that of the traditions of literary taste, the canons of literature, being reversed with success by a popular vote. [...] If literature is to be judged by a plebiscite and if the plebs recognises its power, it will certainly by degrees cease to support reputations which give it no pleasure and which it cannot comprehend. The revolution against taste, once begun, will land us in irreparable chaos.[50]

For Gosse, canonical works of literature appear to materialise in an autonomous space which has little or nothing to do with the broad majority of the population. Thanks to the efforts of a small elite (once more: 'us'), these works used to be acknowledged as great masterpieces, even by those who could not even begin to understand them. Gosse leaves little doubt about the fact that perpetuating this traditional supremacy is a political matter, a question of power: 'popular vote', 'revolt of the mob' and 'plebiscite' are not terms conventionally associated with issues of literary canon formation (or at least weren't at the time when Gosse was writing). The fact that Q. D. Leavis, a card-carrying modernist, sees no problem with citing an arch-Victorian like Gosse to demarcate her own position shows that, despite some fundamental differences, there are just as many fundamental continuities between 'modernist' and 'Victorian' views of Shakespeare's Elizabethan audience. The two periods are united in their desire not to see Shakespeare as a popular dramatist, whether this means a dramatist writing for the lower classes, as for the Victorians, or – this is the modernist bogeyman – as a dramatist writing for the 'masses', i.e. an even larger share of the population.[51]

The debate about Shakespeare's reception during his own lifetime, including those about the role of the cultural minority for his literary production, reflects the need of a cultivated elite, and particularly of a caste of professional critics, to culturally legitimise their own (professional) existence. But it also points towards this elite's increasing awareness of the fact that it constituted a minority whose relevance the majority acknowledged less and less.[52] Against this backdrop, modernism develops its particular version of Shakespeare's popularity. Richard Halpern describes it as follows:

> It is in response to the perceived threat of mass culture as a specifically undifferentiating force that the modernist's conception of Shakespeare takes shape. [...] For Eliot, as for Leavis, Shakespeare's broad popularity overcomes the 'stratifications of public taste' which now results in the cultural isolation of high modernism. Yet – and this is the point – Shakespeare unifies a public sphere without simply erasing boundaries of discrimination, as mass culture is held to do. Shakespearean popularity thus locates a dilemma in modernist thought: the very unification of the public sphere which the modernists desired also held the perceived threat of a chaotic blurring of difference. Shakespeare's overcoming of stratification and his appeal to a unified public has as its terrifying double mass culture's collapse of stratification and its creation of an undifferentiated public. Shakespeare's cultural 'work' in this context is to embody a cultural public space in which distinctions are not so impermeable as to lead to social disintegration – yet not so fragile as to give way altogether.[53]

If anything, Shakespeare's Elizabethan audience embodies this 'cultural public space' even more than the Bard himself does. It is no wonder, then, that the period reflects how Renaissance theatregoers influenced the production of Renaissance drama in a breadth and complexity that is virtually unprecedented – but not without encountering the same problems and issues from which modernist critics had sought to escape by turning to the past in the first place.

The prominent role which the cultivated minority plays in the discourse on Shakespeare's original audiences in the period up to around 1945 has its roots in Victorian traditions of thinking about Renaissance theatregoers. The Victorians had invented the groundling, lower-class by definition and responsible for Shakespearean drama's lapses in morals and good taste. The 'real', expurgated Shakespeare hence belonged to the upper echelons of society, be they Elizabethan or Victorian. While nineteenth-century criticism focusses on a group that has no share in Shakespeare, criticism in the first half of the twentieth century (or at least the school that I have referred to as 'modernist') defines a group to whom alone Shakespeare fully belongs. The Bard and the kind of high culture which he symbolises become more exclusive: access to it is no longer regulated by naming those who do not participate in it, but by naming those who do. This exclusivity, however, is clearly a two-edged sword. If the complexity of Shakespearean drama, both during the Renaissance and in the first half of the twentieth century, is accessible only to a small, cultivated elite, it may be used to explain why the commonweal needs, and should perhaps support and state-fund, a minority of this kind: these are the people capable of fully comprehending Shakespeare, and of explaining him to others. However, this argument works only as long as there is a general consensus about the relevance of Shakespeare, and with him, of high culture. If this consensus becomes unstable and the skills offered by the elite are no longer valued, its very exclusivity is what threatens to render it marginal and irrelevant.

# 6
# Neo-Elizabethanism

Neo-Elizabethanism, the school of Shakespeare criticism discussed in this chapter, continues and intensifies trends already apparent in the modernist focus on the educated few among Shakespeare's first audience. For Wilson, Knights or Greg, the intellectual prowess and aesthetic sophistication of elite theatregoers are seen as a necessary precondition for the complexity of Shakespeare's plays. While Neo-Elizabethanism does not regard Shakespeare's plays primarily as verbal artefacts, but rather as historical documents in the widest possible sense of the term, the nexus it posits between the audience on the one hand and the plays on the other is possibly even closer. The meaning of Shakespeare's plays is seen as largely, sometimes even totally determined by the historical context in which they were written. That context, in turn, is embodied by the Elizabethan audience, who thus offers a privileged, if not in fact the *only* gateway to what a given play 'really' means.

I take the term 'Neo-Elizabethanism' from an article published by Benjamin T. Spencer in 1941. Though rather critical towards its subject, Spencer's definition offers a concise summary of its defining features:

> [Neo-Elizabethanism] has contended that there is but one Shakespeare, that of the Elizabethan [sic]; that not only does the proper understanding of Shakespeare depend upon the corrective awareness of Elizabethan dramatic conventions, symbols, and cultural milieu, but indeed Shakespeare is, and can only be, the sum of what is therein discoverable.[1]

Although Neo-Elizabethanism is a small school of thought rather than a broad movement, its impact on discussions of Shakespeare's early modern audience has been considerable. For the first time in the history of that discourse, early modern theatregoers – all of them, not just the select few – explicitly turn into the scholar's allies and help legitimise his or her interpretation of a given text as historically authentic. This elevates them to a position of unprecedented importance, while critics are inspired with a new kind of (at least rhetorical) modesty. Here is John W. Draper on *Hamlet*:

> Is the modern critic so much keener of discernment that he can see deeper into [a] play than the contemporaries to whose conceptions it was calculated, and deeper into life than the master-dramatist whom he professes to explain? The present writer dares offer no such ambitious program; and, if after a prolonged study of the tragedy [*Hamlet*] in its multiform details and backgrounds, he can but grasp and explain such insight as the dramatist's own lines, *seen in the light of their Elizabethan meaning* [my emphasis], can supply, then he will be well content.[2]

Draper's ostensible modesty cannot however disguise the fact that his scholarly agenda is both comprehensive and innovative in its aims. His research (this is no longer 'criticism' in the narrow sense of the term) attempts a reconstruction of the one original meaning of Shakespeare's plays, a meaning produced – and authenticated – by early modern theatregoers as much as by Shakespeare himself. For the Neo-Elizabethanists, a, or rather, *the* correct reading of Shakespeare takes into account all aspects of his historical situation as far as they are available, the assumption being, as the following pages will show, that there was a collective early modern state of mind which is the key to the meaning of the plays.[3] This 'Elizabethan mind', embodied by the Elizabethan audience, is the sum of the intellectual, social and political factors which shaped the English Renaissance. A thorough familiarity with them is indispensable for any discussion of the plays – clearly, Neo-Elizabethanism is a countermovement to that of New Criticism. A succinct exposition of its goals can be found in the introduction to Draper's *The* Hamlet *of Shakespeare's Audience*:

> There is but one *Hamlet*, and Shakespeare is its prophet, and all others are false. The object of the present study is to set forth, not your *Hamlet*, or mine – what right have we to Shakespeare's own creation? – but Shakespeare's play, if only our diligence can explain it: the Hamlet that he set forth to his own audience, and that we, because of subtle changes in the times and in the language, can discover only by reading the text with a knowledge of these changes. Shakespeare

wrote in a literary and social idiom that his audience could understand; and he who would learn the meaning of the dramatist, things
obvious as daylight to his contemporaries but so timely then that
they are strange and abstruse to us, must be willing to follow the
clues both in the play and in the pertinent writings of the age, no
matter where they lead [...].[4]

Draper, one of the foremost Neo-Elizabethanists, proposes a kind of
historical exoticism: 'strange and abstruse' to a present critic, but all
the more intriguing for it, the Elizabethans are objects of wonder that
require continuous hermeneutical efforts on the part of the latter-born
reader of the plays. Like those focussing on the linguistic complexity
of Shakespeare, he envisions that reader to be a professional, as his
remarks on the comprehensiveness and difficulty of the effort required
make clear.[5]

Draper distinguishes between a 'literary' and a 'social' idiom shared
by Shakespeare and his audience. Although the latter, 'the realm of
mores and ideas', is 'even more elusive' than the former,[6] it is the social
idiom on which he focusses his efforts. The historically conditioned
reactions of early modern theatregoers, he claims, are precisely those
intended by Shakespeare; the dramatist and his audience being in complete accordance with one another because they find themselves in one
and the same historical situation. The emphasis placed on the principle
of theatrical collusion is correspondingly strong: 'A successful play is a
collaboration of dramatist and audience; and in judging a piece critics
must not ignore the audience's part in the performance, its likes and
dislikes, its pent-up feelings that the plot may express and so release.'[7]

On the basis of the collective norms and values he ascribes to both
the Elizabethan audience and the Bard Draper arrives not only at an
interpretation, but at a conclusive evaluation of individual figures in
the plays, which he can then present as the historically authentic one.
His guiding assumption is that the Elizabethans approached fictional
characters just as they did real-life ones. In this way, the niceties of at
least 150 years of character criticism are rendered superfluous:

Since the sources of *Henry IV* give only the slightest suggestion of
Falstaff's character, the present writer proposes to seek his prototype
in contemporary society; and to this end, he presents two hypotheses; that actual Elizabethan conditions furnish ample analogies for
the actions, and so for the character, of Falstaff; and that the audience, knowing such actions and such types of character in daily life,

would see them, not as dramatic conventions, but as a holding of the mirror up to nature, and so judge them, not with nice ethical reasonings, as Bradley supposes, but in such a rough-and-ready fashion, very much as they judged such people and such actions in the world around them.[8]

Draper assumes that the existence of real-life persons of the Falstaff type was a phenomenon specific to the Renaissance, and that this phenomenon was judged in a particular manner by 'the Elizabethans' – a kind of early modern John Bull. His description of this manner as 'rough-and-ready' is reminiscent of Taine, whose carnivalesque depiction of Renaissance Englishmen had sounded a similar note. The subtle shades and gradations in the representation of Falstaff's character noted by later-born critics were not for the Elizabethans. For them, Draper claims, such nuances were overshadowed by

> [...] one thing [they] could not pass over or condone: Falstaff was an arrant coward; he ran away at Gadshill, and at Shrewsbury tried to filch the reward of another's valour. In a brawling age, when one's daily safety on the street depended on being ready with one's weapons, cowardice was universally despised and its outward signs well recognised. Indeed, cowardice is the very crux of Falstaff's character, as an army officer, to which his other traits but appertain; and his cowardice above all must have made the runaway hero of Gadshill and the supposititious slayer of Hotspur a rather despicable figure of fun. Quite contrary, therefore, to the views of Tolman and Bradley, Falstaff's character to an Elizabethan would seem somewhat to improve in Part II and in *Merry Wives*; for the license of the latter plays might be more easily condoned than the poltroonery of Part I.[9]

In a manner similar to the way Falstaff is disambiguated by Draper here, the Elizabethan mindset provides solutions to a number of the more vexing problems in character-centered discussions of Shakespeare's plays. Malvolio 'was detested because the audience saw in him a social type that it despised and an unsolved social problem that it feared',[10] social effrontery. Osric is hated for similar reasons (but also because he uses 'foreign weapons and a foreign swordsmanship'[11]). The enigma of Hamlet is solved as well:

> If a truculent Elizabethan audience [...] had seen in Hamlet only an incompetent dreamer, could he possibly be the hero of a play that

ran through so many quartos? Could this popular hero be depicted in such a fashion as to risk the amused contempt of the Elizabethan public? As a matter of fact, there is very little of either the philosopher or even the student about Shakespeare's Prince of Denmark.[12]

Arguably, the Globe audience must have included would-be social climbers like Malvolio and Osric, students and perhaps even philosophers. They, too, would have been Elizabethans, and arguably they would have sympathised with the figures that 'the Elizabethans', according to Draper, collectively despised. Nevertheless, Neo-Elizabethanism introduces ideas that can seem remarkably modern to scholars working in the wake of the New Historicism, whose blurring of text and context ('the historicity of texts and the textuality of history',[13] in Louis Montrose's famous words) the Neo-Elizabethanists anticipate in many ways, if perhaps with somewhat less rhetorical dexterity. While New Historicists are usually silent on the actual circulators of social energy, preferring to work with conveniently abstract notions of culture and society, Neo-Elizabethanists have no such qualms. For them, the Elizabethan audience is where historical 'context' is located, and it is that audience and context that they refer to in order to legitimise their 'historical' readings of Shakespeare's plays. In order to substantiate his claim that Shylock is meant to be read as a Puritan, Paul N. Siegel writes:

> The connection between the villainous Jewish money-lender of folk tradition whom Shakespeare made a richly colourful figure, the member of an alien, exotic race, and the Elizabethan Puritan usurer is not pointed up by any allusion in the play. However, a contemporary audience, alive to the issues of its own time, does not need the pointers that posterity does.[14]

As a site of meaning, the audience is prioritised over the text, which Siegel openly admits does not call for the reading that he proposes. This opening up of the text results from the fact that Shakespearean drama is treated at least as much as an historical document as it is as a literary artefact – although the term 'document' is perhaps not exactly right here. Neither groundlings nor gallants collectively noted down their reactions to *The Merchant of Venice* and more specifically to the figure of Shylock. The records of actual early modern play-going that remain do not amount to a reliable account of Shakespeare's reception during his own lifetime: the connection between Shylock and Puritanism is made in the scholar's mind. Only in a second step is it then transferred to the collective mind of a hypothetical Elizabethan audience. With this, Renaissance theatregoers take on a completely new role: wielding an unprecedented authority over what counts as 'authentic Shakespeare', they guarantee the correctness of a given interpretation. Of course critics had been citing the 'gallants' as the Bard's intended audience, capable of understanding the more demanding parts of his plays, but the overwhelming majority of the stage's early modern patrons continued to be blamed for his perceived shortcomings. Shakespeare, in turn, continued to need the latter-born critic to recognise these 'weaknesses' as concessions to the audience and restore both his artistic integrity and the plays as he really meant them. The logical and rhetorical manoeuvres characteristic of this approach are turned upside-down by the Neo-Elizabethanists. Author and audience are no longer presented as antagonists, but as equal members of one and the same communication community. Where older criticism had presented Shakespeare's early modern audience as an obstacle to 'really' understanding him – the true Bard only reveals himself once he is liberated from the burden of his concessions to early modern theatregoers – they now become middlemen of a privileged form of access to both text and author: '[T]o consider the Elizabethan audience is our least indirect method of approach to Shakespeare himself.'[15]

This valorisation of the audience does not entail a corresponding devaluation of Shakespeare. It does, however, go hand in hand with certain changes in the period's prevailing conceptions of authorship. In his 1936 study *The Enchanted Glass: The Elizabethan Mind in Literature*, Hardin Craig writes:

> We must abandon to the solace of its advocates the mystical view of creative literature. Those who believe that the poet and the literary genius are independent of time, place and social circumstance and that a God to whom present, past, and future are as one, does actually and directly speak to and through poets and reveal to them ultimate truth and beauty – those holding such doctrines will see no occasion for these remarks. They must perforce be addressed to those who, holding a different opinion as to the nature of genius, believe it to be the possession of ordinary powers to an extraordinary degree and admit that not even Shakespeare and Dante could know and reveal the future as fact or opinion or present those aspects of the past about which they had no information.[16]

Clearly, the Neo-Elizabethanist turn towards the original audience is also a turn against romantic notions of the author-genius. That these two tendencies are mutually dependent had already been noted by E. E. Stoll in 1927. Regarding Shakespeare's witches and ghosts, which criticism had habitually interpreted as concessions either to the superstitions of his audience or to the superstitions of James I, he writes:

> [T]he notion of truckling and complimenting, constantly at hand to save Shakespeare's fame, must in all conscience be used with greater restraint. The favour of the groundlings or of the Queen or King the critic has ever at his elbow to explain away Shakespeare's every divagation in sentiment or art. [...] Shakespeare was a man, an Elizabethan. Omniscience and omnipotence are preserved to him at the expense of principle. Creizenach, the scholar who has written upon Shakespeare with widest knowledge, faces this alternative; and insisting that he could not have believed in witchcraft, admits [...] that according to our ideas he should have shrunk from flattering the vain pedant on the throne even though he thereby secured a good stage effect. But it was ever the case that if the omniscience and impotence of the divinity could be preserved to him, a way would be found to keep the morals. Creizenach excuses Shakespeare by pleading the Renaissance custom of compliment and flattery for kings [...]. Everything by this legerdemain is saved. Shakespeare both basks in the enlightenment of today and keeps the manners and morals of 1600. His thoughts are our thoughts, but his ways are not our ways. [...] And why all this manoeuvring and mystery-mongering, this creating of a need for explanation and then producing the explanation to fit? Simply because of the inability of a scholar or critic to conceive of an art as immortal in which the ideas involved are local and temporary, or to conceive of an immortal artist who is not also a prophet and seer.[17]

'Prophet', 'seer', 'divinity', these are epithets which the Romantics had used to describe the Bard – as well as themselves in their capacity as authors. Stoll's rejection of such idolisation is clearly informed by the anti-Romanticism of literary modernism, as voiced for example in T. S. Eliot's 'Tradition and the Individual Talent' (1919). Modernist views of literature hence influence the discourse on Shakespeare's Elizabethan audience in at least two different ways. They initiate renewed scholarly interest in the cultured minority as the addressees for what is complex and 'difficult' in Shakespeare's plays, and they spur the 'discovery' of the

Elizabethan audience (in its entirety) as a means of disambiguating the Bard: early modern theatregoers knew what Shakespeare *really* meant.

In the previous chapter, I discussed the focus on the 'judicious few' as a means of legitimising the need for university-educated specialists of literature. Neo-Elizabethanism does not single out elite spectators in this manner, but it also uses the Elizabethan audience as a means of increasing its own standing vis-à-vis the academic competition. With the institutionalisation of English as a university subject, Shakespeare criticism becomes more professional and more 'scientific' – a *Wissenschaft*, to use a German term here. Neo-Elizabethanism adapts to this by claiming 'the sanction of scientific and historical objectivity'.[18] As an academic discipline (or, perhaps more precisely, as a major part of an academic discipline, 'English'), Shakespeare criticism competes more directly than ever before with exact science. Neo-Elizabethanism can be seen as an attempt, if not to beat science at its own (empirical) game, then at least to play the game as an equal opponent. Accordingly, Neo-Elizabethanists go to great lengths to distinguish themselves from older criticism with its 'subjective' or 'Romantic' approach. In Draper's *Hamlet,* this iconoclasm is particularly notable:

> [...] [T]he present writer cannot accept the subjective interpretations of Shakespeare's *Hamlet* – cannot accept them, not merely because Professor Bradley and Sir E. K. Chambers, perhaps inadvertently, give their case away by admitting that their theories are not Elizabethan, not merely because these interpretations were late in developing and *suspiciously Romantic* [my emphasis] in their point of view, but also because they are not self-consistent, because they do not accord with the Elizabethan concept of melancholy, because they do not accord with a reasonable interpretation of the minor characters and with the obvious prejudices of Shakespeare's courtly audience [...].[19]

In effect, Neo-Elizabethanism completes a development that starts with the emergence of historical approaches to Shakespeare in the nineteenth century, that is, actual research into his time and place. Once Shakespeare is no longer treated as a more or less a-temporal phenomenon, but as a writer shaped by the historical circumstances in which he lived, it is only logical to approach his original audience the way the Neo-Elizabethanists do. Part of the same historical situation, Renaissance theatregoers can vouch for authenticity of historical interpretation. What the Elizabethan audience made of a play is what Shakespeare intended to be made of it.

## Constructions of non-ambiguity

As the benchmark against which a reading's historical accuracy is measured, the Elizabethan audience is considered to channel and regulate the semantic potential of Shakespeare's plays. Neo-Elizabethanists tend not to be interested in exploring a plurality of meanings; instead, they focus on the one – and only – which they deem historically authentic. Draper confidently announces: 'There is but one *Hamlet*, and Shakespeare is its prophet, and all others are false.'[20] The reader who thinks that the anti-Romantic bias of Neo-Elizabethanism entails a certain soberness as far as prose style and scholarly self-fashioning are concerned is mistaken, however, for Draper continues:

> [The critic in search of Shakespeare's true meaning] must be willing to sacrifice his dearest preconceptions, to refashion his attitudes literary, moral and social, that he may follow the evidence with an objective and single-minded fidelity: Humanly speaking, this is a *tour de force*; but the present writer will risk attempting it in the faith that the object is worthy and the method is just, even though mere human incapacity must make this ideal, like all ideals of scope and value, impossible of complete fulfilment.[21]

The preconditions for approaching a Shakespeare play in the Neo-Elizabethan manner are reminiscent of those of a religious conversion experience: the scholar needs to 'sacrifice his dearest preconceptions' and 'refashion his attitudes'. The process of reading itself resembles a quest. Its object, described in language familiar from Christian liturgy ('worthy', 'just'), needs to be pursued with 'single-minded fidelity'. The scholar turns into a seeker of metaphysical truth. In his study of *Hamlet*, Draper explicitly draws on religious terms and concepts in order to describe the Neo-Elizabethanists' aims:

> [As] in a religion, each critic [of *Hamlet*] has made his own interpretation of the sacred text, and then passed it down, as in a hierarchy, from professor to pupil. Unfortunately, many of these religions have no more to do with their major prophet than have some of the sects of Christianity or Islam [with theirs]. Professor Bradley appears to think that the true interpretation of the play was unknown to the Elizabethans who crowded the theatre, and began only a hundred and fifty years ago 'when the slowly rising sun of Romance began to flush the sky'; and Sir E. K. Chambers likewise declares that his interpretation belongs 'not to his [Shakespeare's] age but to our own'.[22]

Beginning with a comparison between the exegesis of Shakespeare on the one hand and that of religious scripture on the other, Draper soon merges the two formerly distinct activities. The Shakespeare canon itself is made to resemble religious scripture. The concept of authenticity thus becomes even more loaded than it already was, for it turns out to contain a revelatory, religious, and therefore necessarily singular truth. The time and place of the genesis of that truth can become eminently important in this context. The stated aim of Neo-Elizabethanism is a return to the 'origin' of the text, to the historical circumstances under which the latter was produced. Existing traditions of Shakespeare criticism are seen not as preserving or revealing, but as corrupting the true meaning of the text. Established authorities (Chambers or Bradley, for example) are impugned with corresponding vigour. The Neo-Elizabethanists are in some sense the Protestant reformers of Shakespeare criticism, and it is probably no coincidence that this school developed in the United States, a long-established haven for dissenters of various kinds. Their desire to return to some uncorrupted 'origin' of Shakespearean meaning explains what can seem like a rather hazardous insistence on the correctness of the one 'Elizabethan' meaning: on the assumption that all Elizabethans must have reacted to Shakespeare's plays in exactly the same way. This argument is generally more successful when based on what Draper calls the period's 'literary' idiom (though Draper himself is far more involved in the 'social' variant). The work of E. E. Stoll is a good example of this approach. Using literary tradition to channel Shakespeare's perceived polysemy, Stoll, while a great champion of common sense and accessibility, actually presupposes a reader very well-read in the literature of the English Renaissance. This kind of literary education, he claims, came naturally to Shakespeare's first audiences, simply because they were part of what is perhaps best described as the period's literary 'scene' – and hence could not but react to Shakespeare's work as part of an already existing tradition. In a sense, this made things easier. On *Hamlet*, Stoll writes:

> Titus Andronicus had been a revenger before Hamlet, and he too was 'not essentially in madness but mad in craft.' If here Shakespeare saw the unplausibleness [sic] of this he ignored it. Unlike Belleforest or the author of the *Fratricide Punished*, we have seen, he offers no explanation. And if he ignored it, pray, how was the Elizabethan audience to be led to perceive it, or turn it into something psychological, in view of the fact that feigned madness had, in the old play – in any revenge play – in Belleforest himself, been presented as the proper

and regular thing? *Famam sequere* is the precept, nay, the natural principle; and Shakespeare knows that he is observing it, unless he makes his contrary intention unmistakably clear.[23]

In a similar manner, Stoll solves the problem of why Hamlet hesitates to kill his uncle:

> [Hamlet] gives a reason [for delaying his revenge] that is in keeping with other atrocious sentiments and deeds of his in this very play. Indeed, he gives a reason which must already have been offered by the early Hamlet before him, and which, as I take it, no scholar can successfully maintain to have been given otherwise than in perfect good faith. Could, then, the Elizabethan audience, for whom alone the play was written, have understood that the reason presented in all good faith in the old play was now, when retained in the new version, but a shift or a subterfuge?[24]

Stoll puts particular emphasis on the role of convention in the form of dramatic tradition. The medium of this tradition however, is the Elizabethan audience, who has the sort of previous knowledge that allows it to identify the one 'correct' meaning amidst the wealth of possible ones – or rather, whose previous knowledge prevents it from perceiving more than one meaning in the first place. By focussing on the historical context, Stoll therefore returns to the literal meaning of the text:[25] the polysemy which modernist critics in particular had summoned up is eclipsed by the (supposed) unambiguousness of what the text explicitly says. *Hamlet*, at least at first glance, is considerably simplified.

If disambiguation is correctly described as the major goal of Neo-Elizabethanist scholars, not all of them relied on the 'literary idiom' to achieve it. Lilian Winstanley, alongside Draper, is far more interested in socio-historical contexts, as the titles of her books make clear: *Hamlet and the Scottish Succession. Being an Examination of the Relations of the Play of Hamlet to the Scottish Succession and the Essex Conspiracy* (1921) or *Macbeth, King Lear and Contemporary History: being a study of the relation of the play of Macbeth to the personal history of James I, the Darnley murder and the St. Bartholomew Massacre, and also of King Lear as symbolic mythology* (1922). These titles not only anticipate the respective study's results, but also their methodological premises: it is only against the backdrop of the period's politics that Shakespeare's plays can be understood. The Elizabethan audience is imagined as so embedded in this context (arguably, it *is* the context) that the associations which Winstanley describes in her books are virtually unavoidable for each and every spectator. The plays must have had the one single and unambiguous meaning which Winstanley describes as the 'authentic' one. The stage is not so much a moral institution, as Schiller claimed, as a political one. The reasons Winstanley gives for this are as follows:

1. The Elizabethans and Jacobeans had no newspapers and were not allowed the right of discussing political affairs on the public platform. Consequently they expected the stage to play the part of both newspaper and platform. The stage of Shakespeare's day was continually and closely associated with politics.

2. A rigorous censorship was exercised over the stage. It was forbidden to represent contemporary monarchs upon the stage even if they were represented in a favourable light. Any individual, whatever his rank, who found himself criticised upon the stage, could apply to the Court of Star Chamber for a veto, and such applications were frequent. Thus the dramatists had the strongest possible motives (*a*) for representing politics and contemporary history upon the stage, (*b*) for evading the censorship by representing their politics or history in some convenient disguise.[26]

This line of reasoning is as fraught with problems as it is revealing. It is also peculiarly familiar. Even if one hesitates to agree with Winstanley on the first point (to assume that the Elizabethans expected something they did not even know existed is, mildly put, a little odd), the critical orthodoxies of Cultural Materialism and the New Historicism have made it difficult to disagree with her outright. Vulnerable as the tenets of Neo-Elizabethanism may often seem, they also anticipate the most influential critical schools of the last thirty years or so. What remains problematic, however, is the insistence on the one correct meaning of each play. Winstanley is travelling a slippery slope when she claims that the plays got their political 'message' past the censor by way of a 'convenient disguise' – a disguise which apparently did not keep the Elizabethan audience from immediately understanding what was 'really' meant. Was the Master of the Revels really so much less perceptive than the average theatregoer? It is hard to avoid the question of what came first: Shakespeare's encoding of his plays or their decoding by a much later generation of critics. In addition, a drama this cryptic and convoluted presupposes considerable powers of intellect on the part of the audience, which is in turn hard to reconcile with the fact that the Neo-Elizabethanists usually present Renaissance theatregoers as the ruffians which eighteenth- and nineteenth-century criticism had seen them as. And despite the fact that they cite 'the Elizabethans' as the ultimate authority for the one, authentically Elizabethan meaning of a given play, they do not always assume that the early modern audience was socially homogeneous.

John W. Draper presents the Elizabethan audience in a more detailed manner than other critics, not least because it plays a particularly prominent role in his 'authentically Elizabethan' readings of Shakespeare. Like Stoll, he emphasises the primitiveness of Shakespeare's stage, and like Byrne or Beerbohm Tree, he draws on it to explain the lack of psychological realism in the canon. Nevertheless, his Shakespeare is not all simplicity:

> Elizabethan audiences were none too high in average intelligence – if one accepts Hamlet's estimate of the groundlings; and certain conventions of the stage were rather clearly calculated to assist their understanding of plot and character. Soliloquies and asides, for example, must always express the sincere belief of the speakers – even if these beliefs be wrong [...]. [...] This device is particularly useful to set forth feelings and motives that the characters would naturally conceal. In Elizabethan plays, moreover, with their several plots and many roles, a valuable convention decreed either that an important figure at his first entrance should show his social caste and relation to the others by dress or word or action – as the Duke does in the first scene [of *Twelfth Night*], or that he be explained by others just before his entrance as Sir Andrew is by Sir Toby and Maria. Thus, the complicated pattern of the piece is carefully unrolled, and the exposition of the initial elements is clearly and quickly managed; if the groundlings did not understand, they would become noisy and spoil the play for the judicious.[27]

That Draper subscribes to the idea of a split audience sits rather uneasily with the fact that he uses that same audience to prove the essential unambiguousness of Shakespeare's plays. As we have seen, the split audience is generally used to substantiate a view of the plays as complex, sometimes ironic – in any case, as fundamentally plurivalent. Thinking of the Renaissance audience as internally divided, along what faultlines soever, cannot but significantly weaken the claim that they understood any given play in exactly one way. This is especially true when Shakespeare's plays are read, as Draper and Winstanley do, as commentaries on contemporary politics, and if one assumes 'that the Elizabethans attended the theatre for clarification of political problems, that they were concerned not with the consequences of political action, but with politics *per se*, that Shakespeare and his audience assessed the characters in terms of political ends, not means.'[28] This summary of Neo-Elizabethanist orthodoxies comes from one of Draper's sharpest critics, Benjamin T. Spencer; however, if one accepts it as at least partially true, then it is obvious why the split audience hypothesis cannot but cause problems. If *Hamlet* is indeed the treatise on contemporary politics as which Draper presents it, and if the play is *nothing but* this, one wonders how an audience for the most part inattentive and of limited intelligence (Draper's view of the groundlings is thoroughly conventional) would be able to do the play justice. The 'Hamlet of Shakespeare's Audience', which Draper's book of the same title claims to have discovered would then be a *Hamlet* that the majority of Renaissance theatregoers did not understand, and this would undercut the legitimacy Neo-Elizabethans accorded the (supposed) viewpoint of Shakespeare's original audience.

## Specialist versus common-sense approaches

The issue of (non-) understanding is crucial, not just with regard to Elizabethan, but even more so when it comes to (Draper's) contemporary Shakespeare audiences. What Renaissance theatregoers took the play to mean is one thing, but what their interpretation should in turn mean to twentieth-century readers and spectators is another matter altogether. In effect, the latter are put under the tutelage of the scholar-specialist, without the help of whom they can no longer make 'correct' sense of the plays, as Winstanley indicates:

> The moment we attempt to place ourselves at the same angle of vision as an Elizabethan audience we see many things in a different light; many problems solve themselves quite simply; but, on the other hand, many are suggested which do not occur to the modern reader, and which nevertheless surely demand solution if we are to comprehend Shakespeare fully and completely.[29]

If the Shakespeare canon was simple and unequivocal for early modern theatregoers, it isn't for Winstanley's contemporaries, who obviously need a Shakespeare specialist to reconstruct this accessibility. She, in turn, is legitimated by her ability to procure historical authenticity, the 'truth' of both text and author: '[...] Shakespeare's meaning, in so far as it can be learned, is the only true or important meaning, the only meaning that a teacher has any right to ask his classes to spend their time in learning, or that a critic has any right to present before his readers.'[30] But the specialist, sometimes arcane nature of the knowledge of which she disposes is not simply the *raison d'être* of the professional Shakespearean: it is also a threat to the perceived *relevance* of this knowledge outside academia. In effect (though this has historically proven to not be the case), specialists, at least in the humanities, run a theoretical risk of self-abolishment if they specialise too much. Among the critics under discussion here, E. E. Stoll is particularly aware of this circumstance. His critical reactions to an overly academic, intellectual approach to Shakespeare are frequent:

> Elizabethan Drama, says a contemporary neo-Baconian, [...] 'is not the simple, straightforward thing that Mr. Drinkwater supposes it to be; but it is, on the contrary, complex, difficult, symbolic, topical, and double-minded to the last degree.' In that the neo-Baconian finds his satisfaction. The only imaginable way, then, for an audience to find any is themselves to have no inkling of this complexity; and since for them Elizabethan drama was intended, and of Shakespeare's own writing less than half got into print before his death, his complexity was – incredible in an artist – repeatedly thrown away.[31]

Whether they come from the Anti-Stratfordians or from specialists with more substantial academic credentials, Stoll claims that constructions of polysemousness and complexity in Shakespeare generally serve the purposes of those who 'discover' them. Writing against those who see a privileged minority as Shakespeare's intended audience, he insists that the relationship between the dramatist and his audience, in its entirety, was characterised by a basic consent about what made a good drama. This consent is the basis on which the Elizabethan drama develops, and the reason for its outstanding quality: '[The spectators'] taste and the dramatist's and the company's were fairly at one; and that [...] is the secret of the enormous, headlong development of Elizabethan drama.'[32] Implicitly, Stoll is making a counter-argument to Pound's 'Great art is never popular to start with' and similar avant-garde doctrines. The exceptional achievements of English Renaissance drama, for Stoll, result from the fact that they never lose touch with the popular tradition. This positive view of the Elizabethan stage and its patrons goes hand in hand with a clear positioning regarding his own present. Already in his analysis of *Hamlet*, Stoll had drawn parallels between Shakespeare's original audience and a certain segment of twentieth-century American theatregoers:

> Since [Hamlet] exhibits no plan, the reflective reader today may, with Professor Bradley, well shake his head at one so ready to die 'with a sacred duty still undone'; but the unlettered audience is with him now more than ever, and joins in the judgment of audiences long ago at the Globe. If their point of view be taken (and what other are we entitled to take?) Shakespeare here again at the end has not been portraying the impotence of Hamlet's character but has been handling a situation, hedged about with difficulties, with consummate tact.[33]

Stoll's apparently seamless chain of reasoning almost makes one forget that Shakespeare's original audience did not leave us a commentary on *Hamlet*. To claim that an 'unlettered' audience nowadays reacts in just the same manner as it did then is to project the present back onto the Renaissance: Stoll knows how unlettered audiences react today (or so he claims), but he has no first- or even second-hand knowledge of early modern responses. ('Tis all in his mind.) But by constructing a sort of transhistorical community of recipients, Stoll significantly enhances the status of the 'lowbrow' theatregoers of his own time and place. For the critic to do justice to Shakespeare is to take the perspective of exactly this kind of audience. Stoll's championing of the historical alterity of Shakespeare's drama and its original audience is an implicit critique of the avant-garde and its intellectualism. Shakespeare and his audience, he writes, 'had aesthetic interests and conceptions rather different from those current in highbrow circles today'[34] – and, one might add, different from those pursued by many of Stoll's own colleagues. According to him, they have been less than helpful in elucidating Shakespeare for the general public, and he stops short, but only just, of calling them superfluous. Even the play traditionally considered the most complex does not need scholarly commentary, Stoll opines: '*Hamlet* (together with the old *Hamlet*) certainly contains [everything necessary for] it [to be comprehended and relished]; and scholarship [...] is to little purpose except to remove the obstacles in the way – chiefly those of scholarship and criticism.'[35] By denouncing the traditions of criticism in this manner, Stoll of course strengthens his own position as a scholar who 'knows better' than his predecessors. In addition, his common sense-approach contributes significantly to the legitimisation of professional

(Shakespeare) criticism, albeit in a manner that is very different from, even contrary to, that of Draper or Winstanley. In effect, Stoll abandons 'Elizabethanist' approaches (and probably would not have been too happy being discussed as one):

> What are the consequences of this insistence that the only way to Shakespeare is through the strait gate of Elizabethanism? What is Shakespeare's future if, as a recent scholar has put it, 'it is necessary to read and understand that body of erudition to which the poets and dramatists had access'? The most obvious and deplorable consequence will be the discouraging of an interest in Shakespeare among those sensitive and intelligent readers who, responsive though they be to poetic and dramatic idioms and conventions, cannot and do not wish to be Elizabethan specialists. Shakespeare as a central figure in a liberal and humanistic education must be abandoned. For if a meticulous knowledge of Elizabethan psychology, demonology, cosmology, and statecraft is made the *sine qua non* of a reasonable comprehension of Shakespeare's tragic and comic art, then the bard can belong only to a few contending cliques of scholars. And perhaps to them he will be an empty treasure if, thus hoarded, he must cease to be currency among the rest of men.[36]

As a critical school, Neo-Elizabethanism faces problems very similar to those encountered by the authors who focus on an exclusive minority as the intended audience of Shakespeare's highly complex, sometimes outright esoteric plays: the detailed explanation and exegesis supposedly required by the latter threatens to make them – and those who could theoretically provide the information allegedly needed – uninteresting and irrelevant to the broader public. Even more fundamentally, the consensus regarding Shakespeare's iconicity is potentially destabilised, for what use is a national poet inaccessible to a majority of the population? The topicality which Neo-Elizabethanism ascribes to Shakespeare's plays is a hazard to what had traditionally been regarded as their timelessness, particularly where scholars claim a kind of interpretative monopoly and propagate their reading as the only authentic and therefore the only relevant one. In effect, this constitutes a major disempowerment of the common reader. It is precisely at this point that Stoll begs to differ: the Bard's plays emphatically do not call for a specialist reader. Quite to the contrary: the broader the audience and the less exalted its intellectual demands, the more authentic its Shakespeare experience.

If Stoll is less of a Neo-Elizabethanist than Draper or Winstanley, this is also because of his comparably a-political view of the Renaissance stage. Early modern theatregoers interest him not so much in their capacity as however indirect participants in 'current affairs' as bearers of a cultural and literary tradition.[37] Because they are not treated as predominantly political subjects, let alone as a political collective, hence *not as defined primarily by the concerns of their time*, this version of Shakespeare's original customers consolidates rather than destabilises the Bard's cultural prestige. Draper's and Winstanley's use of the audience, by contrast, does not contribute to this iconicity so much as depend on it: whether a given reading of Shakespeare is authentic or not is relevant only once (and when) his canonicity is firmly established.

As opposed to the two last-mentioned scholars, Stoll also subscribes to a view of art as an autonomous sphere. It is the literary tradition within which Shakespeare was writing that explains his drama: there is, broadly speaking, no need of recurring to any *hors-texte*. This is where Draper and Winstanley disagree – and where they incur particularly harsh criticism. Spencer writes:

> Mr. Draper is reading Shakespeare precisely as did Walt Whitman, who felt that the American mind would be chiefly impressed by the feudal element in Shakespeare's plays and not by the private virtues and devotion. In Elizabethan as in Grecian tragedy the utilization of kings implies not necessarily a concern with kingship per se; rather were royal themes and settings employed to enhance the significance of the individuals involved and to heighten the broadly human, as opposed to narrow political, conflicts – as, for instance, in *Antony and Cleopatra*. To regard Shakespeare's plays otherwise is to make them dominantly propaganda; that is, referable above all to current political practices and designed above all to effect political changes.[38]

Spenser's strong critique of Neo-Elizabethanism is not only a plea for the autonomy of art (that autonomy, to him, includes political disinterestedness), but also for the autonomy of the subject: '[The individual imagination] cannot, as Mr. Draper would have it, play the lackey to a monstrous and all-devouring illusion such as "the Elizabethan mind", which demands, as is the custom in these totalitarian days, and [sic] abandonment of all personal liberty, even in the realm of art.'[39] The shift away from the individual that Spencer (in what some might call a rather bourgeois, essentialist manner of thinking) finds so abhorrent is indeed central to Neo-Elizabethanism as a critical school. The figures of the plays are not taken as 'characters', that is, self-contained and (largely) self-explanatory creations of an autonomous artist, but as a series of reflexes to the 'current affairs' of the time when the play was written. The author himself is no longer seen as the essentially time- and placeless genius which the Romantics had celebrated. Given this demystification of the creative act, there is less if any need to present the author as beyond whatever form of reproach. This, in turn, frees the Elizabethan audience for other than apologetic purposes. Neo-Elizabethanism, despite the fact that it is a small and heterogeneous school, demonstrates what these purposes might be. Its revaluation of Renaissance theatregoers contributes to a paradigm change begun by the late-nineteenth-century literary histories and becomes seminal for subsequent developments within Shakespeare criticism. In the second half of the twentieth century, the main function of Renaissance theatre-goers is precisely the one on which Neo-Elizabethanism puts its emphasis: to legitimate any given version of Shakespeare as the authentic one.

# 7
## Shakespeare's Elizabethan Audience in the Second Half of the Twentieth Century

As the preceding chapters have shown, critical commonplaces about Shakespeare's supposedly lower class audience, particularly about the groundlings, reflect the class mentality that informed centuries of Shakespeare criticism. In the course of the twentieth century, this kind of thinking rapidly lost its social acceptability, a development which could not but affect the way in which critics interpreted what they knew, or thought they knew, about Renaissance theatregoers. In his 1949 study *The Populace in Shakespeare*, Brents Stirling stated: 'During the recent past there has been such concern over social and political democracy and, simultaneously, such a growth of Shakespeare scholarship that a merging of the two currents has been inevitable.'[1] This merging manifests itself not only in a growing number of studies on the representation of the populace in Shakespeare's plays, but also, and especially, in the discourse on the Elizabethan audience. The American critic, Alfred Harbage, is a seminal figure. His 1941 monograph *Shakespeare's Audience* is the first book devoted entirely to this topic, and remains a formative influence to this day. Although Harbage's study clearly stands in the tradition of critics like Hazlitt or Ward, it marks a caesura in the discourse on early modern theatregoers. For the first time, their influence on Shakespearean drama is presented as thoroughly positive. Harbage locates the reason for this precisely in the trait that previous criticism had cited to excuse Shakespeare's 'faults': its socially heterogeneous composition. He writes:

> Unlike some other audiences existing in and near his time, Shakespeare's audience was literally popular, ascending through each gradation from potboy to prince. It was the one to which he had been conditioned early and for which he never ceased to write.

It thrived for a time, it passed quickly, and its like has never existed since. It must be given much of the credit for the greatness of Shakespeare's plays. Mere coincidence will not explain why every Elizabethan play addressed to a sector of the people, high or low, learned or unlearned, is inferior in quality; why neither university, nor law school, nor guild hall, nor princely banquet house begat dramatic poetry comparable to what came from the public theatres; or why Blackfriars failed to sustain the level achieved at the Globe. The drama reached its peak when the audience formed a great amalgam, and it began its decline when the amalgam was split in two.[2]

The popular audience, turned into a scapegoat for Shakespeare's perceived shortcomings by centuries of criticism, becomes the ultimate rationale behind the outstanding quality of his plays. Unlike his English predecessors Ward or even Hazlitt, the American Harbage does not temper its diversity by citing the Englishness common to all spectators. What unites the Elizabethan audience is not so much a common nationality as the humanity shared by all. It is because of its heterogeneity that the audience represents the full spectrum of what it means to be human, and thus it provides the basis for Shakespeare's claim to timeless, universal relevance:

An audience so mixed compelled the most discerning of all authors to address himself to men and not to their badges, to men's intelligence and not to its levels. The influence upon the individual exerted by class, whether high or low, is a cramping influence, narrowing the horizon, warping the sympathies, prejudicing the mind. But where all classes are there is no class; there is that common humanity which subtends all. To the kind of audience for which he wrote, and to the fact that he did write for it, we owe Shakespeare's universality.[3]

If the Elizabethan audience represents true community, 'the people' in the most comprehensive meaning of the word, then this is because of rather than despite the differences between spectators, for the disparities between the various groups cancel each other out: '[Shakespeare's work] represents man in the large, and Shakespeare's huge and heterogeneous audience was man in the large.'[4] This turns the early modern theatre not only into an emblem of humankind, but also (and for Harbage, certainly above all) into a political testing-ground. In the opening paragraphs of his study, he already praises it as a 'democratic institution in an intensely undemocratic age',[5] thereby claiming Shakespeare, and with him the Elizabethan drama, for the form of political organisation preferred by his own time and place. That this impulse should come from the United States rather than Britain (or the continent, for that matter), is perhaps only logical given that Shakespeare's relationship to democracy in general, and to the common people more specifically, had already been subject to intense critical discussion there in the nineteenth century. The pressure to align notions of Shakespeare and his theatre with democratic values was greater in the US than on the other side of the Atlantic, and fashioning the Elizabethan audience into an embodiment of Shakespeare's historical alterity, of everything that was 'wrong' with his plays, was not particularly conducive to alleviating it. The alleged heterogeneousness of Renaissance theatregoers was far too similar to the actual heterogeneousness of Americans. The solution, instead, was to turn the early modern audience from historical other to present self – from a hetero-stereotype into an auto-stereotype. 'In most ways', Harbage surmises, '[Shakespeare's audience] must have been remarkably like ourselves, for the plays that please us were written to please them.'[6] The nostrification of Shakespeare reaches an apogee: Just like Shakespeare himself, the Globe and its patrons now anticipate the defining traits and core values of the later-born critic and his world.

Harbage's view of the Globe audience quickly becomes the new orthodoxy, not only where his analysis of the source material is concerned (the accuracy of which does not fall under the scope of this study), but also, and especially, in what concerns his assessment of this material, the judgments he makes. This is already apparent from the fact that critics now frequently characterise the Elizabethan audience as 'democratic' – a term which refers not so much to the social background of early modern theatregoers as to a form of political organisation that was non-existent in early modern England. The period's stage and its patrons are interpreted and evaluated instead of merely described, and it is rather obvious why this view of it and them has proven eminently popular to this day: it meshes perfectly with the official version of life in the Free West. Commentators have frequently drawn a nexus between Harbage's 'democratic' view of the original audience and the self-image propagated by the Allies in the war against fascism.[7] This appears plausible, if perhaps somewhat over-generalised. *Shakespeare's Audience* was published in 1941, the year the United States entered the Second World War. If anything, it must therefore mirror the climate in the years immediately before, that is, those during which it was written – a period in which democracy as a concept was particularly present in the American public discourse. The recession of the Thirties had necessitated a redefinition of the rights and responsibilities of the state, and hence a redefinition of what exactly constituted American democracy. It was becoming increasingly obvious that the economic and social problems the US were facing could not be resolved by relying on traditional values like individualism, self-reliance and liberty alone. The Roosevelt administration therefore propagated a concept of democracy as not or not only a system that permitted the individual a maximum of liberty and self-fulfillment, but as an association of citizens that envisaged themselves as a community. Here is Frances Perkins, US Secretary of Labour from 1933 to 1945:

> When you have been away from this country for a few weeks and land from the steamer, what is that strange enthusiasm that comes over you? It is the people and the mutual confidence of life in America which warm the heart. It is a society of expression, it is a society of hope, which constantly and simply recognizes the dignity and worth of each individual and acts accordingly, a society which, because of this, knows a kind of corporate life. We sense that no one of us alone can realize the benefits of liberty and democracy, but that we can achieve these things together as a corporate body. This accounts for our early established and now quite natural social action in the interest of all, a reciprocal relation between citizens. As a people we have to a remarkable degree both faith in each other and hope in our common achievement. We have a kind of faith and hope of social salvation that by loving our neighbour as ourselves we can all have a good life.[8]

Terms like 'mutual' and 'corporate' point in the same direction as Harbage's 'common humanity' and his idea of the Elizabethan audience as a 'great amalgam'. They present democracy as rooted in community spirit. While it allows for the full realisation of the individual, it also levels the differences between one individual and the other. In effect, democracy is the result of an endeavour made by all, for all. This is very similar to the way Harbage envisions the Elizabethan stage. The 'great amalgam' of spectators is what enables Shakespeare's outstanding achievement: 'where all classes are there is no class', but the 'common humanity' reflected in the Bard's plays. In effect, Harbage claims Shakespeare and his theatre not simply for 'democracy', but for a particular version of it.

Harbage's notion of Shakespeare's theatre proved extremely suitable for the political climate on the other side of the Atlantic as well. With the Education Act of 1944, the British government had taken decisive measures to break down old class barriers, or at least make them more permeable. For the first time in the nation's history, secondary education became available to all. Other measures to turn the 'New Jerusalem' sought by the 1945 Labour government into a classless meritocracy followed, such as the restructuring of state schools into non-selective comprehensives and the expansion of higher education, most notably through the creation of polytechnics and 'redbrick' universities.[9] The idea was, as R. A. Butler said of the Education Act, to 'weld [...] us all into one nation [...], instead of two nations as Disraeli talked about.'[10] This idea(l) proved extremely pertinacious – albeit, despite being embraced across the political spectrum, obviously somewhat elusive. In 1990, John Major still dreamed of turning Britain into a 'genuinely classless society'.[11]

For this kind of society, the Globe audience as depicted by Harbage provided a perfect historical model. Given the formative influence that the idea of a classless meritocracy has exerted at least over the rhetoric of British politics from the end of the Second World War onwards, it is not surprising that Harbage's proto-democratic idyll became more or less entrenched in British Shakespeare criticism after the Second World War. In the words of Richard Wilson, writing in 1993:

> [T]he image of Shakespeare's theatre itself as a democratic forum, where the citizens of England's supposedly organic pre-industrial community met in a classless mutuality which remains a glowing example to the world [has been central to British Shakespeare criticism]. It was a legend which took definitive shape during the Second World War, when Alfred Harbage identified the Globe as a cradle of Anglo-Saxon democracy, the 'theatre of a nation' for which the only price of admission was 'the possession by each spectator of some spiritual vitality',[12] and Laurence Olivier imagined it as a cockney picture palace in *Henry V*, the trailer for D-Day. With its lords and groundlings, this was the concept of the Elizabethan playhouse that became glued in schools in a thousand papier mâché replicas [...] [.] [I]t is a fantasy essential to the stature of the National Poet, who, because he appealed equally to all classes, wrote for 'democracy' and 'Not for an age, but for all time'.[13]

The question, of course, is what 'writing for democracy' actually means. The Greek term δημοκρατία (*dēmokratía*) is commonly translated as 'rule of the people'. In classical antiquity, however, it did not refer to the same form of government that it does in the Western World today, for the *demos*, that part of the people who actually ruled in the democracy of, say, classical Athens, explicitly excluded certain, rather large, parts of the population. Democracy is emphatically not the same as ochlocracy, 'mob rule', the state of affairs in which power rests with all and sundry. To the extent that the late-nineteenth century literary histories can be said to conceive of Shakespeare as a 'democratic' playwright, they tend to adhere to a conservative version of the *demos*, which, by and large, excludes the groundlings from the community of Englishmen (women are very rarely mentioned) which gave rise to his extraordinary plays. In this respect, Harbage differs decisively from his predecessors. Because the standees paid the lowest entrance price available, earlier criticism had habitually thought of them as lower class. But while Harbage does not completely relinquish this idea, his emphasis is of a notably different kind:

> That a penny was a considerable sum of money and that theatregoing was one of the few commercialised pleasures within the workman's means may readily be seen. In fact, the Elizabethan artisan paid so much more proportionately for necessities – food, clothing, fuel – that a penny for pleasure must have been more thoughtfully laid out than even its thirty-one cent equivalent need be at the present time. It is possible, however, that the high cost of living worked in favour of the theatres in one way: if the penny spent on food meant only an additional cucumber or two, one might as well squander it on a play. A play meant over two hours' entertainment in impressive surroundings – entertainment of a quality not to be found in the beer and ballads. Craftsmen, then, with their families, journeymen, and apprentices, must have composed the vast majority of 'groundlings'. Many were skilled, performing functions now allotted to the chemist, architect and engineer. [...] London craftsmen were the best in the country. Those at the Globe had chosen playgoing in preference to boozing and animalbaiting.[14]

In effect, this constitutes a fundamental revaluation of this segment of the audience: groundlings can no longer 'be thought of as a rabble'.[15] Harbage does not mark them as a disruptive factor in the genesis of Shakespearean drama; instead, he identifies them as the players' actual target audience: 'Admission prices were calculated, as prices in general were not, to what workmen could afford to pay.'[16] 'Workmen' thus emerge as the part of the population which primarily sustained the extraordinary achievements of Elizabethan drama.

The book Harbage published roughly a decade after *Shakespeare's Audience, Shakespeare and the Rival Traditions* (1952), makes his remarkably positive view of the mixed audience even more evident. The Globe, in particular, is used as a foil for what Harbage presents as the aristocratic decadence and arrogance of the private theatres and their patrons. Appreciation of democratic principles and concern for the less fortunate members of society are almost entirely limited to the 'public', outdoor theatres.[17] Audiences at the latter also hold superior standards regarding sexual morals:

> The popular drama endorsed the code of sexual rectitude in a way that the coterie drama did not. The illustrations that follow are not intended to prove that public theatres were against sin and the private theatres for it. Officially, of course, both were against it [...]. [...] Although both bodies of drama endorse chastity, only the popular plays are chaste. The others are 'sexy' – in that they serve appetite and curiosity with erotic stimuli, and reveal inadvertently the latitudes of conduct among leisured people for whom a cultivated sensuality has become an escape from boredom.[18]

The drama's law the drama's patrons give: decadent laissez-faire for the Blackfriars' similarly decadent aristocrats, 'the charm of courtship, the dignity of wedded love, and the power of familial affection'[19] for the salt of the earth as assembled at the Globe. The groundlings, as A. J. Cook puts it, accede to working class respectability as Harbage 'pit[s] the proletarian moral soundness that gave birth to Shakespeare against the decadence of elitist tastes [...]'.[20] Established notions about which part of the population had the most beneficial influence on Shakespeare's drama are thus turned on their head.

In the decades that followed, this view was enthusiastically endorsed by Marxist critics. Although they do not, as a group, style early modern theatregoers at the Globe into a working-class audience *avant la lettre*, they strongly emphasise its genuinely popular character. Robert Weimann's *Shakespeare and the Popular Tradition* stresses that the early modern theatre attracted 'an audience from many classes and many social backgrounds',[21] a view later adopted by Walter Cohen[22] and Jean E. Howard,[23] to name only two. In 1989, Alexander Ankist, a (then) Soviet critic, concurred: 'Shakespeare was a representative of the cross-section of English society that was present in his theatre. You had there all the classes of British society and Shakespeare was a man who adapted his art in such a way that the audience of Shakespeare's theatre felt quite at home.'[24]

But despite this emphasis on the social heterogeneity of early modern audiences left-wing critics often present the lower classes as making a special contribution. Weimann thinks of the theatres of Shakespeare's London as 'dependent on large plebeian audiences'.[25] Cohen offers a slightly attenuated version: '[The] popular clientele, concentrated in the pit, was probably the heart of the English public theater audience and the section of it that seems to have determined the financial success or failure of a play.'[26] This popular clientele, of course, are the groundlings, and the revaluation they undergo in this period is quite spectacular. As the ones who 'made' Shakespeare, they turn into potential objects of identification and appropriation. To be like a groundling is to establish a kind of historically authenticated claim to Shakespeare, and, by extension, to the meaning(s) of his work. In what follows, I offer two examples for this: one from literary criticism and one from the theatre.

My example from literary criticism is David Margolies' essay 'Teaching the Handsaw to Fly'. The title alludes to *Hamlet* II, ii, 361f., in which the prince describes himself as being 'but mad north-north-west. When the wind is southerly, I know a hawk from a handsaw.' 'Handsaw' is commonly glossed as a version of heronshaw, i.e. a heron, so that Hamlet would be referring to two species of bird. According to Margolies, however, such ornithological interests are incompatible with the actual composition of the audience and its interests:

> Other authors of the time [...] used hawking images to appeal to an aristocratic audience, and the assumption underlying the interpretation is that Shakespeare writes in an aristocratic frame of reference and draws genteel metaphors. But if we use a 'common' frame of reference instead, that of the apprentices, craftsmen and small traders who made up the bulk of Shakespeare's audience, then 'handsaw' is a carpenter's saw and 'hawk' is a plasterer's hawk, the board on which plasterers carry their plaster. Hamlet says, in the alliterative style of popular sayings, that he can distinguish one tool from another. In short, he is saying that he knows what is obvious, an analytical meaning (even if it requires a footnote) which is consistent with the human experiential understanding of an audience today.[27]

Margolies' preference for the latter reading is rooted in his assumptions about the Elizabethan audience, in fact, it is these assumptions that make a reinterpretation of the famous crux necessary in the first place: early modern apprentices, craftsmen and small traders (these are almost exactly the terms used by Harbage) would not have understood references to falconry, and therefore Shakespeare would not have made them. The crux turns out not to be a crux after all, notwithstanding the fact that Margolies concedes (albeit in brackets) the necessity for a footnote: it means what is 'consistent with the human experiential understanding of an audience today', that is, just what people think it means anyway. This both confirms the timeless relevance of Shakespeare's plays and defines its foundation: the more or less direct accessibility of Shakespearean drama both to non-aristocratic early modern and to non-specialist twentieth-century audiences. The notion that different parts of the audience might have understood the passage in different ways is not taken into consideration. It must mean one thing only so that it, and the text in which it occurs, can be used to claim Shakespeare for a particular social stratum.

Margolies' view of the Elizabethan audience also informs his reading of the Henriad and one of its central critical issues: how to read Henry's break with Falstaff. According to Margolies, to take it for a legitimate, perhaps even laudable return to the duties of a future ruler is a misinterpretation, for the audience assembled in the theatre of Shakespeare's day would never have seen it this way:

> [The] royal-education approach stresses the values appropriate to national unity under intelligent rule. The plays are interpreted in terms of what is relevant to ruling-class interests – order and authority. At the same time they are assumed to be attractive to a popular audience of tradesmen and apprentices who, though they may be very much interested in order, are unlikely to be gripped by the education even of a king. As with *Julius Caesar*, the recognition of a popular element transforms the plays from abstract considerations of kingship to matters of concrete (although dramatically generalised) concern for the audience – the opportunism of rulers, let us say, or the undermining of traditional, collective values by the economic individualism of the bourgeoisie.[28]

In almost Neo-Elizabethanist fashion, Margolies uses Shakespeare's original audience to isolate the 'correct' meaning within a multiplicity of (seemingly) possible ones. Spectators at the Globe apparently realised that new economic developments by and within the 'bourgeoisie' (a somewhat anachronistic term) eroded the period's collectivist ethics, and that this was a problem which directly affected them. In fact, the corruptness of rulers and the destructive effects of proto-capitalism were among their main interests. Clearly, they form a kind of labour movement *avant la lettre*. By foregrounding the importance that a certain social class (allegedly) had for Shakespeare, the Bard himself is claimed for that class – not just as a historical figure, but as a symbol of national identity, a cultural icon. We are all groundlings, but that is just fine – what belonged to a popular audience then belongs to a popular audience now.

Given that it maximises a given production's potential target audience, it is not surprising to find that this line of reasoning is particularly prominent in theatre marketing. The obvious example is the New Globe with its official enthusiasm for all things groundling (witness its 'Groundling – proudly standing since 1599' T-shirt[29]). In its marketing strategy, the standees impersonate the empowerment and sense of participation that the institution routinely promises its patrons.[30] The special relationship between actors and audience is frequently quoted as one of the main reasons (perhaps even *the* main reason) why a return to older ways of building a theatre is legitimate and desirable.[31] In fact, the rhetoric of accessibility and democracy being used to describe actor-audience relations at the Globe can make the invention of the picture frame stage seem like a major (albeit rather persistent) aberration from 'real', 'good' theatre. At the New Globe, 'the meaning of [Shakespeare's] plays is remade each day as a result of the coming together of the actors, the audience, the architecture and the elements both physical and cultural'.[32] One could take this for a reasonably straightforward description of the general principle of theatrical collusion, but no: elsewhere, audiences 'stand [...] outside the performance desperately trying to understand'.[33] That this is not the case at Shakespeare's (New) Globe is deduced from various types of audience intervention, particularly from the fact that the auditors, the standees in particular, make themselves heard: they boo, they hiss, they shout. This is marketed as both authentically early-modern and intrinsically good.

While the New Globe routinely avoids investing 'groundling-dom' with a political significance beyond a vague sense of shareholdership in Shakespeare and the high culture for which he stands (at least outside the New Globe), other ventures have been less shy about this. A case in point is the Halifax-based company Northern Broadsides, more particularly its 'Northern' *Merry Wives of Windsor* called *The Merry Wives*. The production, staged in 1992, a year after the company was founded, spurred considerable controversy among reviewers. To some, a Shakespeare production that employed a clearly non-standard version of English seemed like a profanation of both text and author, 'a piece of karaoke theatre in which Shakespeare provides the orchestra, and the actors have fun providing the voices.'[34] Others considered the venture perfectly legitimate, with one reason being that Northern Broadsides were 'giving Shakespeare back to the groundlings.'[35]

The logic behind this statement says much about the rationale behind the groundlings' rise to acceptability, and indeed something approaching enviability. If to perform Shakespeare in a regionally inflected form of English is to give him back to the groundlings, then it would seem that the latter also spoke non-standard forms of the language. This endows them with all the – in this case positive – traits generally associated with this kind of speaker, such as directness, authenticity, down-to-earthness or warmth. At the same time, 'official' Shakespeare (which at the time was probably intended to be equated with RSC Shakespeare) is brandished as something like an illegitimate appropriation of the Bard, a distortion of what Shakespeare really was 'about'. Authentic Shakespeare is for ordinary people, the groundlings; and the mission of Northern Broadsides is to satisfy that claim. The company's emancipatory self-image is clearly stated (and remains remarkably consistent over the decades): '[Our performance] has a directness and immediacy which is liberating and invigorating, breaking the southern stranglehold on classical performance and making the audience hear afresh.'[36] The groundlings turn into an emblem of this return to the roots: marginalised and defamed by the establishment, anti-hegemonic theatre, just like anti-hegemonic criticism, returns them to the position that is and has always been rightly theirs. They are the true guardians of the Shakespeare heritage.

## The great consensus?

A Shakespeare who belongs to the groundlings is, in a sense, just as exclusive as a Bard who 'really' writes for the gallants, or some other subsection of his audience. In theory, the problem of Shakespeare belonging to some rather than to all persists as long as one assumes that his original audience was essentially heterogeneous and therefore posed various and often conflicting demands on the playwright. In keeping with Marxist theory, this is a view taken by a majority of left-wing critics of the 1980s and 1990s, who in turn like to quote Harbage in support of their tenets. However, Harbage's work only partially warrants this, for he is rather a far cry from seeing spectators at the Globe as some kind of proto-proletariat. While he repeatedly mentions the 'workmen' who flocked to the Globe, he does not take them to have made up the majority of the audience, which he believes to have been composed of

'[c]raftsmen [...] with their families, journeymen and apprentices [...].
Many were skilled, performing functions now allotted to the chemist,
architect and engineer.'[37] If anything, this is an (upper-) middle class
audience, or at least a lower middle-class one if one goes by the 'grocer,
his wife and their young apprentice'[38] of Beaumont's *The Knight of the
Burning Pestle*, whom Harbage names as representative spectators. In
effect, Harbage's proto-democratic Globe does not contain the type
of groundling described by nineteenth-century criticism: the loud,
unmannered ruffian in quest not of art but of mere entertainment.
Harbage may elevate the groundling to respectability, but at the same
time he also elevates him (and with him his wife) socially. That one
might be lower class and respectable at the same time is not necessarily a proposition he is willing to entertain. By levelling the Elizabethan
audience in this manner, Harbage creates the precondition for what he
presents as one of its most decisive characteristics: a comprehensive
unanimity concerning aesthetic as well as moral standards. Especially
in *Shakespeare and the Rival Traditions*, the social heterogeneity of spectators is eclipsed by a far-reaching consensus regarding what is expected
from the stage. In Harbage's view, the period's dramatists profit extensively from this:

> Great works of popular literature establish their own criteria and
> they are best understood where most beloved. But the approach of
> Mr. Bethell[39] and, if he will accept the alliance, of myself assumes
> a rock-bottom agreement between artist and audience. They could
> move about so freely together because the ground underfoot was so
> firm. The plays required the utmost in spontaneity of response, com-
> plete trust in their ethical postulates as well as complete submission
> to their artistic conventions, and could have been written only for
> an audience secure in the knowledge that it would not be betrayed.[40]

In the public theatres of Shakespeare's England, dramatists, spectators
and actors meet as equals. For Harbage, the special quality of the drama
these theatres engendered lies not in its formal elegance or its poetic
language, but in the values it propagates – values endorsed by everyone
alike. Their affirmation of community as an *a priori* value, in turn, is one
of the main reasons why Harbage considers the public theatres morally
superior to the private ones. The great merit of the former is that they
actively support a sense of solidarity and thus counteract the period's
tendencies towards social fragmentation. Where the private theatres
mock the social and political ambitions of the middling sort, the public

ones consciously refuse to badmouth the patrons of the more exclusive establishments.[41] Committed to the interests not of one particular sub-section of the population, but to the commonwealth as a whole, the 'democratic' theatres are distinguished by their avoidance of conflict. For Harbage, this entails a view of Shakespearean drama as essentially constructive and affirmative, not only in the sense that it creates and strengthens community, but also – and this is where the influence of the war effort and the immediate post-war years on Harbage perhaps makes itself felt most clearly – in that the plays, according to him, are meant to convey not scepticism or resignation, but a fundamental optimism:

> It is one thing to be stimulated and another to be disturbed. [...] If *King Lear* had meant to its audience what it is sometimes said to mean, there would have been panic at the Globe. The people there [...] did not want to hear that life is a tale told by an idiot or that clouds of glory trail in the Boar's Head Inn. They were not prepared for a two-hour operation in which old principles were cut away and new ones grafted in. They were too frugal to sacrifice to the day's entertainment the truths they lived by, and accept in exchange sheer loneliness and fear.[42]

Harbage titles the second part of *As They Liked It* 'Pleasurable Reassurance', and this indeed is what he sees as the main aim of Shakespearean drama. The latter thus reflects precisely the absence of conflict which he sees as characteristic of the Elizabethan audience – even if opposing political interests do not go unmentioned. However, they always take the background to what he presents as the Elizabethan audience's fundamental contentment with the status quo. In Harbage's Globe, conflicts need not be negotiated: they do not occur in the first place. The more problematic and difficult aspects of democracy are blanked out as 'the Globe comes to carry the dream of a common culture, transcending the divisiveness of society.'[43]

This vision, albeit not invented by Harbage (in 1933, F. R. Leavis had stressed 'the general advantage [Shakespeare] enjoyed in belonging to a genuinely national culture, to a community in which it was possible for the theatre to appeal to the cultivated and the populace at the same time',[44] and E. E. Stoll often strikes a similar note), proved extremely influential in the decades to come. In a sometimes more, sometimes less watered-down version, the idea of the Globe he proposes is endorsed even by critics whom one would not necessarily associate with an overdue emphasis on social consensus.[45] This assimilation of Shakespeare into a kind of proto-democratic pastoral from the end of the Second World War onwards is closely connected to a change in political norms and values. Until well into the twentieth century, the discourse on Shakespeare's Elizabethan audience reflected essentially anti-democratic attitudes, which in turn directly shaped a predominantly negative idea of Shakespeare's (popular) audience. As societies became themselves more democratic, such attitudes became less acceptable, and hence inefficient in securing Shakespeare's status as a cultural icon. The changed political situation called for a revaluation of precisely the sort which Harbage provided. But while his championing of a proto-democratic Globe is surely no mere lip service, certain ambivalences palpably remain. With his strong emphasis on the unanimity of Shakespeare's Elizabethan audience, Harbage seems to want to suppress any thought of potential class antagonism – both in the Renaissance and also, and perhaps especially, in his own present: 'We are amused at the ease with which [Shakespeare's] work escapes the sectarian and partisan. It now resists Marxist exegesis as readily as in the past it has resisted appropriation by the elites.'[46] Harbage's idea of the Shakespeare canon as a kind of middle ground on which everyone can agree is rooted in his ideal of a society largely free from conflict. If the amusement to which he professes in the passage quoted above has a rather strained ring to it, this may indicate that he himself was aware that many even of his contemporaries would have regarded such a society as essentially Utopian in nature.

Two generations of critics later, such scepticism more or less became the norm. With the politicisation of Shakespeare criticism from the mid-1980s onwards, 'the emphasis in sociocultural analysis shifted from unity, reciprocity and consent to difference, domination, and resistance.'[47] Harbage's views hence could not but come under attack, with reactions ranging from mild bemusement at this 'democratically inclined champion of the theatre'[48] to outright disdain for his perceived espousal of 'universal, essentialist "democracy"'.[49] Harbage's work is increasingly seen as itself conditioned by the time and place of its genesis.[50] His idea of the 'great amalgam' no longer convinces – where he had seen harmony and consent, critics now foreground difference and discord. Louis Montrose writes:

> [...] [D]espite the very broad social appeal of Shakespeare's plays, we should resist any consequent impulse to homogenize Elizabethan culture and society into an organic unity. Shakespeare's plays

played to both courtly and popular audiences, and these audiences constituted frequently overlapping but nevertheless distinct and potentially contradictory sources of socio-economic support and ideological constraint.[51]

Diversity in unity replaces unity in diversity; dissent and political controversy are seen as unavoidable (perhaps even beneficial) features of public life. In contrast to what one might have expected, this does not lead to an outright rebuttal of Harbage. Instead, critics often co-opt him in more or less subtle ways. John Drakakis, in an essay entitled 'Theatre, Ideology, and Institution', opines:

> [I]t would be quite misleading to argue that Harbage's presentation of the evidence accords with the politically quietist myths which demonstrably underpin the reactionary populism of Tillyard and certain of his contemporaries; rather, he directs our attention, almost inadvertently, to the radical potential of the material. A symptomatic reading of Harbage's analysis reveals the problems inherent in any attempt to manufacture a homogeneous Elizabethan audience out of radically antagonistic social groups. But the potential for an analysis in terms of the opposition between the necessary constraints of ideology and the release from it afforded by theatrical performance, problematic though this formulation is, is there [...].[52]

Harbage is certainly no reactionary – but does he really foreground the 'radical potential' of his material? Readers of his *As They Liked It* will find it hard to agree. Harbage may foreground the different backgrounds of Renaissance theatregoers, but what interests him is the theatre's ability to transcend their 'socially disruptive potential'. As dissent turns into a basic, almost metaphysical determinant of human (co-) existence, Shakespeare becomes, to use a rather well-worn phrase, a 'site of cultural struggle and change'.[53] Itself a site of a clash of discourses, Shakespeare's early modern stage necessarily needs a heterogeneous audience. That audience, however, can no longer be imagined as united by anything like a great consensus. In the rare cases where notions of social homogeneity are not discarded, they are considered under completely different auspices. The prime example is Ann Jennalie Cook's 1981 *The Privileged Playgoers of Shakespeare's London*, in which she repudiates virtually all of Harbage's claims about Renaissance theatregoers, particularly those regarding their social backgrounds. According to her, the audience is incorrectly described as socially diverse: '[W]hen all the testimony is considered, it clearly indicates the dominance of one sort of playgoer over all the others: he [sic] was the privileged playgoer.'[54]

The presence of elite spectators in early modern theatres is hardly a new discovery. What is indeed original, however, is the claim that they outnumbered the rest. In a manner typical of this period of Shakespeare criticism, Cook, too, verges towards difference, resistance and domination rather than unity, reciprocity and consent. Who exactly dominated the early modern theatres, however, does not become as clear as Cook's peremptory statements about who did *not* might lead one to expect. Cook is frank about the vagueness of the term 'privileged', which she openly admits to have chosen in an attempt to avoid other, more loaded (albeit possibly more precise) ones.[55] Whether the privileged are rich and titled and educated or whether only one or two of these criteria need to be met remains unclear. Cook points out that those attending the theatres actually needed to have time and money on their hands in order to do so – a fact which earlier critics had tended to handle in a somewhat cavalier manner. Her version of the early modern theatre, in any case, is 'emphatically elitist':[56] 'London's large and lively privileged set ruled the playgoing world quite as firmly as they ruled the political world, the mercantile world, and the rest of the cultural world'.[57]

The total dominance of the privileged has results similar to those that Harbage describes in his publications: they, too, embody a 'great consensus', they, too, endorse the status quo. In effect, both Harbage and Cook claim the Globe for political stasis. But where Harbage attempts to claim Shakespeare for democracy and the proverbial man on the street, Cook foregrounds his dependence on the elites of his period, not only in their capacity as theatregoers, but in their capacity as mentors and sponsors:

> More importantly, surely, than their judgment was the fact that the privileged supported plays and players year after year. They saw performances at school, at Court, in their homes, at theatres, they never abandoned the great public playhouses. They acted as true patrons of the drama, though only a few consciously regarded themselves in this way: playgoing simply formed an accepted part of their lives. [...] With their superior education, their claims to sophistication, their demands for pleasure, and their capricious tastes, these men and women offered a challenge to the finest playwrights of the age. Perhaps those playwrights would not now be considered the finest of any age without the continuing patronage of the privileged.[58]

Cook's idea of the role of early modern elites in the cultural life of their period is clearly shaped by twentieth-century (American) conventions of cultural sponsorship. Although she is wary about making judgments, it is obvious that the term 'elitist' is not one she considers derogative, and her attitude towards those on the other end of the social spectrum is clearly not exactly lenient. She differentiates between deserving and undeserving poor in a manner reminiscent of Victorian practices, and of Margaret Thatcher's attempts at reviving them. People at the bottom of the social scale frequently 'chose crime over privation'; they are 'reprobates' or 'social parasites'.[59] That Cook reproaches Harbage for his 'sentimental faith in the common man'[60] in her introduction is only fitting – it is a faith which she herself would not seem to share.

In the politically impassioned academic climate of the 1980s, this could not but trigger impassioned reactions. Cook is berated for having used her material 'illogically, anachronistically, insensitively and either naively or disingenuously'.[61] The book is brandished as 'the spirit of Reaganomics in theatre criticism, justifying increasing economic inequality by projecting it backwards to make it a "natural" and inescapable condition of culture.'[62] While certainly exaggerated for rhetorical effect, the nexus posited between Cook's view of the Elizabethan audience and Reagan's championing of a supply-side economy cannot be entirely dismissed. Reagonomics are based on a fundamental trust in entrepreneurship. Progress of whatever kind is believed to originate with the upper strata of society – a stance also taken by Cook, who presents the financial and ideational patronage of the privileged as the *sine qua non* of early modern drama. If this tenet eventually fails to draw anything like a scholarly consensus, this is not, however, so much for political reasons as for methodological ones. Butler in *Theatre and Crisis* (1984), Cohen in *Drama of a Nation* (1985)[63] and Gurr in *Playgoing in Shakespeare's London* (1987)[64] all criticise Cook's handling of the data, particularly her 'elastic' use of the term 'privileged', which, according to Butler, 'carr[ies] an inclusive meaning when the size of the body is in question, and an exclusive meaning when habits of playgoing are at stake.'[65] In 1997, Cook herself retracted: 'Too much evidence supports the presence of ordinary folk at the large public playhouses to suggest that they seldom attended.'[66]

## *Mais qui paie?*

The Elizabethan audience, it seems, resists explanation by economics alone. Regardless of this, the economic structure of early modern theatres is the main reason why it rises to critical pre-eminence, for the fact that the Shakespearean stage was a commercial establishment is the basic premise of the socio-historical apology. The much-quoted necessity of pleasing the audience, especially the groundlings, results from the fact that Shakespeare and his company were financially dependent on their continued approval. For the vast majority of critics before Harbage, a negative view of the Elizabethan audience and its alleged demands therefore goes hand in hand with a negative view of the free-market principles which granted them such influence in the first place. Harbage's fundamental revaluation of Renaissance theatregoers, in turn, necessarily entails a similarly fundamental difference in approach towards the economic system that provides them such leverage over the dramatic 'product'. For him, it is because of its commercial nature that the early modern stage becomes a vanguard of democracy: 'In the theatres, the rights of privilege and class melted before the magical process of dropping pennies in a box. Distinctions in admission prices and locations were crude compared with finer distinctions of class; thus, in the pit, the cobbler could look at the carman and realize that he was associating with riffraff.'[67] Democracy and free enterprise emerge as virtually inseparable. The 'great amalgam' which Harbage sees in Shakespeare's Globe audience not only explains the broad range of concerns of Shakespearean drama, even more fundamentally, collective investment is what enables the Bard's extraordinary achievements in the first place:

> The theatrical audience pooled its pennies, and the Elizabethan play as compared with the Elizabethan broadside illustrates the advantages of collective bargaining. Shakespeare's plays were a people's literature in a truer sense than were even the authentic popular ballads; and they were, therefore, less limited.[68]

Harbage's almost romantic belief in the salutary and ultimately levelling effects of capitalism contrasts sharply with the anti-egalitarian tenor of Cook's study forty years later. There, what might be described as the social injustice inherent in capitalism is projected backwards onto the (still only proto-capitalist) Renaissance and thus presented as a natural given of human existence. Unlike Harbage, Cook does not attempt to present capitalism as advantageous to society as a whole; rather, in a text-book display of historical essentialism, her aim is to present the status quo as historically unchanging and therefore unassailable. Generally speaking, it is often virtually impossible to distinguish between a given critic's take on the Elizabethan audience and their view of the economic system exemplified by the Elizabethan stage. Harbage's fundamental optimism enjoys a long critical afterlife. In his extensive study of Shakespeare and the mechanisms of the (cultural) market, *Big-time Shakespeare* (1985), Michael Bristol writes:

> The playhouses make performance available, through direct pur-chase, to a new social constituency of cultural consumers. Affiliation with a corporate body gives way to disposable income as the basic qualification for participation in a cultural event. This confers at least a temporary social equality on all consumers of the same product. The socially undifferentiated consumer of cultural services is the most important invention of the early modern theatre.[69]

The term 'constituency' is significant: it is in their capacity as consumers that early modern theatregoers participate in political life and become empowered as citizens. Early examples of consumer power, the theatres further critical thinking and a sense of citizenship among their patrons. This presupposes a certain capability for critical reflection amongst audiences and, more fundamentally, an essentially positive view of the market as such and of the individual's status within it. Where this is not the case, the Elizabethan audience is credited with a far smaller degree of political agency. In *The Culture of Playgoing in Shakespeare's England* (2001), Paul Yachnin states:

> The players and playgoers would hardly have thought of playgoing as a form of collective protest against aristocratic license; rather, the purpose, or one of the purposes, was the opportunity to participate in an experience of virtual courtliness. A rough analogy from the 1960s is Hugh Hefner's marketing of pornography glamorised by the deluxe Playboy lifestyle, which the subscriber was somehow supposed to be able to acquire by buying the magazine. The modern fashion indus-try is similar, since consumers are encouraged to feel that they are taking part in the glamorous world of superstar designers and models by wearing Calvin Klein's underwear or Cindy Crawford's lipstick. Indeed, the parallel between modern high fashion and Renaissance court culture is worth thinking about further, since we (like our early modern cultural ancestors) can be critical as well as emulative of the excesses and charisma of a Gianni Versace or a Naomi Campbell.[70]

Anything but an embodiment of historical alterity, early modern the-atregoers have become our contemporaries for good, proof of the funda-mental similarity between the English Renaissance on the one hand and the critic's own present on the other. Like the twenty-first century consumer, they pay not for a tangible product (an object) or the rendition of identifiable services, but for something far more abstract: participation in a form of culture (a 'lifestyle') to which they otherwise have no access. But just how 'democratic', 'liberating' or 'emancipatory' is this? It may be true that 'we (like our early modern cultural ancestors) can be critical as well as emulative of the excesses and charisma of a Gianni Versace or a Naomi Campbell', but just how critical, informed and reflective the average consumer is remains a matter of debate. Regarding the early modern age, New Historicist critics in particular have tended to be rather pessimistic about this issue. While they take a highly politicised view of the Elizabethan *stage* (Montrose calls it 'the vanguard of an emergent ideology, that of entrepreneurial capitalism'[71]), they do not credit Elizabethan *audiences* with anything like true political agency. For Harbage, the commercial nature of the Shakespearean playhouse had turned it into an instrument of democratic empowerment. For Greenblatt, by contrast, it is yet another manifestation of the containment ubiquitous in English Renaissance culture. On *2 Henry IV*, he writes:

> Shakespeare does not shrink from any of the felt nastiness implicit in [the] sorting out of the right people and the wrong people; he takes the discursive mode that he could have found in Harman and a hundred other texts and intensifies it, so that the founding of the modern State, like the self-fashioning of the modern prince, is shown to be based upon acts of calculation, intimidation, and deceit. And these acts are performed in an entertainment for which audiences, the subjects of this very state, pay money and applaud.[72]

Elizabethan theatregoers pay for their own ideological indoctrination. The stage is so potent as an instrument of repression because it manages to mask a deeply political undertaking as mere entertainment: 'Shakespeare's theater is powerful and effective precisely to the extent that the audience believes it to be nonuseful and hence nonpractical.'[73] But what *did* Elizabethan audiences think about the theatre? Greenblatt knows as little about this as any critic from Dryden onwards. But just like earlier schools of criticism, the New Historicism needs a certain version of those who frequented the early modern theatres to substantiate its claims. Unlike other critical schools, however, it rarely makes its assumptions about the audience explicit, even though one might think that an emphatically historical approach to Shakespeare might make this all but obligatory. Instead, early modern theatregoers, the actual 'circulators' of 'social energy' are referred to only sporadically – perhaps because there is not all that much to be said about a group of people whose main characteristic seems to be an almost stubborn subservience. Greenblatt, for one, continues:

> [...] [E]ven in *2 Henry IV*, where the lies and the self-serving senti-ments are utterly inescapable, where the illegitimacy of legitimate authority is repeatedly demonstrated, where the whole state seems – to adapt More's phrase – a conspiracy of the great to enrich and protect their interests under the name of commonwealth, even here the audience does not leave the theatre in a rebellious mood.[74]

This audience is the dark side of the 'politically engaged' Shakespeare critic of Greenblatt's own present. In the second half of the twentieth century, the theatregoers of early modernity increasingly function not as a counter-model to the critic's own self-image and not as a backward-looking utopia of a more harmonious, community-oriented form of living, but as a more or less straightforward auto-stereotype: a historical fiction constructed in the critic's own – though not necessar-ily flattering – image. In the course of this process, criticism undertakes a complete reversal of the logical structures that inform the traditional historical apology. In the early stages of Shakespeare criticism the fact that the early modern stage was a profit-driven institution was the rea-son why critics could cite the demands of the early modern audience as the reason behind Shakespeare's 'faults', thus elevating the Bard himself to sacrosanctity. For a critic like Michael Bristol, by contrast, this logic no longer convinces. While the commercial nature of Shakespeare's theatre does endow its customers with some sort of (albeit limited and temporary) agency, it prevents any thought of sacrosanctity on the part of the Bard. Instead, Shakespeare turns into the depersonalised product of an entertainment industry that uses his name as a marketing tool, a brand. Bristol thus dethrones Shakespeare by precisely the same means used to enthrone him in the first place. What had formerly served to deflect blame of whatever kind from Shakespeare onto his Elizabethan audience now figures prominently in precisely the reprove that criti-cism had tried to deflect from the Bard for centuries: that of spinelessly catering to the tastes of an audience that, despite the agency it is now granted, is still not imagined in overly positive ways. Bristol notes:

> Shakespeare has been censured repeatedly for indiscriminate pan-dering to the vulgar tastes of the groundlings. He has also been

denounced for complicity with patriarchy, oppressive state power, and class domination. It might make more sense, however, to follow the lead of Samuel Johnson in condemning Shakespeare as morally unprincipled and opportunistic. The complexity of the plays might then be described not as an artistic achievement but rather as a shrewd strategy to curry favour with as many sectors as possible within a complex multi-cultural market. This would suggest that a Shakespearean work is in effect an industrial rather than an individual product and that its specific form of appearance is in some fundamental way motivated and sanctioned by an ethos of business success. Shakespeare would then be seen as something more like a modern corporate logo or trademark rather than the specific name of an exceptional individual or creative genius. Such a view would, of course, be radically antithetical to the traditional account of Shakespearean authorship.[75]

Bristol is not the first to think through the more problematic aspects of Shakespeare's historical apology. But while generations of critics who did so before him tended to modify their respective conceptions of Elizabethan audiences as a consequence (so as to show Shakespeare's concessions to them in a more positive light), he is not shy to abandon received notions of genius or artistic integrity. Tellingly, however, this debunking of Shakespeare takes the subjunctive. Bristol's revisionism not only goes against the basic claims of more than three hundred years of Shakespeare criticism, but also affects the foundations of his own profession. Why, one could ask, should an entire caste of highly specialised scholars be paid, usually by the state, to occupy themselves with the merchandise an unscrupulous literary entrepreneur threw on the market several centuries ago?

Bristol's iconoclasm marks a climax in the Bard's nostrification, as well as its transmutation: opportunistic and striving for profit, Shakespeare becomes emphatically 'like us'. The moral philosopher that entire generations of critics wanted to see in the Bard disappears, to be replaced by a morally questionable businessman-dramatist. From a symbol of individual genius, Shakespeare turns into a trademark of economic individualism. The implicit reproach Bristol levels at Shakespeare is that of a lack of alterity. Notably, however, this devaluation of Shakespeare does not entail anything like an explicit revaluation of his early modern audience. In this respect, *Big-time Shakespeare* is perhaps more conservative than may be apparent at first glance. Even where the creative individual has 'made the big-time', it is hard to think of him or her as not in some way separate from, and superior to, the masses. Shakespeare at least has artistic potential, even if he squanders it to the groundlings at the Globe. The idea of the author-genius, elevated in however vague a way above the mere mortals who flock to see his work, seems still not entirely dispensable. As long as this is the case, criticism will continue to need Shakespeare's Elizabethan audience – like and unlike him, like and unlike us.

# Appendix: The Grocer's Wife

To talk of conceptions of the women in Shakespeare's first audience in an appendix, a kind of afterthought to the book proper, may seem inelegant, dated, and vaguely patriarchal – yes, they did exist, but they did not matter all that much. Valid as these reproaches may be, the fact remains that scholarly interest in early modern women in their capacity as theatregoers comes late in the discourse on Shakespeare's original audience, and only as a sideline. Until around 1900, critics have little to nothing to say about them – the one possible exception being Queen Elizabeth herself, whose putative presence at the Globe is a common object of critical speculation. The question is what to make of that silence, a silence which contrasts sharply with the early modern period's patent need for discussing the presence of women in the theatres. Shakespeare's contemporaries, particularly those of an anti-theatrical bent, devote considerable attention to this topic.[1] Broadly speaking, their concern is twofold, focussing on the one hand on the danger that the alleged or actual presence of prostitutes in the theatres poses to the moral rectitude of male theatregoers, and, on the other hand, on the danger that the theatre poses to the moral rectitude, and hence the reputation, of female spectators. According to Stephen Gosson's *School of Abuse*, female spectators cannot but become actors in a theatrical environment:

> For this is general, that they which shew themselves openly desire to be seen. It is not [...] your sober countenance, that defendeth your credit, nor your friends which accompany your person, that excuse your folly; nor your modesty at home, that covereth your lightness, if you present your selves in open Theatres. Thought is free; you can forbid no man, that vieweth you, to noate you, and that noateth you, to judge you, for entering to places of suspicion.[2]

These anxieties obviously lose much of their currency after the reopening of the theatres. Women in Restoration audiences are not singled out in the way their Renaissance counterparts were by pre-Civil War commentators, surely not least because the acting profession was no longer an exclusively male domain. The claim that a female spectator is by necessity also an actor is somewhat invalidated by the on-stage presence of actual actresses, who would seem to alleviate the 'burden of visibility' imposed on female audience members.[3] Shakespeare criticism of the long eighteenth century, in any case, patently sees no need to comment specifically on Shakespeare's female customers. The 'rudeness' which it sees as characteristic of the pre-Civil War audience is imagined in gender-neutral terms: critics do not flag the presence of women as a marker of the period's general depravity.

This silence continues long into the nineteenth century. The traits which the period's critics most commonly associate with the newly-invented 'groundlings' clearly go against its ideals of (middle- and upper-class) womanhood. Nevertheless, the standees are not imagined as exclusively or predominantly male, at least not explicitly so. The implicit assumptions of critics, their underlying motives for *not* mentioning female theatregoers, in turn, are another matter altogether, though necessarily a matter of speculation. The silence may be strategic – by eliding the women in his original audience, Shakespeare is claimed as truly available only to men. But this hypothesis is perhaps a little simple, and, quite apart from that, virtually impossible to prove. There are instances where the writer obviously (and ahistorically) conceives of Shakespeare's Elizabethan audience as exclusively male or male-dominated, but they are few and far between. Interestingly, they predominantly stem from critics who prefer the idea of an elite audience. A case in point is L. C. Knights, who assumes that the verbal artistry he describes as the most salient feature of Shakespeare's plays presupposes an audience of '*men* [my emphasis] who were capable of a detached and at the same time vivid interest in words and the kind of pattern into which the dramatist might arrange them'.[4] Similarly, John Dover Wilson claims that Shakespeare wrote especially with 'cultured men of high rank' in mind, the 'dashing young bucks' who also populate the early comedies.[5] More than fifty years earlier, Levin Schücking, another subscriber to the elite audience hypothesis, had already opined that Shakespeare consciously catered to 'the male youth of the English aristocracy'.[6]

All three of course studiously ignore the (in this case indisputable) fact that gentlewomen also frequented the theatres, and that they were an integral part of the court both of Elizabeth I and James I. The insistence on a specifically male target audience seems a little hazardous, in fact – but it is not widespread enough (at least not in a form this explicit) to be treated as much more than a shared idiosyncrasy – an idiosyncrasy, however, that at least in the case of Knights and Wilson emerges precisely at a time when women do begin to enter the picture of Shakespeare's Elizabethan audience. The word 'picture' is in fact peculiarly appropriate, for as if to prove Gosson right, they return as a visual spectacle several decades before they become an actual object of scholarly inquiry.

According to the surviving sources, the mock-Elizabethan audience frolicking in the replica Globe built for the Shakespeare's England exhibition at Earl's Court in 1912 included females, more particularly what eyewitnesses describe as 'orange-girls'.[7] No visual records survive, but given the overall concept of the event, one would be surprised to find that the organisers completely refrained from playing up the term's erotic connotations. The Earl's Court exhibition comes at a time when ideas of Shakespeare's Elizabethan audience begin to diversify and compete with one another, and we know that Poel, for example, strongly objected to its 'merry' kind of Elizabethanism. Interestingly, this merry, intentionally 'popular' type included women, whereas the more high-brow type did not. Poel's stage gallants, it seems, were all male. In this respect, Shakespeare's England at Earl's Court sets a trend: in the years that follow, the more popular or democratic a playwright Shakespeare is imagined to have been, the more prominent a role the women in his audience are given. Within certain limits, this applies both to criticism and to other ventures, most notably, film. My two examples are Harbage's seminal *Shakespeare's Audience* and Olivier's no less influential *Henry V*.

Harbage's 1941 study explicitly includes women among the newly respectable groundlings it envisions as Shakespeare's primary target audience. Drawing on Beaumont and Fletcher's *The Knight of the Burning Pestle*, Harbage's representative spectators are 'a grocer, his wife and their young apprentice',[8] and the wife's presence is not merely for decorative purposes. The middle-class respectability which Harbage ascribes to the Globe audience includes a comparably progressive view of women, and a corresponding regard for 'the charm of courtship, the dignity of wedded love, and the power of familial affection'.[9] The grocer's wife, no doubt, is there because she knows she will hear things about her sex which she is actually going to like. As full electoral rights for women become the norm, their presence at Shakespeare's Globe becomes an asset in fashioning a Bard to suit the demands of this type of society, providing Harbage and those writing in his wake with yet another 'striking proof of its [the Globe's] democratic character.'[10] This logic patently informs Olivier's *Henry V*. The famous opening shots of the Globe audience feature a fair share of female spectators: respectable-looking women in respectable-looking dresses can be seen retiring to the galleries. Clearly, Olivier imagines female theatregoers along very similar lines as Harbage. There is an important difference, however. Harbage does not differentiate between male and female spectators. Olivier, by contrast, does, adding a gender divide to the social distinctions scholarship had traditionally assumed to exist between different parts of the audience. His groundlings (with the exception of a couple of fruit-sellers, of whom shortly) are exclusively male. This may be a concession to the period's notions of female decorum, but it also excludes women from what is arguably one of the central assets of Shakespeare's theatre as depicted by Olivier. If 'the idealized intimacy between player and spectator' indeed 'allows the audience to feel that they, too, are part of the team and that Henry's performance empowers them, projecting the will of the playhouse majority as law',[11] as Martin Butler claims, then this must be especially true for the groundlings with their physical proximity to the stage and their obvious power to disrupt the performance. Butler points out that this empowerment is an illusion: the spectators are customers who pay for the privilege of behaving like masters for a short span of time. The fact remains, however, that Olivier's theatre excludes women from the most potent form of this (felt) shareholdership. As patrons of the galleries, women simply do not get as close to the stage as the men, and their influence on the performance is limited when compared to that of the (all-male) groundlings. If the illusion of empowerment is indeed the commodity brokered by the Globe, then the women pay more, but get less. The film tries to gloss this over by showing the female customers in easy conversation with the men in the pit below – seemingly unbothered by their partial exclusion from the direct democracy of the theatre. Tellingly, it is only as fruit-sellers that women get to enter the pit, as service providers to men rather than 'real' spectators. It may be not much of an exaggeration to claim that the somewhat irrational interest in these orange-girls (as well as in the prostitutes in Shakespeare's audience duly mentioned by virtually every twentieth-century introduction to Shakespeare's theatre) has at its roots a desire to picture women first and foremost as commodities, or providers of commodities, for men – quite apart from the enduring shock value of people munching at the theatre (*Those Nut-cracking Elizabethans!*) and the apparently unbroken mystique of a woman hawking a piece of fruit to a man.

Since the 1940s, as one would expect, the women in Shakespeare's audience have received increasing and increasingly nuanced critical attention. There have been attempts to gauge their reactions to particular plays, and to establish whether and how dramatists factored these reactions into their writing.[12] Perhaps more importantly, their presence in the theatres has been read as indicative of a form of freedom and participation otherwise unavailable to early modern Englishwomen. Jean Howard writes:

> [...] [E]specially for urban women of the 'middling sort', changing cultural practices including but not limited to, the emergence of the public theater, opened space for female behavior which men found genuinely threatening to their construction of proper womanhood. Gosson's unspoken fear was that the practice of female theatergoing, the entry of the middle-class woman into the house of Proteus, could spur her transformation from [a] compliant and powerless fantasy object [...] into [a] transgressive, desiring subject [...].[13]

Obviously, this too is a form of nostrification, of 'inventing' an audience to suit one's needs, even if perhaps one that – at least for the present writer – is particularly hard to acknowledge for what it is: a construct that helps perpetuate Shakespeare's cultural prestige. In the second half of the twentieth century, a Shakespeare whose theatre is an enclave of liberty in a society that otherwise oppresses its women is obviously vastly more attractive than a 'patriarchal Bard'[14] complicit in that oppression. Perhaps this is most obvious in popular Shakespeare films like John Madden's 1998 *Shakespeare in Love*. With the film meant 'to popularize, democratize and universalize Shakespeare',[15] it is certainly no coincidence that Madden's groundlings are made up of men and of women in about equal parts, and that there is virtually no difference in how they comport themselves at the theatre. In the closing scenes of the film, women arguably even turn into something like representative spectators.[16] As William (Romeo) and Viola (Juliet) die their stage deaths, the camera zooms first on Viola's crying nurse, then on two crying prostitutes with their arms (and later, heads) resting on the stage. In a film which has been shown to conceive of authorship 'as an erotic and, ultimately, male prerogative',[17] a representative spectator is not necessarily an empowered spectator though. The women's reactions, it seems, are meant to confirm Shakespeare's potency as a playwright, which in the film's version of poetic genius apparently includes, perhaps even equals, the power to divest others – women – of their self-control. Touchstones of Shakespeare's poetic skills the women may be, his potential equals they certainly are not. With regard to how critics have envisaged the Elizabethan audience as a whole over the centuries, this is certainly nothing new. For much of their critical history, early modern theatregoers have been a mere accessory to Shakespeare, defined by and for him, a means to an end. That this tradition should prove particularly long-lived for the females among them comes perhaps as no surprise.

# Notes

## Introduction: *Those Nut-cracking Elizabethans*

1. William John Lawrence, *Those Nut-cracking Elizabethans: Studies of the Early Theatre and Drama*, London: Macmillan, 1935.
2. William Shakespeare, *The Norton Shakespeare: Hamlet*, Stephen Greenblatt (general ed.), New York: W. W. Norton & Company, 2008, III, ii: 8–12.
3. William Shakespeare, *The Norton Shakespeare: Henry V*, Stephen Greenblatt (general ed.), New York: W. W. Norton & Company, 2008, Prol. III, 25.
4. Jeremy Lopez, 'Imagining the Actor's Body on the Early Modern Stage', *Medieval and Renaissance Drama in England* 20, 2007, 187–203: 189.
5. Michael Dobson, *The Making of the National Poet: Shakespeare, Adaptation and Authorship, 1660–1769*, Oxford: Clarendon Press, 1992.
6. The phrase is, of course, Gary Taylor's. (Gary Taylor, *Reinventing Shakespeare: A Cultural History from the Restoration to the Present*, London: Hogarth Press, 1990).
7. Nova Myhill and Jennifer A. Low, 'Introduction: Audience and Audiences', Nora Myhill and Jennifer A. Low (eds.), *Imagining the Audience in Early Modern Drama, 1558–1642*, New York: Palgrave Macmillan, 2011, 1–17: 2.
8. William Empson 'The Globe Theatre', *Essays on Shakespeare*, Cambridge: Cambridge University Press, 1986, 158–222: 159.
9. Robert Shaughnessy, 'Introduction', Robert Shaughnessy (ed.), *The Cambridge Companion to Shakespeare and Popular Culture*, Cambridge: Cambridge University Press, 2007, 1–5: 2.
10. See E. K. Chambers, *The Elizabethan Stage*, vol. 1, Oxford: Oxford University Press, 1923, esp. 236–307 and related appendices.
11. Ann Jennalie Cook, *The Privileged Playgoers of Shakespeare's London, 1576–1642*, Princeton: Princeton University Press, 1981, 3.
12. E. M. W. Tillyard, *The Elizabethan World Picture*, London: Macmillan, 1943.

## Identity, alterity, authenticity

13. That hetero-stereotype and auto-stereotype are inextricably intertwined is a commonplace of research in the field. Hans Henning Hahn, amongst others, points out that the one in fact conditions the other ('einander bedingen', my translation). See Eva and Hans Henning Hahn, 'Nationale Stereotypen: Plädoyer für eine historische Stereotypenforschung', Hans Henning Hahn (ed.), *Stereotyp, Identität und Geschichte: Die Funktion von Stereotypen in gesellschaftlichen Diskursen* (Mitteleuropa-Osteuropa: Oldenburger Beiträge zur Kultur und Geschichte Ostmitteleuropas, vol. 5), Frankfurt/Main: Peter Lang, 2002, 17–56: 28.
14. Sander L. Gilman, *Difference and Pathology: Stereotypes of Sexuality, Race, and Madness*. Ithaca and London: Cornell University Press, 1985, 20.
15. Gilman, *Difference and Pathology*, 20.

16. Simon Shepherd, Peter Womack, *English Drama: A Cultural History*, Oxford: Blackwell, 1996, 90–91.
17. '[...] Elizabethan culture is the part of Shakespeare which is not us. In the editorial process, the notion of the age and its customs is triggered, as it were, only by those points which would appear anomalous, tasteless or unintelligible without it. A line which strikes everybody as fitting, tasteful and intelligible doesn't require the supplement of history. The age itself is therefore constructed out of everything which transgresses the prevailing canons of fitness, taste and intelligibility – that is, the Elizabethans are set up to be what we are not. This does not necessarily set them up to be what we dislike – on the contrary, [...] it can make them particularly attractive. But it does involve the cultural appropriation of "Elizabethan" drama in the logic of the Other, that figure which, securing my identity by being what I am not, appears as both the antithesis and the reflection of what I am' (Shepherd/Womack, *English Drama*, 92–93).
18. Moody E. Prior, 'The Elizabethan Audience and the Plays of Shakespeare', *Modern Philology* 49, 1951–52, 101–23: 102–03.
19. Amy Rodgers, 'Looking Up to the Groundlings: Representing the Renaissance Audience in Contemporary Fiction and Film', Greg M. Colón Semenza (ed.), *The English Renaissance in Popular Culture: An Age for All Time*, New York: Palgrave Macmillan, 2010, 75–87.
20. See Rodgers and Stephen Purcell's *Popular Shakespeare: Simulation and Subversion on the Modern Stage*, Basingstoke: Palgrave Macmillan, 2009, 158–64. On New Globe audiences more generally, see Paul Prescott, 'Inheriting the Globe: The Reception of Shakespearean Space and Audience in Contemporary Reviewing', Barbara Hodgdon and W. B. Worthen (eds.), *A Companion to Shakespeare and Performance*, Malden and Oxford: Blackwell, 2005, 359–75. See also Christie Carson, 'Democratising the Audience?', Christie Carson and Farah Karim-Cooper (eds.), *Shakespeare's Globe: A Theatrical Experiment*, Cambridge: Cambridge University Press, 2008, 115–26.
21. Michael D. Bristol, *Shakespeare's America, America's Shakespeare*, London/New York: Routledge, 1990, 47.
22. Shepherd/Womack, *English Drama*, 90.
23. On the idea of the audience in the Original Practice movement, see Jeremy Lopez, 'A Partial Theory of Original Practice', *Shakespeare Survey* 61, 2008, 302–17.
24. I direct the interested reader to Andrew Gurr's magisterial *Playgoing in Shakespeare's London*.

# 1 Shakespeare's Elizabethan Audience in Seventeenth- and Eighteenth-century Shakespeare Criticism

1. Jack Lynch writes 'This [the long eighteenth century's] awareness of distance from the sixteenth and seventeenth centuries marks one of the largest shifts in literary and intellectual historiography since the Quattrocento humanists rethought the patristic scheme of periodization in secular terms.' (Jack Lynch, *The Age of Elizabeth in the Age of Johnson*, Cambridge: Cambridge University Press, 2003, 143.)

2. Alexander Pope, 'The Preface of the Editor to the Works of Shakespear [1725]', Rosemary Cowler (ed.), *The Prose Works of Alexander Pope. Vol. II: The Major Works, 1725–1744*, Oxford: Blackwell, 1986, 1–40: 15.
3. Pope, 'Preface', 15.
4. Pope, 'Preface', 15.
5. Pope, 'Preface', 15.
6. Pope, 'Preface', 61: 'The Dates of his plays sufficiently evidence that his productions improved, in proportion to the respect he had for his auditors.'
7. Pope, 'Preface', 16.
8. Alexander Pope, *The Dunciad, The Works of Alexander Pope, Esq; Vol. IV: Containing the Dunciad, with the prolegomena of Scriblerus, and notes variorum*, London: Gilliver and Clarke, 1736, 33.
9. This confirmed the period's belief in the hierarchical formation of taste. What pleased the low was considered 'vulgar', while those elements only an educated taste could appreciate were 'noble'. The task of eighteenth-century critics was to shape contemporary taste in a manner that would allow the 'low' to appreciate the 'noble' – though decidedly not vice versa. (See Don-John Dugas, *Marketing the Bard: Shakespeare in Performance and Print 1660–1740*, Columbia and London: University of Missouri Press, 2006, 2).

## Faults and beauties

10. John Dryden, 'Defence of the Epilogue, or, An Essay in the Dramatique Poetry of the last Age [Epilogue to The Conquest of Granada by the Spaniards]', Alan Roper (ed.), *The Works of John Dryden*, vol. XI, Berkeley: University of California Press, 1978, 203–18: 212.
11. Thomas Seward, 'Preface to the Works of Mr Francis Beaumont, and Mr John Fletcher' [1750], Brian Vickers (ed.), *Shakespeare: The Critical Heritage*, vol. 3: 1733–1752, London/Boston: Routledge and Kegan Paul, 1975, 383–90: 387.
12. Edward Capell, 'Notes and Various Readings to Shakespeare' [1738], Brian Vickers (ed.), *Shakespeare: The Critical Heritage*, vol. 6: 1774–1801, London/Boston: Routledge and Kegan Paul, 1981, 218–72: 234.
13. Dryden, 'Defence of the Epilogue', 205–06.
14. Robert Gould, 'The Play-House: A Satyr' [1685], Brian Vickers (ed.), *Shakespeare: The Critical Heritage*, vol. I: 1623–1692, London/Boston: Routledge and Kegan Paul, 1974, 414–16.
15. Lawrence Echard, 'Prefaces to Terence's Comedies and Plautus's Comedies' [1694], Los Angeles: The University of California (The Augustan Reprint Society), 1968, fol. b1. Echard diagnoses Plautus with the same penchant for quibbles, which he also puts down to the taste of the latter's contemporaries.
16. Nicholas Rowe, 'Some Account of the Life and c. of Mr William Shakespeare' [1709], David Nichol Smith (ed.), *Eighteenth Century Essays on Shakespeare*, Oxford: Clarendon Press, 1963, 2nd edition, 1–22: 13.
17. George Stubbes, 'Some Remarks on the Tragedy of Hamlet' [1763], Brian Vickers (ed.), *Shakespeare: The Critical Heritage*, vol. 3: 1733–1752, London/Boston: Routledge and Kegan Paul, 1975, 40–69: 64.
18. Zachary Grey, *Critical, Historical, and Explanatory Notes on Shakespeare, with Emendations of the Text and Metre*, vol. I., London: Richard Manby, 1754, VII.

19. Samuel Johnson, 'Preface to Shakespeare' [1765], Arthur Sherbo (ed.), *The Yale Edition of the Works of Samuel Johnson, Vol. VII: Johnson on Shakespeare*, New Haven/London: Yale University Press, 1968, 59–113: 74.
20. Lewis Theobald, *Shakespeare Restored; or, a Specimen of the many Errors, As Well Committed, as Unamended, by Mr. Pope in his Late Edition of this Poet: Designed not only to correct the said Edition, but to restore true Reading of Shakespeare in all the Editions ever yet publish'd* [1726], London: Cass, 1971, 64.
21. Joseph Addison, [On Punning], *The Spectator* No. 61, 10 May 1711, Gregory Smith (ed.), *The Spectator*, vol. 1, London/New York: Dent, 1907, 186–89: 186–87.
22. Addison, [On Punning], 188.
23. Charles Gildon, 'An Essay on the Arts, Rise and Progress of the Stage in Greece, Rome and England' [1710], Brian Vickers (ed.), *Shakespeare: The Critical Heritage*, vol. 2: 1693–1733, London/Boston: Dent, 1974, 216–62: 222.
24. Gildon, 'Essay on the Art, Rise and Progress of the Stage', 248.
25. William Guthrie, *An Essay Upon English Tragedy with Remarks upon the Abbe de Blanc's Observations on the English Stage* [1747], London: Cass, 1971, 7.
26. Elizabeth Montagu, *An Essay on the Writings and Genius of Shakespear, compared with the Greek and French Dramatic Poets: With some Remarks Upon the Misrepresentations of Mons. De Voltaire* [1769], London: Cass, 1970, 71.
27. John Brewer, *The Pleasures of the Imagination: English Culture in the Eighteenth Century*, London: Harper Collins, 1997, 144–45, 161–62.
28. Montagu, *Essay on the Writings and Genius of Shakespear*, 14.
29. Benjamin Heath, 'A Revisal of Shakespeare's Text, Wherein the Alterations Introduced Into It by the More Modern Editors and Critics, are Particularly Considered' [1765], Brian Vickers (ed.), *Shakespeare: The Critical Heritage*, vol. 4: 1753–1765, London/Boston: Dent, 1976, 550–64: 558.
30. John Dennis, 'On the Genius and Writings of Shakespeare' [1712], Edward Niles Hooker (ed.), *The Critical Works of John Dennis*, vol. II: 1711–1729, Baltimore: The Johns Hopkins Press, 1943, 1–18: 14.
31. Rowe, *Some Account*, 5.
32. Joseph Addison, [On Taste], *The Spectator* No. 409, 19 June 1712, Gregory Smith (ed.), *The Spectator*, vol. 3, London/New York: Dent, 1907, 270–73: 271–72.
33. Norbert Elias, *The Civilizing Process: The History of Manners*, trans. Edmund Jephcott, vol. 1, New York: Urizen Books, 1978. See also Robert W. Jones, *Gender and the Formation of Taste in Eighteenth-Century Britain: The Analysis of Beauty*, Cambridge: Cambridge University Press, 1998; Denise Gigante, *Taste: A Literary History*, New Haven and London: Yale University Press, 2005, esp. 1–67; For earlier developments in the field of 'civility', see Anna Bryson, *From Courtesy to Civility: Changing Codes of Conduct in Early Modern England*, Oxford: Clarendon, 1998.
34. Though 'taste' is much more widely accepted as a benchmark against which to judge Shakespeare than neoclassicist poetics are, both have non-English origins and thus potentially conflict with nationalistic impulses, a fact which could – and did – work to the considerable advantage of Shakespeare, especially in the second half of the century. William Guthrie, to name but one example, argues: 'We have often been surprized how that word [taste] happens to be applied in Great-Britain to poetry, and can account for it only

by the servility we shew towards every thing which is French. Of all our sensations taste is the most variable and uncertain: Shakespeare is to be tried by a more sure criterion, that of feeling, which is the same in all ages and all climates. To talk of trying Shakespeare by the rules of taste is speaking like the spindle-shanked beau who languished to thresh a brawny coachman'. (*Monthly Review* XX/Nov./Dec. 1765, Brian Vickers (ed.), *Shakespeare: The Critical Heritage*, vol. 5: 1765–1774, London/Boston: Dent, 1979, 211–30: 212.)

35. John Dryden, 'Cleomenes', Alan Roper (ed.), *The Works of John Dryden*, vol. XVI, Berkeley: University of California Press, 1996, 71–165. Prologue spoke by Mr Mountfort, 84–85: 84.

36. Peter Stallybrass and Allon White, *The Poetics and Politics of Transgression*, London: Methuen, 1986, 87. My analysis of Dryden's prologue is much indebted to Stallybrass and White's.

## Nature, the nation and the Elizabethan theatregoer

37. See, for example, Michèle Willems, 'Shakespeare', Roger Paulin (ed.), *Great Shakespeareans Vol. III: Voltaire, Goethe, Schlegel, Coleridge*, London: Continum, 2011, 5–43. See also Kathryn Prince, 'Shakespeare and English Nationalism', Fiona Ritchie and Peter Sabor (eds.), *Shakespeare in the Eighteenth Century*, Cambridge: Cambridge University Press, 2012, 277–94.

38. Vickers, 'Introduction', *Shakespeare: The Critical Heritage*, vol. 2: 1693–1733, 1–21: 7. On Shakespeare and neoclassicism, see also Jack Lynch, 'Criticism of Shakespeare', Fiona Ritchie and Peter Sabor (eds.), *Shakespeare in the Eighteenth Century*, Cambridge: Cambridge University Press, 2012, 41–77.

39. Jean Marsden, *The Re-Imagined Text: Shakespeare, Adaptation and Eighteenth-Century Literary Theory*, Lexington: University Press of Kentucky, 1995, 53.

40. Jonathan Bate, *The Genius of Shakespeare*, London: Picador, 1997, 183.

41. Bate, *The Genius of Shakespeare*, 174.

42. Johnson, 'Preface', 67. For recent research on Johnson and Shakespeare, see Eric Rasmussen and Aaron Santesso (eds.), *Comparative Excellence: New Essays on Shakespeare and Johnson* (AMS Studies in the Eighteenth Century, 52), New York: AMS Press, 2007.

43. John Dryden, 'Prologue to Love Triumphant', Alan Roper (ed.), *The Works of John Dryden*, vol. XVI, Berkeley: University of California Press, 1996, 169–72: 171. Brian Vickers' introduction to Volume 6 of *Shakespeare: The Critical Heritage* dates the emergence of the pragmatic argument against the three unities to the last quarter of the eighteenth century. Dryden's criticism, in this respect at least, is decidedly avant-garde. (Cf. Brian Vickers, 'Introduction', Brian Vickers (ed.), *Shakespeare: The Critical Heritage*, vol. 6: 1774–1801, London/Boston: Dent, 1981, 1–86, 16.)

44. 'A nice Observation of the Rules is a Confinement a great Genius cannot bear, which naturally covets Liberty. And tho' the French, whose Genius as well as Language is not strong enough to rise to the majesty of Poetry, are easier reduc'd within the Discipline of Rules, and have perhaps of late years more exactly observ'd 'em, yet I never met with any Englishman who wou'd prefer their Poetry to ours.' Charles Gildon, 'Some Reflections on Mr Rymer's Short View of Tragedy and an Attempt at a Vindication of Shakespeare, in an Essay

directed to John Dryden, Esq' [1694], Brian Vickers (ed.), *Shakespeare: The Critical Heritage*, vol. 2: 1693–1733, London/Boston: Dent, 1974, 63–85: 70.

45. Thomas Davies, *Dramatic Miscellanies: Consisting of Critical Observations on several Plays of Shakespeare: with a Review of his principal Characters, and those of various eminent Writers, as represented by Mr. Garrick, and other celebrated Comedians. With Anecdotes of Dramatic Poets, Actors & c.* [London 1783], vol. II, New York: AMS Press, 1973, 22–23.

46. Davies, *Dramatic Miscellanies*, vol. II, 23–24.

47. Guthrie, *Essay Upon English Tragedy*, 9.

48. Thomas Warton is a rare exception: 'Shakespeare's aim was to collect an audience, and for this purpose all the common expedients were necessary. No dramatic writer of his age has more battles or ghosts. His representations abound with the usual appendage of mechanical terror, and he adopts all the superstitions of the theatre.' (Thomas Warton, *The History of English Poetry, from the Close of the Eleventh to the Commencement of the Eighteenth Century*, vol. III, London: J. Dodsley, 1781, 361–62).

49. Arthur Murphy writing in *Gray's-Inn Journal* No. 8, 17 November 1753, Brian Vickers (ed.), *Shakespeare: The Critical Heritage*, vol. 4: 1753–1765, 84–109: 87.

50. Rowe, *Some Account*, 7.

51. Montagu, *Essay on the Writings and Genius of Shakespear*, 20.

52. John Upton, *Critical Observations on Shakespeare* [Second Edition 1748], Brian Vickers (ed.), *Shakespeare: The Critical Heritage*, vol. 3, 290–323: 299. Similarly, Francis Gentleman criticises what he perceives as an attempt to flatter James I – Shakespeare's reference to the king's healing powers in *Macbeth*. See Francis Gentleman, *The Dramatic Censor; or, Critical Companion* [1770], Brian Vickers (ed.), *Shakespeare: The Critical Heritage*, vol. 5, 373–409: 384.

53. Similar views of the Elizabethan age can be found in Stubbes' *Remarks on the Tragedy of Hamlet*, which lauds the 'virtuous Plainness of our Fore-fathers' (56), as well as in Nicholas Rowe's prologue to his 1714 *Tragedy of Jane Shore*: 'Their [the Elizabethans'] words no shuffling, double-meaning knew, / Their speech was homely, and their hearts were true. / In such an age, immortal Shakespeare wrote, / By no quaint rules or hampering critics taught.' (*The Tragedy of Jane Shore*, Harry William Pedicord (ed.), London: Edward Arnold, 1975, 9.)

54. Johnson, 'Preface', 123. Johnson opines: 'This fault the barbarity of his age cannot extenuate, for it is always a writer's duty to make the world better, and justice is a virtue independent on time and place.'

55. Capell, *Notes and Various Readings to Shakespeare*, 71.

56. Montagu, *Essay on the Writings and Genius of Shakespear*, 286.

57. Marcus Walsh, *Shakespeare, Milton and Eighteenth-Century Literary Editing: The Beginnings of Interpretative Scholarship*, Cambridge: Cambridge University Press, 1997, 124.

## The audience as *topos*

58. Lewis Theobald, 'Preface to Edition of Shakespeare', David Nichol Smith (ed.), *Eighteenth-Century Essays on Shakespeare*, Oxford: Clarendon Press, 1733, 63–91: 73.

59. Johnson, 'Preface', 83.

60. Samuel Johnson, 'Proposals for Printing, by Subscription, the Dramatick Works of William Shakespeare, Corrected and Illustrated by Samuel Johnson, London, June 1, 1756', Arthur Sherbo (ed.), *The Yale Edition of the Works of Samuel Johnson*, vol. VII, New Haven: Yale University Press, 1968, 51–58: 52–53.
61. As Margareta de Grazia has pointed out in her seminal *Shakespeare Verbatim*, '[...] [W]hile salvaging the past differences that his own universal standards could not comprehend, Malone's historicism still permitted those standards to appear universally valid' (Margareta De Grazia, *Shakespeare Verbatim: The Reproduction of Authenticity and the 1790 Apparatus*, Oxford: Clarendon Press, 1991, 115–16.).
62. Moody Prior, 'The Elizabethan Audience and the Plays of Shakespeare', *Modern Philology* 49, 1951–52, 101–23: 107–08.

## 2   'No man of genius ever wrote for the mob': Shakespeare's Elizabethan Audience and Romantic Shakespeare Criticism

1. Jonathan Bate, *Shakespeare and the English Romantic Imagination*, Oxford: Clarendon Press, 1986, 8.
2. Charles Lamb is as case in point: 'It may seem a paradox, but I cannot help being of [sic] opinion that the plays of Shakespeare are less calculated for performance on a stage, than those of almost any other dramatist whatever. Their distinguished excellence is a reason that they should be so. There is so much in them, which comes not under the province of acting, with which eye, and tone, and gesture, have nothing to do.' (*On the Tragedies of Shakespeare* [1811], Joan Coldwell (ed.), *Charles Lamb on Shakespeare*, Gerrards Cross: Smythe, 1978, 24–42: 28.)
3. The Romantic apotheosis of the author implies a corresponding apotheosis of his book, which Gary Taylor describes as follows: 'Books abstract, impersonalize, idealize; what had been an interaction between a cast and an audience became instead a kind of message left by an untrenchable author for any and all possible readers. The text became a thing, a perfect, timeless thing, and any attempt to transform it back into an action came to be regarded as a transgression; any actualisation diminishes the ideal by confining it to a particular time and place and person.' (Taylor, *Reinventing Shakespeare*, 108)
4. Jonathan Arac, 'The Impact of Shakespeare', Marshall Brown (ed.), *The Cambridge History of Literary Criticism*, vol. 5: Romanticism, Cambridge: Cambridge University Press, 2000, 272–95: 281.
5. Charles Lamb, 'G. F. Cooke in *Richard the Third*', Joan Coldwell (ed.), *Charles Lamb on Shakespeare*, Gerrards Cross: Smythe, 1978, 18.
6. William Wordsworth, 'Essay, Supplementary to the Preface to *The Excursion*' [1815], W. J. B. Owen (ed.), *Wordsworth's Literary Criticism*, London: Routledge, 1974, 192–218: 198.
7. William Wordsworth, 'Preface to Lyrical Ballads' [1802], W. J. B. Owen (ed.), *Wordsworth's Literary Criticism*, London: Routledge, 1974, 68–95: 70–71.
8. '[A] multitude of causes, unknown to former times', Wordsworth states, 'are now acting with a combined force to blunt the discriminating powers of

the mind, and unfitting it for all voluntary exertion to reduce it to a state of almost savage torpor. The most effective of these causes are the great national events which are daily taking place, and the increasing accumulation of men in cities, where the uniformity of their occupations produces a craving for extraordinary incident, which the rapid communication of intelligence hourly gratifies.' (Wordsworth, 'Preface to Lyrical Ballads', 73.)

## Coleridge and Shakespeare's Elizabethan audience

9. Samuel Taylor Coleridge, *Lectures 1808–1819 On Literature*, vol. I in R. A. Foakes (ed.), *The Collected Works of Samuel Taylor Coleridge*, vol. V, London: Routledge and Kegan Paul, 1987, 212.

10. Coleridge, *Lectures 1808–1819 On Literature*, vol. 1, 353.

11. Samuel Taylor Coleridge, *The Friend*, Barbara Rooke (ed.), *The Collected Works of Samuel Taylor Coleridge* vol. IV.i and IV.ii, London: Routledge and Kegan Paul, 1969, IV.i, 218.

12. '"Shakespeare combined the poet and the gentleman" and "No man of genius ever wrote for the mob" [...] were precisely the kind of things that Coleridge's gentle audiences liked to hear.' Jonathan Bate, 'Introduction', Jonathan Bate (ed.), *The Romantics on Shakespeare*, London: Penguin Shakespeare Library, 1992, 1–36: 19.

13. Coleridge, *Lectures 1808–1819 On Literature*, vol. I, 229.

14. Coleridge, *Lectures 1808–1819 On Literature*, vol. I, 229.

15. Coleridge, *Lectures 1808–1819 On Literature*, vol. I, 228.

16. Coleridge, *Lectures 1808–1819 On Literature*, vol. I, 229.

17. Coleridge, *Lectures 1808–1819 On Literature*, vol. II, 362.

18. Coleridge, *Lectures 1808–1819 On Literature*, vol. II, 273.

19. Coleridge, *Lectures 1808–1819 On Literature*, vol. II, 272.

20. Jonathan Bate, 'The Politics of Romantic Shakespeare Criticism: Germany, England, France', *European Romantic Review* 1, 1990, 1–26: 16.

## Jacobin Jacobeans: Hazlitt

21. Taylor, *Reinventing Shakespeare*, 148.

22. Taylor, *Reinventing Shakespeare*, 150.

23. William Hazlitt, *Lectures on the Dramatic Literature of the Age of Elizabeth* [1818], P. P. Howe (ed.), *The Complete Works of William Hazlitt*, after the edition of R. A. Waller and Arnold Glover, vol. 6: *Lectures on the English Comic Writers and Lectures on the Age of Elizabeth*, London and Toronto: Dent, 1931, 175.

24. Hazlitt, *Dramatic Literature of the Age of Elizabeth*, 176–77.

25. 'The vulgar Elizabethan barbarians of the previous age do not exist for Hazlitt. Shakespeare's auditors are members of a great and characteristically English age, and they are men first before they are Elizabethans.' (Prior, 'The Elizabethan Audience and the Plays of Shakespeare', 180.)

26. Hazlitt, *Dramatic Literature of the Age of Elizabeth*, 180.

27. William Hazlitt, 'What is the People?' [1818], P. P. Howe (ed.), *The Complete Works of William Hazlitt*, after the edition of R. A. Waller and Arnold Glover, vol. 7: *Political Essays, with Sketches of Public Characters*, London/Toronto: Dent, 1932, 259–81: 269.

28. That this is not without its conceptual difficulties is obvious from a passage in *Characters of Shakespear's Plays* in which Hazlitt elaborates on the less than democratic forces behind great writing: 'The principle of poetry is a very anti-levelling principle. [...] It presents a dazzling appearance. It shows its head turreted, crowned, and crested. Its front is gilt and blood-stained. [...] Kings, priests, nobles are its train-bearers, tyrants and slaves its executioners. [...] Poetry is right-royal. It puts the individual for the species, the one above the infinite many, might before right. (P. P. Howe (ed.), *The Complete Works of William Hazlitt*, after the edition of R. A. Waller and Arnold Glover, vol. 4: *The Round Table and Characters of Shakespear's Plays*, London/Toronto: Dent, 1930, 214–15.)

## The Elizabethan audience in nineteenth-century American Shakespeare criticism

29. Walt Whitman, 'A Thought on Shakespeare' [1886], Floyd Stovall (ed.), *Prose Works 1892, Vol. II: Collect and Other Prose*, New York: New York University Press, 1964, 556–58: 558.

30. Walt Whitman, 'Democratic Vistas' [1871], Floyd Stovall (ed.), *Prose Works 1892, Vol. II: Collect and Other Prose*, New York: New York University Press, 1964, 361–426: 388.

31. Richard Grant White, *Studies in Shakespeare* [1885], Boston: Houghton Mifflin, 1893, 6th edition, 20.

32. Brander Matthews, *Shakspere as a Playwright*, New York/London: Longmans, Green, 1913, 274.

33. Matthews, *Shakspere as a Playwright*, 274.

34. George Bancroft, 'On the Progress of Civilization, or Reasons Why the Natural Association of Men of Letters is With the Democracy' [1838], Peter Rawlings (ed.), *Americans on Shakespeare 1776–1914*, Aldershot: Ashgate, 70–71: 70.

35. Ralph Waldo Emerson, *Representative Men: Seven Lectures*, Alfred R. Ferguson, Joseph Slater and Ronald A. Bosco (eds.), *The Collected Works of Ralph Waldo Emerson*, vol. IV, Cambridge (Massachusetts)/London: Harvard University Press, 1987, 109.

36. Emerson, *Representative Men*, 114–15.

37. Emerson, *Representative Men*, 110–11.

38. Emerson, *Representative Men*, 113.

39. Emerson, *Representative Men*, 124–25.

40. '[Emerson claims that] without education, individualism can only produce weak and oppressive forms of social and political life. Great men educate, they lead the individual out of privatism, out of inauthentic and uncritical affiliation with tradition or with mass culture.' (Bristol, *Shakespeare's America, America's Shakespeare*, 129.)

41. George Wilkes, *Shakespeare: From an American Point of View; Including an Inquiry as to his Religious Faith and his Knowledge of Law: With the Baconian Theory Considered*, London: Sampson Low, Marston, 1877, 315.

42. Wilkes, *Shakespeare*, 120.

43. Wilkes, *Shakespeare*, 101.

44. Taylor, *Reinventing Shakespeare*, 202.

45. Wilkes, *Shakespeare*, 2.
46. Wilkes, *Shakespeare*, 154.
47. Henry N. Hudson, *Lectures on Shakespeare*, vol. 1, New York: Baker and Scribner, 1848, 18–19.
48. Wilkes, *Shakespeare*, 218.
49. Matthews, *Shakspere as a Playwright*, 308.
50. Delia Bacon, 'William Shakespeare and His Plays, an Enquiry Concerning Them' (1856), Peter Rawlings (ed.), *Americans on Shakespeare 1776–1914*, Aldershot: Ashgate, 1999, 169–99: 191.
51. Joseph C. Hart, *The Romance of Yachting: Voyage the First* [1848], Peter Rawlings (ed.), *Americans on Shakespeare 1776–1914*, Aldershot: Ashgate, 1999, 140–50: 149.
52. Hart, *The Romance of Yachting*, 141.

# 3   Enter the Groundlings

1. Charles Darwin, *The Origin of Species* [1859], Gillian Beer (ed.), Oxford: Oxford University Press, 1996, 145.
2. Shakespeare, *Hamlet*, III, ii: 8–12.
3. *The Oxford English Dictionary: Being a Corrected Re-Issue with an Introduction, Supplement, and Bibliography of a New English Dictionary on Historical Principles. Founded Mainly on the Materials Collected by The Philological Society.* Volume IV: F–G. Oxford: Oxford University Press, 1933, *s.v.* 'groundling'.
4. Thomas Dekker, *The Guls Hornbook and the Belman of London* [1609], R. B. McKerrow (ed.), London: De la More, 1904, 47.
5. John Fletcher and Philip Massinger, *The Prophetess* [1622], George Walton Williams (ed.), *The Dramatic Works in the Beaumont and Fletcher Canon*, vol. IX, Cambridge: Cambridge University Press, 1994, 221–318: 238.
6. Shepherd/Womack, *English Drama*, 111.
7. G. H. Lewes, 'Shakespeare's Critics: English and Foreign', *Edinburgh Review* 90, 1849, 46–47: 46–47.
8. Shepherd/Womack, *English Drama*, 111.
9. Shepherd/Womack, *English Drama*, 111–12.
10. John Addington Symonds, *Studies of the Greek Poets* [1873], London: Black, 1920, 3rd edition, 233.
11. Herbert Weir Smyth, *Greek Melic Poets* [1903], New York: Biblo and Tannen, 1963, l, vii.

## Groundlings, pit and carnival

12. Shepherd/Womack, *English Drama*, 112.
13. Marc Baer, *Theatre and Disorder in Late Georgian London*, Oxford: Clarendon Press, 1992, 53.
14. Shepherd/Womack, *English Drama*, 115.
15. Baer, *Theatre and Disorder*, 143.
16. Shepherd/Womack, *English Drama*, 112.
17. Baer, *Theatre and Disorder*, 182. On 'counter-theatricality' during the OP riots, see also Elaine Hadley, 'The Old Price Wars: Melodramatizing the

Public Sphere in Early-Nineteenth-Century England', *PMLA* 107, 1992, 524–37.

18. Taine's *Histoire de la literature anglaise* (1863, English translation 1872) was the first major work of literary historiography since Thomas Wharton's unfinished and, by the 1870s, certainly outdated *History of English Poetry* (1774–1781). Adolphus Ward's *History of English Dramatic Literature to the Death of Queen Anne* only came out in 1875; just like Wharton, Ward limited himself to the drama. George Saintsbury's 1898 *Short History of English Literature* was the first English attempt at a comprehensive overview of English literature.

19. Hippolyte A. Taine, *History of English Literature* [1872], translated from the French by H. van Laun, two Volumes in One, New York: Holt, 1886, 226.

20. Early modern sumptuary laws would of course have put a check on such unregulated self-display. Taine's Elizabethans are clearly Elizabethans of the mind.

21. Taine, *History*, 223. No mention is made of the (apparently less spectacular) galleries. The Elizabethan theatre as Taine describes it is made up of the extremely privileged and the masses, with no middle ground in between.

22. Taine, *History*, 223.

23. Taine, *History*, 223–24.

24. Taine, *History*, 223.

25. Mikhail Bakhtin, *Rabelais and His World*, translated by Helene Iswolsky, Cambridge, Massachusetts: Massachusetts Institute of Technology Press, 1968, 7.

26. Bakhtin, *Rabelais and His World*, 3.

27. Baer, *Theatre and Disorder*, 53.

28. Taine, *History*, 227–28. ('Billingsgate' is 'le langage des halles' in the French original.)

29. These are the four passages that Minto in his 1874 *Characteristics of English Poets from Chaucer to Shirley* (London: Blackwood, 1885, 2nd edition, 301) quotes as traditionally considered the most objectionable ones.

30. Frederick S. Boas, *Shakspere and his Predecessors*, London: Murray, 1896, 459–60.

31. Algernon Charles Swinburne, *A Study of Shakespeare*, Sir Edmund Gosse, C.B. and Thomas James Wise (eds.), *The Complete Works of Algernon Charles Swinburne*, Prose Works vol.1 (= Complete Works vol. XI), New York: Russell & Russell, 1968, 1–222: 76–77.

32. Maurice Morgann, *Shakespearian Criticism*, Daniel A. Fineman (ed.), Oxford: Clarendon Press, 1972, 154.

33. Morgann, *Shakespearian Criticism*, 238.

34. Morgann, *Shakespearian Criticism*, 282. Already for Morgann, the groundlings are no longer exclusively defined by their whereabouts in the theatre. ('the gallery Where the groundlings are now seated').

35. Shepherd/Womack, *English Drama*, 121.

36. Bakhtin, *Rabelais and His World*, 34: 'The carnival spirit offers the chance to have a new outlook on the world, to realize the relative nature of all that exists, and to enter a completely new order of things.'

37. George Saintsbury, *A History of Elizabethan Literature*, London: Macmillan, 1901, 170.

## Dumb shows and noise

38. F. A. Bather, 'The Puns of Shakespeare', Charles Halford Hawkins/Winchester College Shakspere Society (eds.), *Noctes Shaksperianae: A Series of Papers by Late and Present Members*, Winchester/London: Warren, 1887, 69–91: 82.
39. A. C. Bradley, *Oxford Lectures on Poetry*, London: Macmillan, 1950, 363–64.
40. Bradley, *Oxford Lectures on Poetry*, 364–65.
41. George Augustus Sala, *Twice Round the Clock*, London: Houlston and Wright, 1859, 271.
42. *Stage-Land: Curious Habits and Customs of its Inhabitants*, London 1889, 3, cited from Tetzeli von Rosador, 'Victorian Theories', 101–02.
43. See e.g. Robert Bridges, *The Influence of the Audience on Shakespeare's Drama* [1907] (= Collected Essays Papers & c. of Robert Bridges, vol. 1), London: Milford, 1927, 21–23.
44. G. H. Lewes, 'Charles Kean in *The Corsican Brothers*', George Rowell (ed.), *Victorian Dramatic Criticism*, London: Methuen, 1971, 97–99: 98–99.
45. Charles Dickens, *'The Amusements of the People' and Other Papers: Reports, Essays and Reviews 1834–51* (= *Dickens' Journalism Vol. 2*), Michael Slater (ed.), London: Dent, 1997, 56.
46. Bradley, *Oxford Lectures on Poetry*, 365.
47. Henry Mayhew, *London Labour and the London Poor. In Four Volumes. Vol. 1: The London Street-Folk (partial)* [1861], New York: Dover Publications, 1968, 15.
48. While Bradley consistently uses the groundlings to rationalise the presence of seemingly undesirable passages in Shakespeare, his views on the Elizabethan audience *in its entirety* fluctuate. Sometimes, the Elizabethans are presented as the great integrators of seemingly irreconcilable extremes: 'Into this most mysterious and inward of his works [*Hamlet*], it would seem, the poet flung, as if in derision of his cultured critics, well-nigh every stimulant of popular excitement he could collect: [...] five deaths on the open stage, three appearances of a ghost, two of a mad woman, a dumbshow, two men raving and fighting in a grave at a funeral, the skulls and bones of the dead, a clown bandying jests with a prince, songs at once indecent and pathetic, marching soldiers, a fencing-match, then a litter of corpses, and explosions in the first Act [sic] and explosions in the last. And yet out of this sensational material – not in spite of it, but out of it – he made the most mysterious and inward of his dramas, which leaves us haunted by thoughts beyond the reaches of our souls; and he knew that the very audience that rejoiced in ghosts and explosions would listen, even while it was waiting for the ghost, to that which the explosion had suggested, – a general disquisition, twenty-five lines long, on the manner in which one defect may spoil a noble reputation. In this strange harmony of discords, surely unexampled before or since, we may see at a glance the essence of Elizabethan drama, of its poet, and of its audience.' (*Oxford Lectures on Poetry*, 372).
49. Hadley, 'Old Price Wars', 532.
50. Hadley, 'Old Price Wars', 533.

## 'Wretched beings': The Elizabethan audience and Victorian morality

51. Bridges, 'Influence', 1–2.
52. Bridges, 'Influence', 2.

53. Bridges, 'Influence', 2.
54. Bridges, 'Influence', 4.
55. Bridges, 'Influence', 6.
56. Bridges, 'Influence', 4.
57. Bridges, 'Influence', 7.
58. Bridges, 'Influence', 6.
59. A. C. Bradley, *Shakespearean Tragedy: Lectures on Hamlet, Othello, King Lear, Macbeth* [1904], London: Macmillan, 1937, second edition, 395.
60. Note the phrase 'roared with laughter', which likens the groundlings to animals. Also, compare Taine: '[T]he sixteenth century is like a den of lions.' (*History*, 228).
61. John W. Hales, *Notes and Essays on Shakespeare*, London: Bell, 1884, 288–89.
62. Hales, *Notes and Essays*, 289.
63. Hales, *Notes and Essays*, 290.
64. Matthew Arnold, 'George Sand', R. H. Super (ed.), *Philistinism in England and America* (= *The Complete Prose Works of Matthew Arnold*, Vol. X), Ann Arbor: University of Michigan Press, 1974, 187–89: 188.
65. According to Arnold, 'the eternal spirit of the Populace' may surface even in the Barbarian or the Philistine – 'every time that we snatch up a vehement opinion in ignorance and passion, every time that we long to crush an adversary by sheer violence, every time that we are envious, every time that we are brutal, every time that we adore mere power or success, every time that we add our voice to swell a blind clamour against some unpopular personage, every time that we trample savagely on the fallen [...].' (Matthew Arnold, *Culture and Anarchy* [1869], R. H. Super (ed.), (= The Complete Prose Works of Matthew Arnold, Vol. V), Ann Arbor: University of Michigan Press, 85–256: 144–45.).
66. Gissing's *The Nether World* (1889) is a good case in point. In the chapter 'Io Saturnalia!', Gissing describes the grounds around the Crystal Palace – from a point of view in which aesthetics seamlessly merge with morality: 'Not one in a thousand shows the elements of taste in dress; vulgarity and worse glares in all but every costume. Observe the middle-aged women; it would be small surprise that their good looks had vanished, but whence comes it they are animal, repulsive, absolutely vicious in ugliness? Mark the men in their turn: four in every six have visages so deformed by ill-health that they excite disgust; their hair is cut down to within half an inch of the scalp; their legs are twisted out of shape by evil conditions of life from birth upwards. Whenever a youth and a girl come along arm-in-arm, how flagrantly shows the man's coarseness!' (George Gissing, *The Nether World: A Novel* [1889], John Goode (ed.), Brighton: The Harvester Press, 1982, 109–10.)
67. Mayhew, *London Labour and the London Poor*, 41–42.
68. Kurt Tetzeli von Rosador, 'Henry Mayhews Vielstimmigkeit', Henry Mayhew, *Die Armen von London. Ein Kompendium der Lebensbedingungen und Einkünfte derjenigen, die arbeiten wollen, derjenigen, die nicht arbeiten können, und derjenigen, die nicht arbeiten wollen*, Frankfurt/Main: Eichhorn, 1996, 361–38: 376–77. Translations from Tetzeli are mine.
69. Tetzeli, 'Henry Mayhews Vielstimmigkeit', 277.

70. As Dan Bivona and Roger Henkle point out, the images of poverty (particularly *female* poverty) constructed by Mayhew and other social observers 'may tell us as much about what it meant to be male and middle class in the nineteenth century as they tell us about what it meant to be poor'. (Dan Bivona and Roger B. Henkle, *The Imagination of Class: Masculinity and the Victorian Urban Poor*, Columbus: The Ohio State University Press, 2006, 5.).
71. Bridges, 'Influence', 28–29.
72. Bradley, *Oxford Lectures on Poetry*, 392.

## A nation of groundlings?

73. Edward Dowden, *Introduction to Shakespeare*, London: Blackie, 1893, 44.
74. James Anthony Froude, *History of England from the Fall of Wolsey to the Death of Elizabeth*, vol. 1, Leipzig: F. A. Brockhaus, 1861, 43.
75. Ward, *A History of English Dramatic Literature to the Death of Queen Anne*, vol. 1, 273–74.
76. Boas, *Shakspere and his Predecessors*, 35.
77. Hales, *Essays and Notes*, 145–47.
78. The perceived vitality and impulsiveness of the Elizabethans contrasts rather sharply with what the Victorians sometimes saw as their own rather dull and cerebral ways. Edward Dowden writes: 'To many, at the present time, the sanity and the strength of Shakspere would assuredly be an influence that might well be called religious. The Elizabethan drama is thoroughly free from lassitude, and from that lethargy of heart, which most of us have felt at one time or another. Those whose lot falls in a period of doubt and spiritual alteration, between the ebb and the flow, in the welter and wash of the waves, are, – because they lack the joyous energy of a faith – peculiarly subject to this mood of barren lethargy. And it is not alone in the mystic, spiritual life of the soul that we may suffer from coldness or aridity. [...] To this mood of barren world-weariness the Elizabethan drama comes with no direct teaching, but with the [sic] vision of life. Even though death end all, these things at least are – beauty and force, purity, sin, and love, and anguish and joy. These things are, and therefore life cannot be a little idle whirl of dust. [...] The vision of life rises before us; and we know that the vision represents a reality. These things, then, being actual, how poor and shallow a trick of the heart is cynicism!' (Edward Dowden, *Shakspere: A Critical Study of his Mind and Art* [1875], London: Routledge & Kegan Paul, 1948, 3rd edition, 29–30.). This, Shepherd and Womack feel, is 'a statement of cultural need so naked that it's almost touching' (*English Drama*, 105).
79. Charles Halford Hawkins, 'The Stage-Craft of Shakspere', Winchester College Shakspere Society/Charles Halford Hawkins (eds.), *Noctes Shaksperianae*, Winchester/London: Warren, 1887, 121–65: 131.
80. Ward, *History*, 480–81.
81. Thomas Seccombe and J. W. Allen, *The Age of Shakespeare (1579–1631)*, vol. II: Drama, London: George Bell & Sons, 1903, 41–42.
82. Ward, *History*, 469.
83. George Dawson, *Shakespeare and Other Lectures*, London: Kegan Paul, Trench & Co., 1888, 106.

## 4  Childish and Primitive: Shakespeare's Elizabethan Audience and the Turn-of-the-century Theatrical Avant-garde

1. John Dover Wilson, *The Elizabethan Shakespeare: Annual Shakespeare Lecture of the British Academy*, London: Humphrey Milford, 1929, 20–21.
2. Muriel St. Clare Byrne, 'Shakespeare's Audience', *A Series of Papers on Shakespeare and the Theatre: Together with Papers on Edward Alleyn and Early Records Illustrating the Personal Life of Shakespeare, by Members of the Shakespeare Association, 1925–1926*, London: Oxford University Press, 1927, 186–216: 199.
3. '[Shakespeare's audience] possessed [...] a vivid imagination. Shakespeare could address to it not in vain the injunction, "Work, work your thoughts!" Probably in three scenes out of five the place and surroundings of the action were absolutely invisible to its eyes. In a fourth it took the barest symbol for reality. A couple of wretched trees made the Forest of Arden for it, five men with ragged foils the army that conquered at Agincourt: are we stronger than it, or weaker? It heard Romeo say "Look, love, what envious streaks / Do lace the severing clouds in yonder east", and to its mind's eye, they were there. It looked at a shabby old balcony, but as it listened it saw the swallows flitting round the sun-lit battlements of Macbeth's castle, and our pitiful sense of grotesque incongruity never troubled it.' (A. C. Bradley, 'Shakespeare's Theatre and Audience' [1902], *Oxford Lectures on Poetry*, London: Macmillan, 1950, 361–93: 391).
4. Byrne, 'Shakespeare's Audience', 200.
5. Byrne, 'Shakespeare's Audience', 200.
6. Byrne, 'Shakespeare's Audience', 202–03.
7. George Pierce Baker, *The Development of Shakespeare as a Dramatist* [1907], New York: AMS Press, 1965, 13.
8. Georg Brandes, *William Shakespeare: A Critical Study* [1898], London: William Heinemann, 1917, 102.)
9. 'J'ai vu, l'autre jour, une petite fille qui se cachait derrière un paravent et qui s'assit sur le plancher. "Que fais-tu?" lui dit sa mère. "Viens donc frapper à la porte", répondit-elle, "je suis chez moi, voici ma maison, je reçois aujourd'hui". Or, cette imagination enfantine et naïve nous donne la clef de l'imagination populaire élisabéthaine.' (Charles J. Sisson, *Le Goût Public et le Théâtre Elisabéthain jusqu'à la Mort de Shakespeare*, Dijon: Darntière [c. 1914], 94 [my translation]).
10. Max J. Wolff, *William Shakespeare: Studien und Aufsätze*, Leipzig: Seemann, 1903, 357.
11. Levin Ludwig Schücking, *Character Problems in Shakespeare's Plays: A Guide to the Better Understanding of the Dramatist* [1922], Gloucester (Massachusetts): Peter Smith, 1959, 11.
12. Schücking, *Character Problems*, 37.
13. Schücking, *Character Problems*, 37. The German original even attests the audience 'den bestimmenden Einfluß' ('the decisive influence') on Shakespeare, a statement which the translation obviously felt a need to attenuate. Levin Ludwig Schücking, *Die Charakterprobleme bei Shakespeare: Eine Einführung in das Verständnis des Dramatikers*, Leipzig: Tauchnitz, 1919, 33.

14. Bill Ashcroft, 'Primitive and Wingless: The Colonial Subject as Child', Wendy S. Jackson (ed.), *Dickens and the Children of Empire*, Basingstoke: Palgrave, 2000, 184–202: 185.

15. Cecil Rhodes, for example, had the following to offer on suffrage in the colonies: 'As to the question of voting, we say that the natives are in a sense citizens, but not altogether citizens – they are still children [...]. Now, I say the natives are children. They are just emerging from barbarism. [...]. To us annexation was an obligation, whereas to the natives it will be a positive relief, for they will be freed from a seething cauldron of barbarian atrocities.' (Cecil Rhodes, *Cecil Rhodes: His Political Life and Speeches,* F. Verschoyle (ed.), London: Chapman & Hall, 1900, 380, 383, 396. The passage is also quoted in Ashcroft, *op. cit.*) The image is metonymical: The 'seething cauldron of barbarian atrocities' is also the cauldron in which missionaries are cooked to be eaten by cannibalistic natives. The latter are in effect being freed from what makes them so threatening to the colonisers in the first place.

## Making pictures

16. Tree was quite clear about this: 'I take it that the entire business of the stage is – illusion. As the entire aim of all art is illusion, to gain this end all means are fair. [...] Illusion, then, is the first and last word of the stage; all that aids illusion is good, all that destroys illusion is bad.' (Herbert Beerbohm Tree, *Thoughts and Afterthoughts*, London and New York: Cassell and Company, 1913, 57.)

17. Cary M. Mazer, *Shakespeare Refashioned: Elizabethan Plays on Edwardian Stages*, Ann Arbor: UMI Research Press, 1980, 8.

18. Byrne, 'Shakespeare's Audience', 203.

19. 'There is no evidence that [the Elizabethans] visualised the swallows flitting around the sunlit battlements of Dunsinane as Bradley suggests. Shakespeare's injunction "Work, work your thoughts" implies that they could work them but it does not imply that they did. If human nature is any guide to the nature of the Elizabethan audience we may be fairly sure that it did not exercise its imagination unless it was forced to.' (Byrne, 'Shakespeare's Audience', 203.)

20. 'The Edwardian traditionalists believed that the fictive reality on the stage was an intrinsic feature of their dramatic text. If Shakespeare was not able to create such a verisimilar world on the stage, this was, according to the traditionalist, the fault of his theatre, not of his dramatic vision.' (Mazer, *Shakespeare Refashioned*, 10.)

21. Tree, *Thoughts*, 60.

22. Roberta E. Pearson and William Uricchio, 'How Many Times Shall Caesar Bleed in Sport: Shakespeare and the Cultural Debate about Moving Pictures', *Screen* 31, 1990, 243–61: 258.

23. Harley Granville-Barker, *Prefaces to Shakespeare*, vol. I.: *Hamlet, King Lear, The Merchant of Venice, Antony and Cleopatra, Cymbeline*, London: Batsford, 1958, 384–85.

24. Influential theatre critics had castigated the excesses of pictorial realism from the late nineteenth century onwards – for the very reason that they impeded rather than furthered 'real' imagination. Sidney Lee is a case in point:

'The unintellectual playgoer, to whom Shakespeare will never really prove attractive, has little or no imagination to exercise, and he only tolerates a performance in the theatre when little or no demand is made on the exercise of the imaginative faculty. "The groundlings," said Shakespeare for all time, "are capable of [appreciating – SL] nothing but inexplicable dumb shows and noise." They would be hugely delighted nowadays with a scene in which two real motor cars, with genuine chauffeurs and passengers, race uproariously across the stage. That is realism in its nakedness. That is realism reduced to its first principles. Realistic "effects", however speciously beautiful they may be, invariably tend to realism of that primitive type, which satisfies the predilections of the groundling, and reduces drama to the level of the cinematograph.' (Sidney Lee, *Shakespeare and the Modern Stage: With Other Essays*, London: Murray, 1906, 23). Here, the spectator who enjoys pictorial realism is not the counterpart to the 'childish' Elizabethans – he is himself 'unintellectual', perhaps even 'primitive'. Given that most of these spectators were middle-class, Lee's remarks can indeed be read as a manifestation of anti-philistinism, as Richard Halpern claims in Shakespeare *Among the Moderns* (Ithaca and London: Cornell University Press, 1997, 64). Lee's groundlings are indeed clearly no longer lower class. That they should be able to turn bourgeois with such ease demonstrates the remarkable elasticity of the concept. While the term remains pejorative, it now includes a component decidedly not covered by its conventional usage.

25.  'As we, when a play has no hold on us, may fall to thinking about the scenery, the [Elizabethan] stage might be an obvious bare stage. But are we conscious of the scenery when a play really moves us? If we are, there is something very wrong with the scenery, which should know its place as a background. The audience was not conscious of curtain and balcony when Burbage played Hamlet. That conventional background faded as does our painted illusion, and they certainly did not deliberately conjure up in its place mental pictures of Elsinore.' (Granville-Barker, *Prefaces to Shakespeare*, I, 9).

26.  Richard W. Schoch, 'Pictorial Shakespeare', Stanley Wells and Sarah Stanton (eds.), *The Cambridge Companion to Shakespeare on Stage*, Cambridge: Cambridge University Press, 59–75: 59.

27.  This is a quotation from John Addington Symonds which Poel leaves unattributed in the print version of the talk. Mazer interprets this as follows: '[...] [S]o well did it [the passage from Symonds] represent Poel's views that he represented it as his own [...].' (Mazer, *Shakespeare Refashioned*, 56). Poel quotes Symonds in *Shakespeare in the Theatre*, London: Sidgwick and Jackson, 1913, 9; as well as in *Some Notes on Shakespeare's Stage and Plays*, Manchester: Manchester University Press, 1916, 11.

28.  Mazer, *Shakespeare Refashioned*, 80–81.

29.  Mazer, *Shakespeare Refashioned*, 83.

30.  Marion F. O'Connor, 'Theatre of the Empire: "Shakespeare's England" at Earl's Court, 1912', Marion F. O'Connor and Jean E. Howard (eds.), *Shakespeare Reproduced: The Text in History and Ideology*, New York and London: Methuen, 1987, 68–98: 87.

31.  *Pall Mall Gazette*, 17 May 1912, 3, cited from O'Connor, 'Theatre of the Empire', 88.

32. Poel, *Shakespeare in the Theatre*, 208–09.
33. *The Times*, 12 July 1912, 8, cited from O'Connor, 'Theatre of the Empire', 93.
34. Halpern, *Shakespeare Among the Moderns*, 27.

### Telling stories, asking questions

35. Byrne, 'Shakespeare's Audience', 204.
36. Byrne, 'Shakespeare's Audience', 204.
37. '[...] [H]ow easy it would have been to have provided a more reasonable ground for Othello's jealousy. If in the break of the second act his vessel had been delayed a week by the storm, those days of anxiety and officious consolation would have given the needed opportunity, and the time-contradictions might also have been avoided. The tragedy of OTHELLO is intolerably painful; and that not merely because we see Othello being grossly deceived, but because we are ourselves constrained to submit to palpable deception. The whole thing is impossible: it is just as Mr Bradley [A. C. Bradley, *Shakespearean Tragedy: Lectures on Hamlet, Othello, King Lear, Macbeth* [1904], London: Macmillan, 1937, 423–25] points out: Iago's calumnies postulate certain events; but if the time indispensable for those events had been allowed, then his incredible lies must have been exposed. [...] Exasperation is the word that I should choose to express the state of feeling which the reading of the OTHELLO induces in me: and seeing how cleverly everything is calculated to this effect, I conclude that it was Shakespeare's intention, and that what so hurts me was only a pleasurable excitement to his audience, whose gratification was relied on to lull their criticism.' (Robert Bridges, 'The Influence of the Audience on Shakespeare's Drama' [1907], *Collected Essays Papers & c. of Robert Bridges*, vol. 1, London: Oxford University Press, 1927, 24.)
38. Byrne, 'Shakespeare's Audience', 206.
39. Baker, *The Development of Shakespeare*, 13.
40. Baker, *The Development of Shakespeare*, 280.
41. Harley Granville-Barker, 'From *Henry V* to *Hamlet* (Revised Edition of the British Academy Annual Shakespeare Lecture on May 13, 1925)', Harley Granville-Barker, *More Prefaces to Shakespeare*, Princeton: Princeton University Press, 1974, 135–67: 138–39.
42. Granville-Barker, 'From *Henry V* to *Hamlet*', 141.
43. The term was coined by F. S. Boas in *Shakespeare and His Predecessors* (London: Murray, 1896).
44. Byrne, 'Shakespeare's Audience', 206–07.
45. Byrne, 'Shakespeare's Audience', 208.
46. William Archer, *English Dramatists of To-Day*, London: Sampson Low & Co, 1882, 9, 11.
47. Bernard Shaw, *The Quintessence of Ibsenism: Now Completed to the Death of Ibsen*, London: Constable, 1913, 191–92.
48. Schücking, *Character Problems*, 26.
49. Schücking, *Character Problems*, 26.
50. Shaw, *The Quintessence of Ibsenism*, 198.
51. Bernard Shaw, *Shaw on Shakespeare: An Anthology of Bernard Shaw's Writings on the Plays and Production of Shakespeare*, Edwin Wilson (ed. and introd.), London: Cassell, 1962, 75.

52. Granville-Barker, 'From *Henry V* to *Hamlet*', 147.
53. Shaw, *Shaw on Shakespeare*, 2.
54. Byrne, 'Shakespeare's Audience', 212–14.
55. Byrne, 'Shakespeare's Audience', 207.
56. Shaw, *Shaw on Shakespeare*, 2.
57. Byrne, 'Shakespeare's Audience', 209–10.
58. Poel, *Shakespeare in the Theatre*, 146.
59. Harley Granville-Barker, *Prefaces to Shakespeare*, vol. II: *Othello, Coriolanus, Romeo and Juliet, Julius Caesar, Love's Labour's Lost*, London: Batsford, 1958, 392.

## 5 The Rediscovery of the Judicious Few

1. Even Levin Schücking, a vocal proponent of the 'primitiveness' of Shakespeare's theatre in *Character Problems in Shakespeare's Plays*, readjusted his focus. Contributing to a controversy waged in *The Times Literary Supplement* regarding the duration of Shakespeare's plays on stage, he writes: '[...] [I]t needs not much imagination to picture the Elizabethan dramatist to oneself reading – like Molière – to an illustrious gathering of his distinguished protectors those "tragical speeches" in full which had to be cut together so miserably at the performance in the theatre. Prince Hamlet, at any rate, [...] seems to have in mind a similar custom in addressing the player with the words "I heard thee speak me a speech once, but it was never acted." Does not this utterance point unmistakably to the possibility of private readings of dramatic literature in aristocratic society? However, the author's principal intention, irrespectively of the theatre audience, must have been to create for the future reader. The reason why it was so imperfectly realized in Shakespeare's case is to be looked for in his psychology.' (Levin L. Schücking, 'Stage or Study', *The Times Literary Supplement*, 16 May 1936, 420.)
2. John Dover Wilson, *The Elizabethan Shakespeare: Annual Shakespeare Lecture of the British Academy*, London: Humphrey Milford, 1929, 24.
3. A notable exception is John Middleton Murry. In *Shakespeare*, written during his Marxist phase, he vehemently opposes the idea of Shakespeare as a sort of honorary aristocrat: 'Shakespeare did not need to consort continually with young noblemen in order to create [aristocratic] characters; nor did he create them to please such an audience: he was merely embodying the conditions of the finest natural workings of his own mind.' (John Middleton Murry, *Shakespeare*, London: Cape, 1936, 121.) While he remains thoroughly conventional in his ideas of what the groundlings were like and liked (Caliban is 'the servant-monster that makes the groundlings goggle', 137), he refuses to draw the conclusion proposed by many of his peers. Shakespeare admittedly made concessions to the groundlings in some places, but 'surely it was a better way than being hand-fed by the aristocracy, gratification for dedication [...]'. (190).
4. H. S. Bennett, *Shakespeare's Audience: Annual Shakespeare Lecture of the British Academy*, London: Milford, 1944, 3.
5. Bennett, *Shakespeare's Audience*, 9.

6. Bennett, *Shakespeare's Audience*, 13.
7. Bennett, *Shakespeare's Audience*, 7.
8. Sir Arthur Quiller-Couch and John Dover Wilson, 'Introduction', William Shakespeare, *Love's Labour's Lost*, John Dover Wilson, Sir Arthur Quiller-Couch (eds.), Cambridge: Cambridge University Press, 1923, VII–XXXIX: XXXIV.
9. Oscar James Campbell, '*Love's Labour's Lost* Re-Studied', *Studies in Shakespeare, Milton and Donne: By Members of the English Department of the University of Michigan*, New York: Haskell House, 1925, 3–45.
10. Sir Arthur Quiller-Couch, 'Introduction', William Shakespeare, *Twelfth Night or What You Will*, Sir Arthur Quiller-Couch (ed.), Cambridge: Cambridge University Press, 1930, VII–XXVIII.
11. Leslie Hotson, *The First Night of Twelfth Night*, London: Hart-Davis, 1954.
12. Peter Alexander, '*Troilus and Cressida*, 1609', *The Library* 9, 1929, 267–86.
13. William Witherle Lawrence, *Shakespeare's Problem Comedies*, New York: Macmillan, 1931.
14. Oscar James Campbell, *Comicall Satyre and Shakespeare's Troilus and Cressida*, San Marino (Cal.): Huntington Library & Art Gallery, 1938.
15. Gerald Eades Bentley, 'Shakespeare and the Blackfriars Theatre', *Shakespeare Survey* 1, 1948, 38–50: 46–48.
16. John Dover Wilson, *The Essential Shakespeare* [1932], Cambridge: Cambridge University Press, 1962, 30–31.
17. Darrell Figgis, *Shakespeare: A Study*, London: J. M. Dent & Sons, 1911, 81.
18. Henry N. Paul, *The Royal Play of Macbeth: When, Why and How It Was Written by Shakespeare*, New York: Macmillan, 1950, 3.
19. Paul, *The Royal Play of Macbeth*, 3.
20. Paul, *The Royal Play of Macbeth*, 2.
21. L. C. Knights, 'Education and the Drama in the Age of Shakespeare', T. S. Eliot (ed.), *The Criterion 1922–1939*, vol. XI: October 1931- July 1932, London: Faber and Faber, 1967, 599–625: 607–08.
22. Knights, 'Education and the Drama', 612.
23. Knights, 'Education and the Drama', 621.
24. Knights, 'Education and the Drama', 619.
25. Knights, 'Education and the Drama', 619.
26. This is not meant as a proposition on the actual degree of difficulty that an academic or non-academic reader faces when reading Shakespeare. That this particular view of the plays at this particular point in time was not exactly disadvantageous to the profession seems obvious, however.
27. Knights, 'Education and the Drama', 623–24.

## The problem of irony

28. Knights, 'Education and the Drama', 607–08.
29. Knights, 'Education and the Drama', 607–08.
30. Gerald Gould, 'A New Reading of *Henry V*', *The English Review* 29, 1919, 42–55: 42.
31. Gould, 'A New Reading of *Henry V*', 44.
32. W. W. Greg, 'Hamlet's Hallucination', *The Modern Language Review* 12, 1917, 393–421: 415–17.

33. Lukas Erne, *Shakespeare as Literary Dramatist*, Cambridge: Cambridge University Press, 2003.
34. Greg, 'Hamlet's Hallucination', 419–20.
35. W. W. Greg, 'Re-Enter Ghost. A Reply to Mr J. Dover Wilson', *Modern Language Review* 14, 1919, 353–69: 354–55.
36. Greg, 'Re-Enter Ghost', 355.
37. Northrop Frye, *Anatomy of Criticism: Four Essays*, Princeton: Princeton University Press, 1957, 41.
38. Compare Frye in *The Anatomy of Criticism*: 'The Romantic standards, in English literature, were in the main carried on by the Victorians, indicating a continuity of mode; the long anti-Romantic revolt that began around 1900 [...] indicated a shift to the ironic. In the new mode the fondness for the small closely-knit group, the sense of the esoteric, and the nostalgia for the aristocratic that has produced such very different phenomena as the royalism of Eliot, the fascism of Pound, and the cult of chivalry in Yeats, are all in a way part of a reversion to high mimetic standards. The sense of the poet as courtier, of poetry as the service of a prince, of the supreme importance of the symposium or elite group, are among the high mimetic conceptions reflected in twentieth-century literature [...].' (63)
39. See also Gary Taylor in *Reinventing Shakespeare*: 'By redefining Shakespeare as a complex of problems, critics and scholars redefined themselves as problem solvers. Like science, criticism was a set of techniques for eliciting solutions from the controlled examination of artificial objects. Expectant authors, at the same time, saw themselves as problem setters. Their works aspired to furnish material for questions in the university examinations of the future. James Joyce anticipated that *Finnegans Wake* would keep scholars busy for hundreds of years; readers setting out across *The Waste Land* were escorted by a party of poker-faced endnotes and some suggestions for further reading. Such texts demand and reward professional readers.' ( 245)

## The cultured few and the unified public sphere

40. Ezra Pound, *The Selected Letters of Ezra Pound 1907–1941* [1950], D. D. Paige (ed.), New York: James Laughlin, 1971, 101.
41. Wyndham Lewis is an exception, for he basically refuses the idea of any kind of positive rapport between Shakespeare and his audiences. While aware of the demands and restraints placed upon him by the fact that he wrote for a living, Shakespeare, according to Lewis, effectively despised those who paid his way: 'Shakespeare and the rest were hired entertainers, and not hierophants, they had to be supple and in some sense vulgar: and were as much in search of that terrible néant, "what the public wants" (only it was on the whole a little better public), as is any journalist to-day. And it is no doubt true that the artist, unless he is in some way godsman [sic] instead of Lord Leicester's merely, or Lord Northcliffe's, is coaxed or beaten off, and never allowed fully to possess, the perfection of expression. To a Shakespeare, these sad compromises and shifts, necessitated by the stupid and mean egotisms of his audience (whose tastes or lack of taste it is his unpleasant duty to learn by heart and have at his fingers' ends) can hardly endear them to him. [...] Nor would his audiences of gentlemen and ladies appeal to him much

more than his pit. In fact, with their pretentious arrogance, greater power to interfere with him, and with the eternal cheap effrontery of the *enfant gaté*, they might appeal to him at most times even less. As a showman, his remarks would not, as is generally supposed, be addressed to the mere "rotten-breathed" of his audience, the many-headed multitude, only. The crowd of his more elegant clients were "many-headed", too. Their breath probably did not smell especially sweet to the author of *Timon*. What is Shakespeare supposed to have thought of Lord Leicester's guests? He saw a good deal of them. He must have thought a good deal in consequence.' (Wyndham Lewis, *The Lion and the Fox: The Role of the Hero in the Plays if Shakespeare* [1927], London: Methuen, 1951, 172.)

42. F. R. Leavis, *Mass Civilisation and Minority Culture,* Cambridge: Minority Press, 1930, 25.

43. T. S. Eliot, *The Use of Poetry and the Use of Criticism: Studies in the Relation of Criticism to Poetry in England*, London: Faber and Faber, 1933, 153.

44. Taylor, *Reinventing Shakespeare*, 245.

45. Eliot, *The Use of Poetry*, 51–52.

46. Lawrence, *Shakespeare's Problem Comedies*, 14–15.

47. Bennett, *Shakespeare's Audience*, 14–15.

48. Q. D. Leavis, *Fiction and the Reading Public* [1932], London: Chatto and Windus, 1965, 85.

49. Leavis, *Fiction and the Reading Public*, 264.

50. Sir Edmund Gosse, *Questions at Issue*, cited in Q. D. Leavis, *Fiction and the Reading Public*, 190.

51. Gary Taylor comments: 'Virginia Woolf would no doubt have regarded Lady Monkswell [a Victorian socialite] as a moron; Q. D. Leavis and Robert Bridges would have been as contemptuous of one another as they both were of the bulk of Shakespeare's audience. Two different cultural elites were colliding. Monkswell represented a relatively closed old elite defined by social status and based largely on inherited wealth, the Leavises represented a more open-ended elitism, a new cultural meritocracy accessible to anyone with intelligence who could secure the right kind of education. Each elite excluded, by definition, most members of the other. But the hostility between them should not obscure the fact that in the early twentieth century both groups cooperated in reshaping Shakespeare. For their different reasons, they both insisted that Shakespeare the old popular playwright did not belong to the populace.' (*Reinventing Shakespeare*, 249.)

52. Richard Halpern writes: '[I]f Shakespeare's plays offered high modernists a language for articulating their anxieties about mass culture, they also registered an historical diminution of the literary space in which modernist protest could be heard. The reduction of modernism's literary public was itself seen as the splitting of what had been a relatively unified literary sphere into mass culture on the one hand and high-modernist and avantgardist cultures on the other. Within this context, Shakespeare's status as a broadly popular playwright allowed modernism to chart its own relative cultural isolation. [...] Of course, not all modernists regarded Shakespearean popularity as the sign of their own marginalization. [...] But for the more conservative, elitist, or esoteric strains of modernism, Shakespeare embodied a now-unattainable cultural reach. Thus his specter occupied both ends of high modernism's

paralysing engagement with mass culture. The Roman plays embodied fears of mob rule and mass politics, while the example of Shakespeare's popularity only highlighted the apparent disappearance of a cultural public forum within which modernist protest might have some effect.' (Halpern, *Shakespeare Among the Moderns*, 53–54.)

53. Halpern, *Shakespeare Among the Moderns*, 62–63.

# 6 Neo-Elizabethanism

1. Benjamin T. Spencer, 'This Elizabethan Shakespeare', *The Sewanee Review* 49, 1941, 536–53: 537.
2. John W. Draper, *The Hamlet of Shakespeare's Audience* [1939], New York: Octagon Books, 1966, VII.
3. Draper, *Hamlet*, VII.
4. Draper, *Hamlet*, VII–IX.
5. 'To collect all the Elizabethan writings pertinent to a long and complex play like *Hamlet* is truly counsel of perfection; to take to oneself completely the Elizabethan attitude, or varying class attitudes, toward life is sometimes more than one can hope of the imagination; and to see all the minutiae of the text in the light of all these pertinent ideas and facts and also all the rest of the play, puts no moderate strain on the most inclusive mind, but the effort is a challenge and an adventure; and, in this challenge and this adventure, the present writer asks the reader to participate in a spirit of co-operation, and where necessary, of indulgence.' (Draper, *Hamlet*, p. VIII–IX.) Obviously, Draper and his hypothetical reader are not exactly equals in this undertaking.
6. Draper, *Hamlet*, VIII.
7. John W. Draper, *The Twelfth Night of Shakespeare's Audience*, Stanford: Stanford University Press, 1952, 96.
8. John W. Draper, 'Sir John Falstaff', *Review of English Studies* 8, 1932, 414–24: 415.
9. Draper, 'Sir John Falstaff', 422–23.
10. Draper, *Twelfth Night*, 96.
11. Draper, *Hamlet*, 80.
12. Draper, *Hamlet*, 71–72.
13. Louis Montrose, 'Professing the Renaissance: The Poetics and Politics of Culture', H. Aram Veeser (ed.), *The New Historicism*, New York and London: Routledge, 1989, 15–36: 20.
14. Paul N. Siegel, 'Shylock and the Puritan Usurers', Arthur D. Matthews and Clark M. Emery (eds.), *Studies in Shakespeare*, Coral Gables: University of Miami Press, 1953, 129–38: 129.
15. Lilian Winstanley, *Hamlet and the Scottish Succession: Being an Examination of the Relations of the Play of Hamlet to the Scottish Succession and the Essex Conspiracy*, Cambridge: Cambridge University Press, 1921, 1. Incidentally, Carl Schmitt's recently famous 'Hamlet or Hecuba' is the preface to his daughter Anima's translation of Winstanley's study into German (*Hamlet, Sohn der Maria Stuart*, Pfullingen: Günther Neske, 1952). See Andreas Höfele, 'Hamlet in Plettenberg: Carl Schmitt's Shakespeare', *Shakespeare Survey* 65, 2012, 378–97.

16. Hardin Craig, *The Enchanted Glass: The Elizabethan Mind in Literature* [1936], Oxford: Blackwell, 1950, 62–63.
17. Elmer Edgar Stoll, *Shakespeare Studies: Historical and Comparative in Method*, New York: Macmillan, 1927, 249–51.
18. Spencer, 'This Elizabethan Shakespeare', 537.
19. Draper, *Hamlet*, 186.

### Constructions of non-ambiguity

20. Draper, *Hamlet*, VII.
21. Draper, *Hamlet*, VIII.
22. Draper, *Hamlet*, VII.
23. Elmer Edgar Stoll, *Hamlet: An Historical and Comparative Study*, Minneapolis: Research Publications of the University of Minnesota, 1919, 46–47.
24. Stoll, *Hamlet*, 56.
25. This is yet another instance of the essentially Protestant nature of Neo-Elizabethanism: Just like Luther and Tyndale, Stoll's aim is to rescue the literal sense out of a thicket of allegorical, typological and anagogical interpretations.
26. Lilian Winstanley, *Macbeth, King Lear and Contemporary History: Being a Study of the Relations of the Play of Macbeth to the Personal History of James I, the Darnley Murder and the St Bartholomew Massacre and also of King Lear as Symbolic Mythology*, Cambridge: Cambridge University Press, 1922, 3–4.
27. Draper, *Twelfth Night*, 5.
28. Spencer, 'This Elizabethan Shakespeare', 539.

### Specialist versus common-sense approaches

29. Winstanley, *Hamlet*, 3.
30. Draper, *Hamlet*, 5.
31. Elmer Edgar Stoll, *Shakespeare and Other Masters* [1940], New York: Russell & Russell, 1962, 3.
32. Stoll, *Shakespeare and Other Masters*, 95.
33. Stoll, *Hamlet*, 42.
34. Stoll, *Shakespeare and Other Masters*, 202.
35. Stoll, *Shakespeare and Other Masters*, 188.
36. Spencer, 'This Elizabethan Shakespeare', 544–45.
37. Spencer, 'This Elizabethan Shakespeare', 546–47.
38. Spencer, 'This Elizabethan Shakespeare', 542.
39. Spencer, 'This Elizabethan Shakespeare', 545.

## 7   Shakespeare's Elizabethan Audience in the Second Half of the Twentieth Century

1. Brents Stirling, *The Populace in Shakespeare*, New York: Columbia University Press, 1949, 64.
2. Alfred Harbage, *Shakespeare's Audience*, New York: Columbia University Press, 1941, 159.
3. Harbage, *Shakespeare's Audience*, 162.

4. Harbage, *Shakespeare's Audience*, 163.
5. Harbage, *Shakespeare's Audience*, 11.
6. Alfred Harbage, *As They Liked It: An Essay on Shakespeare and Morality*, New York: Columbia University Press, 1947, 3.
7. 'Harbage's view might be seen as influenced by democratic sentiments prominent in the war against fascism.' (David Margolies, 'Teaching the Handsaw to Fly: Shakespeare as a Hegemonic Instrument', Graham Holderness (ed.), *The Shakespeare Myth*, Manchester: Manchester University Press, 1988, 42–53: 53).
8. Frances Perkins, 'What Is Worth Working For in America?', Robert P. Lane (ed.), *Proceedings of the National Conference of Social Work, 1941*, New York: Columbia University Press, 1941, cited in Clarke A. Chambers, *The New Deal at Home and Abroad*, New York: Free Press Macmillan, 1965, 75–83: 77.
9. Andrew Adonis, Stephen Pollard, *A Class Act: The Myth of Britain's Classless Society*, London: Hamish Hamilton, 1997, 28.
10. Cited in Nicholas Timmins, *The Five Giants: A Biography of the Welfare State*, London: HarperCollins, 2001, 2nd edition, 92.
11. *Today* newspaper, 24 November 1990.
12. Alfred Harbage, *Shakespeare and the Rival Traditions*, New York: Columbia University Press, 1952, 25.
13. Richard Wilson, *Will Power: Essays on Shakespearean Authority*, New York: Harvester, 1993, 23.
14. Harbage, *Shakespeare's Audience*, 60–61.
15. Harbage, *Shakespeare's Audience*, 64.
16. Harbage, *Shakespeare's Audience*, 64.
17. Harbage, *Shakespeare and the Rival Traditions*, 270.
18. Harbage, *Shakespeare and the Rival Traditions*, 190.
19. Harbage, *Shakespeare and the Rival Traditions*, 222.
20. Ann Jennalie Cook, 'Audiences: Investigation, Interpretation, Invention', John D. Cox, David Scott Kastan (eds.), *A New History of Early English Drama*, New York: Columbia University Press, 1997, 305–20: 316.
21. Robert Weimann, *Shakespeare and the Popular Tradition in the Theater: Studies in the Social Dimension of Dramatic Form and Function*, Robert Schwarz (ed.), Baltimore: The Johns Hopkins University Press, 1978, xvi. The German original (*Shakespeare und die Tradition des Volkstheaters: Soziologie – Dramaturgie – Gestaltung*) was published in 1975.
22. Walter Cohen, *Drama of a Nation: Public Theater in Renaissance England and Spain*, Ithaca: Cornell University Press, 1985, 168 and *passim*.
23. Jean E. Howard, *The Stage and Social Struggle in Early Modern England*, London: Routledge, 1994, 13.
24. John Elsom (ed.), *Is Shakespeare Still Our Contemporary?*, London: Routledge, 1989, 159–60. The passage quoted is a contribution Ankist made to a section called 'Is Shakespeare a Feudal Propagandist?'
25. Weimann, *Shakespeare and the Popular Tradition*, 170.
26. Cohen, *Drama of a Nation*, 168.
27. Margolies, 'Teaching the Handsaw to Fly', 42.
28. Margolies, 'Teaching the Handsaw to Fly', 45.
29. http://www.shakespearesglobe.com/shop/product/groundling-t-shirt/1567, accessed 7 October 2014.

30. Jeremy Lopez, 'A Partial Theory of Original Practice', *Shakespeare Survey* 61, 2008, 302–17.
31. Claire van Kampen, 'Music and Aural Texture at Shakespeare's Globe', Christie Carson, Farah Karim-Cooper (eds.), *Shakespeare's Globe: A Theatrical Experiment*, Cambridge: Cambridge University Press, 2008, 79–89: 80.
32. Christie Carson, 'Democratising the Audience?', Christie Carson, Farah Karim-Cooper (eds.), *Shakespeare's Globe: A Theatrical Experiment*, Cambridge: Cambridge University Press, 2008, 115–26: 122.

    Proponents of the particularly democratic nature of the New Globe often claim that there are no barriers between actors and audience, a statement that is perhaps somewhat optimistic. Pauline Kiernan's claim that 'there is no physical or psychological dividing line between the playgoers and the players' (*Staging Shakespeare at the New Globe*, Basingstoke: Macmillan, 1999, 4), for example, is significantly undercut when, less than twenty pages later, she quotes an audience member as saying that the actors on stage 'look like giants'. (19)

33. Carson, 'Democratising the Audience?', 122.
34. John Peter, [Review], *The Sunday Times*, 13 December 1992, cited from Peter Holland, *English Shakespeares: Shakespeare on the English Stage in the 1990s*, Cambridge: Cambridge University Press, 1997, 151.
35. Simon Shepherd, Peter Womack, *English Drama: A Cultural History*, Oxford: Blackwell, 1996, 110.
36. This quote is from 2003 (http://www.northern-broadsides.co.uk/Pages/about_us.htm, accessed 31 October 2003). The page also contained a quote from John Prescott describing Northern Broadsides' production style as 'factory floor Shakespeare' – yet another link to working class culture, and of course also an indication of the company's political allegiances. More than a decade later (12 September 2014), the company's 'About' page has changed considerably. It now foregrounds Shakespeare's 'timeless resonance' and 'universal exploration of the human condition'. The production style itself is described as accessible and 'no frills'. There is no testimonial from Ed Miliband.

## The great consensus?

37 Harbage, *Shakespeare's Audience*, 60.
38. Harbage, *Shakespeare's Audience*, 155.
39. Harbage is referring to S. L. Bethell, *Shakespeare and the Popular Dramatic Tradition*, London: Staples Press, 1944. Just like Harbage, Bethell claims there is a nexus between Shakespeare's popular audience and the particular qualities of his drama.
40. Harbage, *Shakespeare and the Rival Traditions*, XIV.
41. 'The attack upon the citizens by the writers of Blackfriars and Paul's inspired a defense by the writers of the Globe, the Fortune, and the Red Bull, rather than a counterattack upon the gentry. The playwrights were speaking not for a class but for the whole community, and they persisted in portraying gentleness in the gentry, and nobleness in the nobility, where such qualities ought to be found and sometimes were.' Harbage, *Shakespeare and the Rival Traditions*, 277.
42. Harbage, *As They Liked It*, 117.

43. Shepherd/Womack, *English Drama*, 119.
44. F. R. Leavis, 'Joyce and "The Revolution of the Word"', *Scrutiny* Vol. II No. 2, 1933, 193-200: 199.
45. Two examples may suffice here. Germaine Greer writes: 'The playhouses [...] were [...] the only places where all the denizens of London, from the meanest pickpocket to the grandest functionary, could foregather and actually experience their membership of a *community* [my emphasis]. Even the largest churches did not afford the same spectacular possibilities, for the pulpit was raised above the congregation who stood all on one plane. In the theatre the audience could see itself as a tapestry of faces, surging below in the pit and rising on the tiers around the wooden walls, with the actor on his promontory, the projecting stage, at their mercy' (Germaine Greer, *Shakespeare*, Oxford: Bloomsbury Publishing, 1986, 19). Even Stephen Greenblatt states: 'The Shakespearean theatre depends upon a felt community.' (Stephen Greenblatt, 'The Circulation of Social Energy', *Shakespearean Negotiations: The Circulation of Social Energy in Renaissance England*, Oxford: Clarendon Press, 1988, 1–20: 5.)
46. Harbage, *Shakespeare's Audience*, 162–63.
47. Louis Montrose, *The Purpose of Playing: Shakespeare and the Cultural Politics of the Elizabethan Theatre*, Chicago: University of Chicago Press, 1996, 8.
48. Anthony B. Dawson, Paul Yachnin, *The Culture of Playgoing in Shakespeare's England: A Collaborative Debate*, Cambridge: Cambridge University Press, 2001, 89.
49. John Drakakis, 'Theatre, Ideology and Institution: Shakespeare and the Roadsweepers', Graham Holderness (ed.), *The Shakespeare Myth*, Manchester: Manchester University Press, 1988, 26–41: 35.
50. Gurr describes Harbage as 'work[ing] in the 1930s and 1940s when the political climate encouraged him to identify Shakespeare as a truly "popular" playwright appealing to a whole and united nation' (Andrew Gurr, *Playgoing in Shakespeare's London*, Cambridge: Cambridge University Press, 1987, 3). Jamieson mentions 'Harbage's democratic assumptions of the American forties' (Michael Jamieson, 'Shakespeare in Performance', Stanley Wells (ed.), *Shakespeare: A Bibliographical Guide*, Oxford: Oxford University Press, 1990, 37–68: 45).
51. Montrose, *The Purpose of Playing*, 177.
52. Drakakis, *Theatre, Ideology and Institution*, 35–36.
53. Alan Sinfield, 'Introduction: Reproductions, Interventions', Jonathan Dollimore and Alan Sinfield (eds.), *Political Shakespeare: New Essays in Cultural Materialism*, Manchester: Manchester University Press, 1985, 130–33: 131.
54. Ann Jennalie Cook, *The Privileged Playgoers of Shakespeare's London, 1576–1642*, Princeton: Princeton University Press, 1981, 8.
55. Cook, *Privileged Playgoers*, 8–9.
56. Montrose, *The Purpose of Playing*, 47.
57. Cook, *Privileged Playgoers*, 167.
58. Cook, *Privileged Playgoers*, 167.
59. Cook, *Privileged Playgoers*, 241.
60. Cook, *Privileged Playgoers*, 4.
61. Margolies, 'Teaching the Handsaw to Fly', 53.

62. Margolies, 'Teaching the Handsaw to Fly', 53.
63. Cohen, *Drama of a Nation*, 168: 'Although this controversy will most likely not be soon resolved, the hypothesis of primarily elite spectators represents no more than an abstract possibility, and one fraught with logical and empirical problems.'
64. Gurr, *Playgoing in Shakespeare's London*, 4: 'Cook's is a more plausible stereotype than Harbage's but still a thorough oversimplification.'
65. Butler, *Theatre and Crisis*, 295.
66. Cook, 'Audiences: Investigation, Interpretation, Invention', 306, 317.

### *Mais qui paie?*

67. Harbage, *Shakespeare's Audience*, 12.
68. Harbage, *Shakespeare's Audience*, 161–62.
69. Michael D. Bristol, *Big-time Shakespeare*, London and New York: Routledge, 1996, 37.
70. Dawson/Yachnin, *The Culture of Playgoing*, 53.
71. Montrose, *The Purpose of Playing*, 87.
72. Stephen Greenblatt, 'Invisible Bullets', *Shakespearean Negotiations*, 21–65: 52–53.
73. Greenblatt, 'The Circulation of Social Energy', 18.
74. I quote from an early version in Jonathan Dollimore und Alan Sinfield (eds.), *Political Shakespeare: New Essays in Cultural Materialism*, Manchester: Manchester University Press, 1985, 18–47: 41. In *Shakespearean Negotiations*, the passage has been slightly modified (55): '[...] [E]ven with *2 Henry IV*, where the lies and the self-serving sentiments are utterly inescapable, where the illegitimacy of legitimate authority is repeatedly demonstrated, where the whole state seems, to adapt More's phrase, a conspiracy of the great to enrich and protect their interests under the name of commonwealth, even here the state, watchful for signs of sedition on the stage, was not prodded to intervene.' The Elizabethan audience has become a *quantité négligeable*.
75. Bristol, *Big-time Shakespeare*, 50–51.

## Appendix: The Grocer's Wife

1. For an overview see Gurr, *Playgoing in Shakespeare's London*, 56–59.
2. Stephen Gosson, 'To the Gentlewomen Citizens of London', *The School of Abuse*, London: Thomas Woodcoke, F2–F3.
3. This is not meant to imply that female audience members necessarily ceased to attract male attention. Samuel Pepys describes what is clearly a case of male 'noting' directed at an audience member rather than at an actress: '[...] to the King's to The Mayds Tragedy; but vexed all the while with two talking ladies and Sir Ch. Sidly [Sir Charles Sedley], yet pleased to hear their discourse, he being a stranger; and one of the ladies would, and did, sit with her mask on all the play; and being exceeding witty as ever I heard a woman, did talk most pleasantly with him; but was, I believe, a virtuous woman and of quality. He would fain know who she was, but she would not tell. Yet did give him many pleasant hints of her knowledge of him, by that means setting his brains at work to find out who she was; and did give him leave to use all means to find out who she was but pulling off her mask. He was mighty

witty; and she also making sport with him very inoffensively, that a more pleasant rencontre I never heard. But by that means lost the pleasure of the play wholly, to which now and then Sir Ch. Sidlys exceptions against both words and pronouncing was very pretty. So home and to office; did much business; then home to supper and to bed.' (Samuel Pepys, *The Diary of Samuel Pepys* [1667], Robert Latham and William Matthews (eds.), London: Bell 1974, 71–72 (18 February 1667).

4. Knights, *Education and the Drama*, 619.
5. Wilson, *The Elizabethan Shakespeare*, 22.
6. The German phrase is 'die männliche Jugend des englischen Adels'. (Gustav Rümelin, 'Für wen dichtete Shakespeare?', *Shakespearestudien*, Stuttgart: J. G. Cotta, 1866, 32–49: 41. My translation.)
7. See, for example, Charles Whitworth, *The Making of a National Theatre*, Westport: Hyperion Press, 1951, 95.
8. Harbage, *Shakespeare's Audience*, 155.
9. Harbage, *Shakespeare and the Rival Traditions*, 222.
10. Harbage, *Shakespeare and the Rival Traditions*, 222.
11. Martin Butler, 'Translating the Elizabethan Theatre: The Politics of Nostalgia in *Henry V*', Shirley Chew and Alistair Stead (eds.), *Translating Life: Studies in Transpositional Aesthetics*, Liverpool: Liverpool University Press, 1999, 75–97: 90.
12. See Richard Levin, 'Women in the Renaissance Theatre Audience', *Shakespeare Quarterly* 40, 1989, 165–74.
13. Howard, *The Stage and Social Struggle*, 92.
14. See Kathleen McLuskie's 'The Patriarchal Bard: Feminist Criticism and Shakespeare: *King Lear* and *Measure for Measure*', Jonathan Dollimore and Alan Sinfield (eds.), *Political Shakespeare: New Essays in Cultural Materialism*, Manchester: Manchester University Press, 1985, 88–108.
15. Sarah Mayo, '"A Shakespeare for the People"? Negotiating the Popular in *Shakespeare in Love* and Michael Hoffman's *A Midsummer Night's Dream*', *Textual Practice* 17, 2003, 295–315: 303.
16. Mayo would seem to disagree here. She writes: 'The most telling responses among the audience of the inaugural performance of *Romeo and Juliet* are those of the puritan preacher, who was earlier to be heard decrying the playhouses as hotbeds of sin on a Bankside street corner, and Hugh Fennyman the moneylender, whose initial interest in the theatre did not stretch beyond recouping his debts. Both are redeemed by the drama: the puritan is utterly enraptured, and laughs, weeps and kisses his hands at the players in praise, while Hugh Fennyman forgets all fiscal considerations under the influence of Shakespeare's poetry.' These reactions, she claims, are indicative of the film's modernist agenda, according to which art redeems all. (312)
17. Courtney Lehmann, 'Dancing in a (Cyber) Net: "Renaissance Women", Systems Theory, and the War of the Cinemas', *Renaissance Drama* 34, 2005, 121–61: 122.

# Bibliography

Addison, J. ([10 May 1711] 1907) *The Spectator* 61 in G. Smith (ed.) *The Spectator*, vol. 1 (London and New York: Dent), pp. 186–89.

———, ([19 June 1712] 1907) *The Spectator* 409 in G. Smith (ed.) *The Spectator*, vol. 3 (London and New York: Dent), pp. 270–73.

Adonis, A. and S. Pollard (1997) *A Class Act: The Myth of Britain's Classless Society* (London: Hamish Hamilton).

Alexander, P. (1929) '*Troilus and Cressida*, 1609', *The Library* 9: 267–86.

Arac, J. (2000) 'The Impact of Shakespeare' in M. Brown (ed.) *The Cambridge History of Literary Criticism*, vol. 5: Romanticism (Cambridge: Cambridge University Press), pp. 272–95.

Archer, W. (1882) *English Dramatists of To-Day* (London: Sampson Low & Co).

Arnold, M. ([1884] 1974) 'George Sand' in R. H. Super (ed.) *Philistinism in England and America* (= *The Complete Prose Works of Matthew Arnold*, Vol. X) (Ann Arbor: University of Michigan Press), pp. 187–9.

———, ([1869] 1994) *Culture and Anarchy*, R. H. Super (ed.), (= The Complete Prose Works of Matthew Arnold, Vol. V) (Ann Arbor: University of Michigan Press) pp. 85–256.

Ashcroft, B. (2000) 'Primitive and Wingless: The Colonial Subject as Child' in W. S. Jackson (ed.) *Dickens and the Children of Empire* (Basingstoke: Palgrave), pp. 184–202.

Bacon, D. ([1856] 1999) 'William Shakespeare and His Plays, an Enquiry Concerning Them' in P. Rawlings (ed.) *Americans on Shakespeare 1776–1914* (Aldershot: Ashgate), pp. 169–99.

Baer, M. (1992) *Theatre and Disorder in Late Georgian London* (Oxford: Clarendon Press).

Baker, G. P. ([1907] 1965) *The Development of Shakespeare as a Dramatist* (New York: AMS Press).

Bakhtin, M. (1968) *Rabelais and His World* (Cambridge, Massachusetts: Massachusetts Institute of Technology Press).

Bancroft, G. ([1838] 1999) 'On the Progress of Civilization, or Reasons Why the Natural Association of Men of Letters is With the Democracy' in P. Rawlings (ed.) *Americans on Shakespeare 1776–1914* (Aldershot: Ashgate), pp. 70f.

Bate, J. (1986) *Shakespeare and the English Romantic Imagination* (Oxford: Clarendon).

———, (1990) 'The Politics of Romantics Shakespeare Criticism: Germany, England, France', *European Romantic Review* 1: 1–26.

———, (1992) 'Introduction' in J. Bate (ed.) *The Romantics on Shakespeare* (London: Penguin), pp. 1–36.

———, (1997) *The Genius of Shakespeare* (London: Picador).

Bather, F. A. (1887) 'The Puns of Shakespeare' in C. H. Hawkins and Winchester College Shakspere Society (eds.) *Noctes Shaksperianae: A Series of Papers by Late and Present Members* (Winchester/London: Warren), pp. 69–91.

Bennett, H. S. (1944) *Shakespeare's Audience: Annual Shakespeare Lecture of the British Academy* (London: Milford).

Bentley, G. E. (1948) 'Shakespeare and the Blackfriars Theatre', *Shakespeare Survey* 1: 38–50.

Bethell, S. L. (1944) *Shakespeare and the Popular Dramatic Tradition* (London: Staples Press).

Bivona, D. and R. B. Henkle (2006) *The Imagination of Class: Masculinity and the Victorian Urban Poor* (Columbus: The Ohio State University Press).

Boas, F. S. (1896) *Shakspere and his Predecessors* (London: Murray).

Bradley, A. C. ([1902] 1950) 'Shakespeare's Theatre and Audience' in *Oxford Lectures on Poetry* (London: Macmillan), pp. 361–93.

———, ([1904] 1937) *Shakespearean Tragedy: Lectures on Hamlet, Othello, King Lear, Macbeth* (London: Macmillan).

———, (1950) *Oxford Lectures on Poetry* (London: Macmillan).

Brandes, G. ([1898] 1917) *William Shakespeare: A Critical Study* (London: William Heinemann).

Brewer, J. (1997) *The Pleasures of the Imagination: English Culture in the Eighteenth Century* (London: Harper Collins).

Bridges, R. ([1907] 1927) 'The Influence of the Audience on Shakespeare's Drama' in *Collected Essays Papers & c. of Robert Bridges*, vol. 1 (London: Oxford University Press).

Bristol, M. D. (1990) *Shakespeare's America, America's Shakespeare* (London and New York: Routledge).

———, (1996) *Big-Time Shakespeare* (London and New York: Routledge).

Bryson, A. (1998) *From Courtesy to Civility: Changing Codes of Conduct in Early Modern England* (Oxford: Clarendon).

Butler, M. (1999) 'Translating the Elizabethan Theatre: The Politics of Nostalgia in *Henry V*' in S. Chew and A. Stead (eds.) *Translating Life: Studies in Transpositional Aesthetics* (Liverpool: Liverpool University Press), pp. 75–97.

Byrne, M. St. C. (1927) 'Shakespeare's Audience' in *A Series of Papers on Shakespeare and the Theatre: Together with Papers on Edward Alleyn and Early Records illustrating the Personal Life of Shakespeare, by Members of the Shakespeare Association, 1925–1926* (London: Oxford University Press), pp. 186–216.

Campbell, O. J. (1925) '*Love's Labour's Lost* Re-Studied' in *Studies in Shakespeare, Milton and Donne: By Members of the English Department of the University of Michigan* (New York: Haskell House), pp. 3–45.

———, (1938) *Comicall Satyre and Shakespeare's* Troilus and Cressida (San Marino (Cal.): Huntington Library & Art Gallery).

Capell, E. ([1738] 1981) 'Notes and Various Readings to Shakespeare' in B. Vickers (ed.) *Shakespeare: The Critical Heritage*, vol. 6: 1774–1801 (London and Boston: Routledge and Kegan Paul), pp. 218–72.

Carson, C. (2008) 'Democratising the Audience?' in C. Carson and F. Karim-Cooper (eds.) *Shakespeare's Globe: A Theatrical Experiment* (Cambridge: Cambridge University Press), pp. 115–26.

Chambers, C. A. (1965) *The New Deal at Home and Abroad* (New York: Free Press Macmillan).

Chambers, E. K. (1923) *The Elizabethan Stage*, vol. 1 (Oxford: Oxford University Press).

Cohen, W. (1985) *Drama of a Nation: Public Theater in Renaissance England and Spain* (Ithaca: Cornell University Press).

Coleridge, S. T. (1969) *The Friend*, vol. I in B. Rooke (ed.) *The Collected Works of Samuel Taylor Coleridge*, vol. IV (London: Routledge and Kegan Paul).

———, (1987) *Lectures 1808–1819: On Literature*, vol. I in R. A. Foakes (ed.) *The Collected Works of Samuel Taylor Coleridge*, vol. V (London: Routledge and Kegan Paul).

———, (1987) *Lectures 1808–1819: On Literature*, vol. II in R. A. Foakes (ed.) *The Collected Works of Samuel Taylor Coleridge*, vol. V (London: Routledge and Kegan Paul).

Cook, A. J. (1981) *The Privileged Playgoers of Shakespeare's London, 1576–1642* (Princeton: Princeton University Press).

———, (1997) 'Audiences: Investigation, Interpretation, Invention' in J. D. Cox, D. S. Kastan (eds.) *A New History of Early English Drama* (New York: Columbia University Press), pp. 305–20.

Craig, H. ([1936] 1950) *The Enchanted Glass: The Elizabethan Mind in Literature* (Oxford: Blackwell).

Darwin, C. ([1859] 1996) *The Origin of Species* (Oxford: Oxford University Press).

Davies, T. ([1783] 1973) *Dramatic Miscellanies: consisting of Critical Observations on several Plays of Shakespeare: with a Review of his principal Characters, and those of various eminent Writers, as represented by Mr. Garrick, and other celebrated Comedians: With Anecdotes of Dramatic Poets, Actors & c.*, vol. II (New York: AMS Press).

Dawson, A. B. and P. Yachnin (2001) *The Culture of Playgoing in Shakespeare's England: A Collaborative Debate* (Cambridge: Cambridge University Press).

Dawson, G. (1888) *Shakespeare and Other Lectures* (London: Kegan Paul, Trench & Co.).

Dekker, T. ([1609] 1904) *The Guls Hornbook and the Belman of London*, R. B. McKerrow (ed.) (London: De la More).

Dennis, J. ([1712] 1943) 'On the Genius and Writings of Shakespeare' in E. N. Hooker (ed.) *The Critical Works of John Dennis*, vol. II: 1711–1729 (Baltimore: The Johns Hopkins Press), pp. 1–18.

Dickens, C. (1997) *Dickens' Journalism*, vol. 2: 'The Amusements of the People' and Other Papers: Reports, Essays and Reviews 1834–51, M. Slater (ed.) (London: Dent).

Dobson, M. (1992) *The Making of the National Poet: Shakespeare, Adaptation and Authorship, 1660–1769* (Oxford: Clarendon Press).

Dowden, E. ([1875] 1948) *Shakspere: A Critical Study of his Mind and Art* (London: Routledge & Kegan Paul).

———, (1893) *Introduction to Shakespeare* (London: Blackie).

Drakakis, J. (1988) 'Theatre, Ideology and Institution: Shakespeare and the Roadsweepers' in G. Holderness (ed.) *The Shakespeare Myth* (Manchester: Manchester University Press) pp. 26–41.

——— and A. Sinfield (eds.) (1985) *Political Shakespeare: New Essays in Cultural Materialism* (Manchester: Manchester University Press).

Draper, J. W. (1932) 'Sir John Falstaff', *Review of English Studies* 8, 414–24.

———, ([1939] 1966) *The Hamlet of Shakespeare's Audience* (New York: Octagon Books).

———, (1952) *The Twelfth Night of Shakespeare's Audience* (Stanford: Stanford University Press).

Dryden, J. (1978) 'Defence of the Epilogue, or, An Essay on the Dramatique Poetry of the last Age [Epilogue to *The Conquest of Granada by the Spaniards*]' in A. Roper (ed.) *The Works of John Dryden*, vol. XI (Berkeley: University of California Press), pp. 203–18.

———, (1996) *Cleomenes* in A. Roper (ed.) *The Works of John Dryden*, vol. XVI (Berkeley: University of California Press), pp. 71–165.

———, (1996) 'Prologue to *Love Triumphant*' in A. Roper (ed.) *The Works of John Dryden*, vol. XVI (Berkeley: University of California Press) pp. 169–72.

Dugas, D. J. (2006) *Marketing the Bard: Shakespeare in Performance and Print 1660–1740* (Columbia and London: University of Missouri Press).

Echard, L. ([1694] 1968) *Prefaces to Terence's Comedies and Plautus's Comedies* (Los Angeles: The Augustan Reprint Society).

Elias, N. (1978) *The Civilizing Process: The History of Manners*, vol. 1, E. Jephcott (trans.) (New York: Urizen Books).

Eliot, T. S. (1933) *The Use of Poetry and the Use of Criticism: Studies in the Relation of Criticism to Poetry in England* (London: Faber and Faber).

Elsom, J. (ed.) (1989) *Is Shakespeare Still Our Contemporary?* (London: Routledge).

Emerson, R. W. (1987) 'Representative Men: Seven Lectures' in A. R. Ferguson, J. Slater and R. A. Bosco (eds.) *The Collected Works of Ralph Waldo Emerson*, vol. IV (Cambridge (Massachusetts) and London: Harvard University Press).

Empson, W. (1986) 'The Globe Theatre' in *Essays on Shakespeare* (Cambridge: Cambridge University Press), pp. 158–222.

Erne, L. (2003) *Shakespeare as Literary Dramatist* (Cambridge: Cambridge University Press).

Figgis, D. (1911) *Shakespeare: A Study* (London: J. M. Dent & Sons).

Fletcher, J. and P. Massinger ([1622] 1994) *The Prophetess* in G. W. Williams (ed.) *The Dramatic Works in the Beaumont and Fletcher Canon*, vol. IX (Cambridge: Cambridge University Press), pp. 221–318.

Froude, J. A. (1861) *History of England from the Fall of Wolsey to the Death of Elizabeth*, vol. 1 (Leipzig: F. A. Brockhaus).

Frye, N. (1957) *Anatomy of Criticism: Four Essays* (Princeton: Princeton University Press).

Gentleman, F. ([1770]) *The Dramatic Censor; or, Critical Companion* in B. Vickers (ed.) *Shakespeare: The Critical Heritage*, vol. 5: 1765–1774 (London and Boston: Routledge and Kegan Paul), pp. 373–409.

Gigante, D. (2005) *Taste: A Literary History* (New Haven and London: Yale University Press).

Gildon, C. ([1694] 1974) 'Miscellaneous Letters and Essays on Several Subjects in Prose and Verse' in B. Vickers (ed.) *Shakespeare: The Critical Heritage*, vol. 2: 1693–1733 (London and Boston: Routledge and Kegan Paul), pp. 63–85.

———, ([1710] 1974) 'An Essay on the Arts, Rise and Progress of the Stage in Greece, Rome and England' in B. Vickers (ed.) *Shakespeare: The Critical Heritage*, vol. 2: 1693–1733 (London and Boston: Routledge and Kegan Paul), pp. 216–62.

Gilman, S. L. (1985) *Difference and Pathology: Stereotypes of Sexuality, Race, and Madness* (Ithaca and London: Cornell University Press).

Gissing, G. ([1889] 1982) *The Nether World: A Novel*, J. Goode (ed.) (Brighton: The Harvester Press).

Gosson, S. (1579) *The School of Abuse* (London: Thomas Woodcoke).

Gould, G. (1919) 'A New Reading of *Henry V*', *The English Review* 29: 42–55.

Gould, R. ([1685] 1974) 'The Play-House: A Satyr' in B. Vickers (ed.) *Shakespeare: The Critical Heritage*, vol. 1: 1623–1692 (London and Boston: Routledge and Kegan Paul), pp. 414–16.

Granville-Barker, H. (1958) *Prefaces to Shakespeare*, vol. I.: *Hamlet, King Lear, The Merchant of Venice, Antony and Cleopatra, Cymbeline* (London: Batsford).

———, (1958) *Prefaces to Shakespeare*, vol. II: *Othello, Coriolanus, Romeo and Juliet, Julius Caesar, Love's Labour's Lost* (London: Batsford).

———, ([1925] 1974) 'From *Henry V* to *Hamlet* (Revised Edition of the British Academy Annual Shakespeare Lecture on May 13, 1925)' in H. Granville-Barker (ed.) *More Prefaces to Shakespeare* (Princeton: Princeton University Press), pp. 135–67.

Grazia, M. de (1991) *Shakespeare Verbatim: The Reproduction of Authenticity and the 1790 Apparatus* (Oxford: Clarendon Press).

Greenblatt, S. (1988) 'The Circulation of Social Energy' in *Shakespearean Negotiations: The Circulation of Social Energy in Renaissance England* (Oxford: Clarendon Press), pp. 1–20.

———, (1988) 'Invisible Bullets' in *Shakespearean Negotiations: The Circulation of Social Energy in Renaissance England* (Oxford: Clarendon Press), pp. 21–65.

Greer, G. (1986) *Shakespeare* (Oxford: Bloomsbury Publishing).

Greg, W. W. (1917) 'Hamlet's Hallucination', *The Modern Language Review* XII: 393–421.

———, (1919) 'Re-Enter Ghost: A Reply to Mr J. Dover Wilson', *Modern Language Review* XIV: 353–69.

Grey, Z. (1754) *Critical, Historical, and Explanatory Notes on Shakespeare, with Emendations of the Text and Metre*, vol. I (London: Printed for the author, and sold by Richard Manby).

Gurr, A. (1987) *Playgoing in Shakespeare's London* (Cambridge: Cambridge University Press).

Guthrie, W. ([1747] 1971) *An Essay Upon English Tragedy with Remarks upon the Abbe de Blanc's Observations on the English Stage* (London: Cass).

———, ([1765] 1979) [Article in *Monthly Review* XX] in B. Vickers *Shakespeare: The Critical Heritage*, vol. 5: 1765–1774 (London and Boston: Routledge and Kegan Paul), pp. 211–30.

Hadley, E. (1992) 'The Old Price Wars: Melodramatizing the Public Sphere in Early-Nineteenth-Century England', *PMLA* 107: 524–37.

Hahn, E. and H. H. (2002) 'Nationale Stereotypen: Plädoyer für eine historische Stereotypenforschung' in H. H. Hahn (ed.) *Stereotyp, Identität und Geschichte: Die Funktion von Stereotypen in gesellschaftlichen Diskursen*, vol. 5 (Frankfurt/Main: Peter Lang), pp. 17–56.

Hales, J. W. (1884) *Notes and Essays on Shakespeare* (London: Bell).

Halpern, R. (1997) *Shakespeare Among the Moderns* (Ithaca and London: Cornell University Press).

Harbage, A. (1941) *Shakespeare's Audience* (New York: Columbia University Press).

———, (1947) *As They Liked It: An Essay on Shakespeare and Morality* (New York: Columbia University Press).

———, (1952) *Shakespeare and the Rival Traditions* (New York: Columbia University Press).

Harding, D. P. ([1954] 1973) 'Shakespeare the Elizabethan' in C. T. Prouty (ed.) *Shakespeare: Of an Age and For All Time: The Yale Shakespeare Festival Lectures* (New York: Shoe String Press), pp. 11–32.

Hart, J. C. ([1848] 1999) 'The Romance of Yachting: Voyage the First' in P. Rawlings (ed.) *Americans on Shakespeare, 1776–1914* (Aldershot: Ashgate), pp. 140–50.

Hawkins, C. H. (1887) 'The Stage Craft of Shakspere', in C. H. Hawkins/ Winchester College Shakspere Society (eds.) *Noctes Shaksperianae* (Winchester/ London: Warren), pp. 121–65.

Hazlitt, W. ([1817] 1930) *Characters of Shakespear's Plays* in P. P. Howe (ed.) *The Complete Works of William Hazlitt*, vol. 4: *The Round Table* and *Characters of Shakespeare's Plays* (London and Toronto: Dent).

———, ([1818] 1931) *Lectures on the Dramatic Literature of the Age of Elizabeth* in P. P. Howe (ed.) *The Complete Works of William Hazlitt*, vol. 6: Lectures on the English Comic Writers and Lectures on the Age of Elizabeth (London and Toronto: Dent).

———, ([1818] 1932) 'What is the People?' in P. P. Howe (ed.) *The Complete Works of William Hazlitt*, vol. 7: Political Essays, with Sketches of Public Characters (London and Toronto: Dent), pp. 259–81.

Heath, B. ([1765] 1976) 'A Revisal of Shakespeare's Text, Wherein the Alterations Introduced Into It By the More Modern Editors and Critics, are Particularly Considered' in B. Vickers (ed.) *Shakespeare: The Critical Heritage*, vol. 4: 1753–1765 (London and Boston: Routledge and Kegan Paul), pp. 550–64.

*Henry V* (1994), dir. L. Olivier (United Kingdom: Rank Film Distributors).

Höfele, A. (2012) 'Hamlet in Plettenberg: Carl Schmitt's Shakespeare', *Shakespeare Survey* 65: 378–97.

Holland, P. (1997) *English Shakespeares: Shakespeare on the English Stage in the 1990s* (Cambridge: Cambridge University Press).

Hotson, L. (1954) *The First Night of Twelfth Night* (London: Hart-Davis).

Howard, J. E. (1994) *The Stage and Social Struggle in Early Modern England* (London and New York: Routledge).

Hudson, H. N. (1848) *Lectures on Shakespeare*, vol. 1 (New York: Baker and Scribner).

Jamieson, M. (1990) 'Shakespeare in Performance' in S. Wells (ed.) *Shakespeare: A Bibliographical Guide* (Oxford: Oxford University Press), pp. 37–68.

Johnson, S. ([1765] 1968) 'Preface to Shakespeare' in A. Sherbo (ed.) *The Yale Edition of the Works of Samuel Johnson*, vol. VII: Johnson on Shakespeare (New Haven and London: Yale University Press), pp. 59–113.

———, (1968) 'Proposals for Printing, by Subscription, the Dramatick Works of William Shakespeare, Corrected and Illustrated by Samuel Johnson, London, June 1, 1756' in A. Sherbo (ed.) *The Yale Edition of the Works of Samuel Johnson*, vol. VII: Johnson on Shakespeare (New Haven and London: Yale University Press), pp. 51–58.

Jones, R. W. (1998) *Gender and the Formation of Taste in Eighteenth-Century Britain: The Analysis of Beauty* (Cambridge: Cambridge University Press).

Kampen, C. van (2008) 'Music and Aural Texture at Shakespeare's Globe' in C. Carson, F. Karim-Cooper (eds.) *Shakespeare's Globe: A Theatrical Experiment* (Cambridge: Cambridge University Press), pp. 79–89.

Kiernan, P. (1999) *Staging Shakespeare at the New Globe* (Basingstoke: Macmillan).

Knights, L. C. ([1932] 1967) 'Education and the Drama in the Age of Shakespeare' in T. S. Eliot (ed.) *The Criterion 1922–1939*, vol. XI: October 1931–July 1932 (London: Faber and Faber), pp. 599–625.

Lamb, C. (1978) '[On *Richard III*]' in J. Coldwell (ed.) *Charles Lamb on Shakespeare* (Gerrards Cross: Smythe), pp. 17–21.

———, ([1811] 1978) 'On the Tragedies of Shakespeare' in J. Coldwell (ed.) *Charles Lamb on Shakespeare* (Gerrards Cross: Smythe), pp. 24–42.

Lawrence, W. W. (1931) *Shakespeare's Problem Comedies* (New York: Macmillan).

Lawrence, W. J. (1935) *Those Nut-Cracking Elizabethans: Studies of the Early Theatre and Drama* (London: The Argonaut Press).

Leavis, F. R. (1930) *Mass Civilisation and Minority Culture* (Cambridge: Minority Press).

———, (1933) 'Joyce and "The Revolution of the Word"', *Scrutiny* Vol. II No. 2: 193–20.

Leavis, Q. D. ([1932] 1965) *Fiction and the Reading Public* (London: Chatto and Windus).

Lee, S. (1906) *Shakespeare and the Modern Stage: With Other Essays* (London: Murray).

Lehmann, C. (2005) 'Dancing in a (Cyber) Net: "Renaissance Women", Systems Theory, and the War of the Cinemas', *Renaissance Drama* 34: 121–61.

Levin, R. (1989) 'Women in the Renaissance Theatre Audience', *Shakespeare Quarterly* 40: 165–74.

Lewes, G. H. ([1852] 1971) 'Charles Kean in *The Corsican Brothers*' in G. Rowell (ed.), *Victorian Dramatic Criticism* (London: Methuen), pp. 97–99.

———, (1849) 'Shakespeare's Critics: English and Foreign', *Edinburgh Review* 90: 46–47.

Lewis, W. ([1927] 1951) *The Lion and the Fox: The Role of the Hero in the Plays of Shakespeare* (London: Methuen).

Lopez, J. (2007) 'Imagining the Actor's Body on the Early Modern Stage', *Medieval and Renaissance Drama in England* 20: 187–203.

———, (2008) 'A Partial Theory of Original Practice', *Shakespeare Survey* 61: 302–17.

Lynch, J. (2003) *The Age of Elizabeth in the Age of Johnson* (Cambridge: Cambridge University Press).

———, (2012) 'Criticism of Shakespeare' in F. Ritchie and P. Sabor (eds.) *Shakespeare in the Eighteenth Century* (Cambridge: Cambridge University Press), pp. 41–77.

Margolies, D. (1988) 'Teaching the Handsaw to Fly: Shakespeare as a Hegemonic Instrument' in G. Holderness (ed.) *The Shakespeare Myth* (Manchester: Manchester University Press), pp. 42–53.

Marsden, J. I. (1995) *The Re-Imagined Text: Shakespeare, Adaptation and Eighteenth-Century Literary Theory* (Lexington: University Press of Kentucky).

Matthews, B. (1913) *Shakspere as a Playwright* (New York / London: Longmans, Green).

Mayhew, H. ([1861] 1968) *London Labour and the London Poor: In Four Volumes*, vol. 1: The London Street-Folk (partial) (New York: Dover Publications).

Mayo, S. (2003) '"A Shakespeare For the People"? Negotiating the Popular in *Shakespeare in Love* and Michael Hoffman's *A Midsummer Night's Dream*', *Textual Practice* 17: 295–315.

Mazer, C. M. (1980) *Shakespeare Refashioned: Elizabethan Plays on Edwardian Stages* (Ann Arbor: UMI Research Press).

McLuskie, K. (1985) 'The Patriarchal Bard: Feminist Criticism and Shakespeare: *King Lear* and *Measure for Measure*' in J. Dollimore and A. Sinfield (eds.) *Political Shakespeare: New Essays in Cultural Materialism* (Manchester: Manchester University Press), pp. 88–108.

Minto, W. ([1874] 1885) *Characteristics of English Poets from Chaucer to Shirley* (London: Blackwood).

Montagu, E. ([1769] 1970) *An Essay on the Writings and Genius of Shakespear, compared with the Greek and French Dramatic Poets: With some Remarks upon the Misrepresentations of Mons. De Voltaire* (London: Cass).

Montrose, L. (1989) 'Professing the Renaissance: The Poetics and Politics of Culture' in H. A. Veeser (ed.) *The New Historicism* (New York and London: Routledge), pp. 15–36.

——, (1996) *The Purpose of Playing: Shakespeare and the Cultural Politics of the Elizabethan Theatre* (Chicago: University of Chicago Press).

Morgann, M. (1972) *Shakespearian Criticism* (Oxford: Clarendon Press).

Murphy, A. ([1753] 1976) [Contribution to *Gray's-Inn Journal* 8] in B. Vickers (ed.) *Shakespeare: The Critical Heritage*, vol. 4: 1753–1765 (London and Boston: Routledge and Kegan Paul), pp. 84–109.

Murry, J. M. (1936) *Shakespeare* (London: Cape).

Myhill, N. and J. A. Low (2011) 'Introduction: Audience and Audiences' in *Imagining the Audience in Early Modern Drama, 1558–1642* (New York: Palgrave Macmillan), pp. 1–17.

O'Connor, M. F. (1987) 'Theatre of the Empire: "Shakespeare's England" at Earl's Court, 1912' in M. F. O'Connor and J. E. Howard (eds.) *Shakespeare Reproduced: The Text in History and Ideology* (New York and London: Methuen), pp. 68–98.

Oxford English Dictionary (1933) *The Oxford English Dictionary: Being a Corrected Re-Issue with an Introduction, Supplement, and Bibliography of A New English Dictionary on Historical Principles. Founded mainly on the Materials collected by The Philological Society*, Volume IV: F–G. (Oxford: Oxford University Press), *s.v.* 'groundling'.

Paul, H. N. (1950) *The Royal Play of Macbeth: When, Why and How It Was Written by Shakespeare* (New York: Macmillan).

Pearson, R. E. and W. Uricchio (1990) 'How Many Times Shall Caesar Bleed in Sport: Shakespeare and the Cultural Debate about Moving Pictures', *Screen* 31: 243–61.

Pepys, S. ([1667] 1974) *The Diary of Samuel Pepys*, vol. VIII: 1667, R. Latham and W. Matthews (eds.) (London: Bell).

Poel, W. (1913) *Shakespeare in the Theatre* (London: Sidgwick and Jackson).

——, (1916) *Some Notes on Shakespeare's Stage and Plays* (Manchester: Manchester University Press).

Pope, A. ([1725] 1986) 'The Preface of the Editor to the Works of Shakespear' in R. Cowler (ed.) *The Prose Works of Alexander Pope*, vol. II: The Major Works, 1725–1744 (Oxford: Blackwell), pp. 1–40.

——, (1736) *The Dunciad: The Works of Alexander Pope, Esq*, vol. IV: Containing the Dunciad, with the prolegomena of Scriblerus, and notes variorum (London: Gilliver and Clarke).

Pound, E. ([1950] 1971) *The Selected Letters of Ezra Pound 1907–1941*, D. D. Paige (ed.) (New York: James Laughlin).

Prescott, P. (2005) 'Inheriting the Globe: The Reception of Shakespearean Space and Audience in Contemporary Reviewing' in B. Hodgdon and W. B. Worthen (eds.) *A Companion to Shakespeare and Performance* (Malden and Oxford: Blackwell), pp. 359–75.

Prince, K. (2012) 'Shakespeare and English Nationalism' in F. Ritchie and P. Sabor (eds.) *Shakespeare in the Eighteenth Century* (Cambridge: Cambridge University Press), pp. 277–94.

Prior, M. E. (1951) 'The Elizabethan Audience and the Plays of Shakespeare', *Modern Philology* 49: 101–23.

Purcell, S. (2009) *Popular Shakespeare: Simulation and Subversion on the Modern Stage* (Basingstoke: Palgrave Macmillan).

Quiller-Couch, Sir A. (1930) 'Introduction', in William Shakespeare, *Twelfth Night or What You Will*, A. Quiller-Couch (ed.) (Cambridge: Cambridge University Press), pp. VII–XXVIII.

Quiller-Couch, Sir A. and J. D. Wilson (1923) 'Introduction' in William Shakespeare, *Love's Labour's Lost*, Sir A. Quiller Couch and J. D. Wilson (eds.) (Cambridge: Cambridge University Press), pp. VII–XXXIX.

Rasmussen, E. and A. Santesso (eds.) (2007) *Comparative Excellence: New Essays on Shakespeare and Johnson* (AMS Studies in the Eighteenth Century, 52) (New York: AMS Press).

Rhodes, C. (1900) *Cecil Rhodes: His Political Life and Speeches*, F. Verschoyle (ed.) (London: Chapman & Hall).

Rodgers, A. (2010) 'Looking Up to the Groundlings: Representing the Renaissance Audience in Contemporary Fiction and Film' in G. M. Colón Semenza (ed.) *The English Renaissance in Popular Culture: An Age for All Time* (New York: Palgrave Macmillan), pp. 75–87.

Rowe, N. ([1709] 1963) 'Some Account of the Life and c. of Mr William Shakespeare' in D. N. Smith (ed.) *Eighteenth Century Essays on Shakespeare* (Oxford: Clarendon Press), pp. 1–22.

———, (1975) *The Tragedy of Jane Shore*, H. W. Pedicord (ed.) (London: Edward Arnold).

Rümelin, G. (1866) 'Für wen dichtete Shakespeare?' in *Shakespearestudien* (Stuttgart: J. G. Cotta), pp. 32–49.

Saintsbury, G. (1898) *A Short History of English Literature* (London: Macmillan).

———, (1901) *A History of Elizabethan Literature* (London: Macmillan).

Sala, G. A. (1859) *Twice Round the Clock* (London: Houlston and Wright).

Schoch, R. W. (2002) 'Pictorial Shakespeare' in S. Wells and S. Stanton (eds.) *The Cambridge Companion to Shakespeare on Stage* (Cambridge: Cambridge University Press), pp. 59–75.

Schücking, L. L. ([1922] 1959) *Character Problems in Shakespeare's Plays: A Guide to the Better Understanding of the Dramatist* (Gloucester (Massachusetts): Peter Smith).

———, (1919) *Die Charakterprobleme bei Shakespeare: Eine Einführung in das Verständnis des Dramatikers* (Leipzig: Tauchnitz).

———, (16 May 1936) 'Stage or Study', *The Times Literary Supplement* 420.

Seccombe, T. and J. W. Allen (1903) *The Age of Shakespeare (1579–1631)*, vol. II: Drama (London: George Bell & Sons).

Seward, T. ([1750] 1975) 'Preface to the Works of Mr Francis Beaumont, and Mr John Fletcher' in B. Vickers (ed.) *Shakespeare: The Critical Heritage*, vol. 3: 1733–1752 (London and Boston: Routledge and Kegan Paul), pp. 383–90.

*Shakespeare in Love* (1998), dir. J. Madden (UK/US: Universal Pictures/ Miramax Films).

Shakespeare, W. (2008) *The Norton Shakespeare*, S. Greenblatt (general ed.) (New York: W. W. Norton & Company).

Shaughnessy, R. (2007) 'Introduction' in R. Shaughnessy (ed.) *The Cambridge Companion to Shakespeare and Popular Culture* (Cambridge: Cambridge University Press), pp. 1–5.

Shaw, B. (1913) *The Quintessence of Ibsenism: Now Completed to the Death of Ibsen* (London: Constable).

———, (1962) *Shaw on Shakespeare: An Anthology of Bernard Shaw's Writings on the Plays and Production of Shakespeare*, Edwin Wilson (ed.) (London: Cassell).

Shepherd, S. and P. Womack (1996) *English Drama: A Cultural History* (Oxford: Blackwell).

Siegel, P. N. (1953) 'Shylock and the Puritan Usurers' in A. D. Matthews and C. M. Emery (eds.) *Studies in Shakespeare* (Coral Gables: University of Miami Press), pp. 129–38.

Sinfield, A. (1985) 'Introduction: Reproductions, Interventions' in J. Dollimore and A. Sinfield (eds.) *Political Shakespeare: New Essays in Cultural Materialism* (Manchester: Manchester University Press), pp. 130–33.

Sisson, C. J. (1914) *Le Goût Public et le Théâtre Elisabéthain jusqu'à la Mort de Shakespeare*, (Dijon: Darntière).

Smyth, H. W. ([1903] 1963) *Greek Melic Poets* (New York: Biblo and Tannen).

Spencer, B. T. (1941) 'This Elizabethan Shakespeare', *The Sewanee Review* 49: 536–53.

Stallybrass, P. and A. White (1986) *The Poetics and Politics of Transgression* (London: Methuen).

Stirling, B. (1949) *The Populace in Shakespeare* (New York: Columbia University Press).

Stoll, E. E. (1919) *Hamlet: An Historical and Comparative Study* (Minneapolis: Research Publications of the University of Minnesota).

———, (1927) *Shakespeare Studies: Historical and Comparative in Method* (New York: Macmillan).

———, ([1940] 1962) *Shakespeare and Other Masters* (New York: Russell & Russell).

Stubbes, G. ([1763] 1975) 'Some Remarks on the Tragedy of Hamlet' in B. Vickers (ed.) *Shakespeare: The Critical Heritage*, vol. 3: 1733–1752 (London and Boston: Routledge and Kegan Paul), pp. 40–69.

Swinburne, A. C. ([1880] 1968) *A Study of Shakespeare* in Sir E. Gosse, C. B. and T. J. Wise (eds.) *The Complete Works of Algernon Charles Swinburne*, Prose Works Vol.1 (= Complete Works Vol. XI) (New York: Russell & Russell), pp. 1–222.

Symonds, J. A. ([1873] 1920) *Studies of the Greek Poets*, (London: Black).

Taine, H. A. ([1872] 1886) *History of English Literature* (New York: Holt).

Taylor, G. (1990) *Reinventing Shakespeare: A Cultural History from the Restoration to the Present* (London: Hogarth Press).

Tetzeli von Rosador, K. (1977) 'Victorian Theories of Melodrama', *Anglia* 95: 87–114.

———, (1996) 'Henry Mayhews Vielstimmigkeit' in H. Mayhew (ed.) *Die Armen von London: Ein Kompendium der Lebensbedingungen und Einkünfte derjenigen, die arbeiten wollen, derjenigen, die nicht arbeiten können, und derjenigen, die nicht arbeiten wollen* (Frankfurt/Main), pp. 361–81.

Theobald, L. ([1733] 1963) 'Preface to Edition of Shakespeare' in D. N. Smith (ed.) *Eighteenth-Century Essays on Shakespeare* (Oxford: Clarendon Press), pp. 63–91.

———, ([1726] 1971) *Shakespeare Restored; or, a Specimen of the many Errors, As Well Committed, as Unamended, by Mr. Pope in his Late Edition of this Poet: Designed not only to correct the said Edition, but to restore true Reading of Shakespeare in all the Editions ever yet publish'd* (London: Cass).

Tillyard, E. M. W. (1943) *The Elizabethan World Picture* (London: Macmillan).

Timmins, N. (1995) *The Five Giants: A Biography of the Welfare State* (London: Harper Collins).

*Today* Newspaper (24 November 1990).

Tree, H. B. (1913) *Thoughts and Afterthoughts* (London and New York: Cassell and Company).

Upton, J. ([1748] 1975) *Critical Observations on Shakespeare* in B. Vickers (ed.) *Shakespeare: The Critical Heritage*, vol. 3: 1733–1752 (London and Boston: Routledge and Kegan Paul), pp. 290–323.

Vickers, B. (1981) 'Introduction' in B. Vickers (ed.) *Shakespeare: The Critical Heritage*, vol. 6: 1774–1801 (London and Boston: Routledge and Kegan Paul), pp. 1–86.

———, (1974) 'Introduction' in B. Vickers (ed.) *Shakespeare: The Critical Heritage*, vol. 2: 1693–1733 (London and Boston: Routledge and Kegan Paul), pp. 1–21.

Walsh, M. (1997) *Shakespeare, Milton and Eighteenth-Century Literary Editing: The Beginnings of Interpretative Scholarship* (Cambridge: Cambridge University Press).

Ward, A. W. (1875) *A History of English Dramatic Literature to the Death of Queen Anne*, vol. 1 (London: Macmillan).

Warton, T. (1781) *The History of English Poetry, from the Close of the Eleventh to the Commencement of the Eighteenth Century*, vol. III (London: J. Dodsley).

Weimann, R. (1978) *Shakespeare and the Popular Tradition in the Theater: Studies in the Social Dimension of Dramatic Form and Function*, R. Schwarz (ed.) (Baltimore: The Johns Hopkins University Press).

White, R. G. ([1885] 1893) *Studies in Shakespeare* (Boston: Houghton Mifflin).

Whitman, W. ([1886] 1964) 'A Thought on Shakespeare' in F. Stovall (ed.) *Prose Works 1892*, vol. II: Collect and Other Prose (New York: New York University Press), pp. 556–58.

———, ([1871] 1964) 'Democratic Vistas' in F. Stovall (ed.) *Prose Works 1892*, vol. II: Collect and Other Prose (New York: New York University Press), pp. 361–426.

Whitworth, C. (1951) *The Making of a National Theatre* (Westport: Hyperion Press).

Wilkes, G. (1877) *Shakespeare: From an American Point of View; Including an Inquiry as to his Religious Faith and his Knowledge of Law: With the Baconian Theory Considered* (London: Sampson Low, Marston).

Willems, M. (2011) 'Shakespeare' in R. Paulin (ed.) *Great Shakespeareans*, vol. III: Voltaire, Goethe, Schlegel, Coleridge (London: Continuum), pp. 5–43.

Wilson, J. D. (1929) *The Elizabethan Shakespeare: Annual Shakespeare Lecture of the British Academy* (London: Humphrey Milford).

———, ([1932] 1962) *The Essential Shakespeare* (Cambridge: Cambridge University Press).

Wilson, R. (1993) *Will Power: Essays on Shakespearean Authority* (New York: Harvester).

Winstanley, L. (1921) *Hamlet and the Scottish Succession: Being an Examination of the Relations of the Play of Hamlet to the Scottish Succession and the Essex Conspiracy* (Cambridge: Cambridge University Press).

———, (1922) *Macbeth, King Lear and Contemporary History: Being a Study of the Relations of the Play of Macbeth to the Personal History of James I, the Darnley Murder and the St Bartholomew Massacre, and also of King Lear as Symbolic Mythology* (Cambridge: Cambridge University Press).

Wolff, M. J. (1903) *William Shakespeare: Studien und Aufsätze* (Leipzig: Seemann).

Wordsworth, W. ([1815] 1974) 'Essay, Supplementary to the Preface to *The Excursion*' in W. J. B. Owen (ed.) *Wordsworth's Literary Criticism* (London: Routledge), pp. 192–218.

———, ([1800, 1802] 1974) 'Preface to Lyrical Ballads' in W. J. B. Owen (ed.) *Wordsworth's Literary Criticism* (London: Routledge), pp. 68–95.

# Index

Lightning Source UK Ltd.
Milton Keynes UK
UKOW06n2304150915

258706UK00002B/5/P